THE NOVELIST AS PHILOSOPHER

Studies in French Fiction, 1935–1960

THE NOVELIST AS PHILOSOPHER

———✭———

Studies in French Fiction
1935–1960

by

JOHN CRUICKSHANK
ERNEST BEAUMONT
CECIL JENKINS
MARTIN ESSLIN
JOHN WEIGHTMAN
GEOFFREY HARTMAN
MAURICE CRANSTON
CARLOS LYNES

Edited by
JOHN CRUICKSHANK

London
OXFORD UNIVERSITY PRESS
NEW YORK TORONTO
1962

Oxford University Press, Amen House, London E.C.4

GLASGOW NEW YORK TORONTO MELBOURNE WELLINGTON
BOMBAY CALCUTTA MADRAS KARACHI LAHORE DACCA
CAPE TOWN SALISBURY NAIROBI IBADAN ACCRA
KUALA LUMPUR HONG KONG

© Oxford University Press 1962

Printed in Great Britain

CONTENTS

INTRODUCTION

    SOME ASPECTS OF FRENCH FICTION, 1935–1960
    by John Cruickshank   3

PRECURSORS

    GEORGES BERNANOS by Ernest Beaumont   29
    ANDRÉ MALRAUX by Cecil Jenkins   55

SUCCESSORS

    RAYMOND QUENEAU by Martin Esslin   79
    JEAN-PAUL SARTRE by John Weightman   102
    SAMUEL BECKETT by Martin Esslin   128
    MAURICE BLANCHOT by Geoffrey Hartman   147
    SIMONE DE BEAUVOIR by Maurice Cranston   166
    JEAN CAYROL by Carlos Lynes   183
    ALBERT CAMUS by John Cruickshank   206
    ALAIN ROBBE-GRILLET by John Weightman   230

INDEX   253

NOTE

The essays forming this symposium were all specially written for it and have not been previously published in this country. Apart from a few formal requirements, the contributors were left entirely free to express their personal views and indulge their private enthusiasms. The result, I hope, is a symposium which has achieved variety and liveliness within a clear general framework.

I should like to take this opportunity of thanking the various contributors for their ready co-operation and near-punctuality. It is also a pleasure to record my gratitude to the Oxford University Press for a great deal of help and encouragement in this project.

Acknowledgement is made to the publishers concerned for permission to quote from the works of Raymond Queneau, published by Gallimard & Cie, Paris, and Samuel Beckett and Alain Robbe-Grillet, published by Les Éditions de Minuit, Paris.

J. C.

Southampton.
February 1962

INTRODUCTION

SOME ASPECTS OF FRENCH FICTION
1935-1960
BY JOHN CRUICKSHANK

———————✯———————

THE novelists whose work is discussed in these essays do not form a distinct school or movement. It must be admitted, too, that they are not the only writers of importance who have contributed to the development of French fiction during the last twenty-five years. Considerable differences of artistic achievement, as well as of individual temperament, exist between some of them (between Bernanos and Sartre, or between Queneau and Robbe-Grillet, for example). And yet, from several points of view, all possess a certain general 'family likeness' which is not easily extended to Gide and Mauriac, even though some might argue that it could include Montherlant and Julien Green. This 'family likeness', in the broadest sense, existing between the writers discussed later, arises mainly from the fact that their novels, and the attitudes they adopt to the novelist's function and responsibilities, suggest to the critic a series of questions concerning the nature of the relationship between philosophy and literature. Any thorough assessment of their work must include some exploration of that ill-defined area (what Malraux calls 'ce domaine un peu trouble') where philosophy and fiction appear to meet. It is an area which all these novelists have occupied with varying degrees of conscious purpose and artistic success. I would add, however, that the fact of taking up this position has been connected, in their work, with other attitudes and tendencies as well. Yet while some of these features have been widely shared by most serious novelists of the present century, others seem to be particularly distinctive aspects of French fiction since the nineteen-thirties.

It has become a commonplace to say that general agreement exists less today than ever before concerning the validity of many traditional moral beliefs and practices. In the past, almost universal assent was given to the theory that virtue should be rewarded and vice punished. Even more important is the fact, emphasized some years ago by David Daiches,[1] that near-unanimity existed about what actually constituted virtue and vice. This is obviously no longer the case. Absolutes and abstractions command little intellectual loyalty. Political and social events during the last twenty-five years, together with the accelerating pace of scientific discovery, have destroyed or seriously undermined belief in most of the traditional humanist assumptions. A whole conception of man, accepted in much the same form over a long period of time, has now been called in question. Even in the nineteen-twenties Duhamel, in his *Vie et aventures de Salavin*, presented us with a typical modern hero whom he described as being 'a man deprived of any metaphysics'.

What is now the extreme fragmentation of belief, and often the destruction of belief, has been reflected in much modern writing. The literature of this century has registered, above all, the breakdown of a settled, established intellectual and moral order. In providing the age with a nihilistic rhetoric it has also explored, on occasions, the possibility of a new coherence. A marked divorce has arisen, as a result, between writers and readers. A common body of reference seems to be lacking. This fact is not to be explained, as has sometimes been suggested, by the existence today of a much larger, and therefore more diversified, reading public. Lack of contact between reader and writer does not arise simply because these French novelists describe a social world which many of their readers do not share. On the contrary, a divorce exists because these novelists hold very distinct and special views about the nature of experience and what it means to be a human being against the background of such experience.

Because agreed standards and shared assumptions are largely absent, recent French fiction disturbs many ordinary readers, and

[1] See David Daiches, *The Novel and the Modern World* (Chicago, Chicago University Press, 1939), pp. 7–11.

is meant to disturb them. The desire to entertain and reassure has gone. Novels of disquiet reflect an age of anxiety. Bernanos, for example, attacked many intellectual assumptions and the pharisaism of much public morality. In his *Journal d'un curé de campagne* (1936), quite apart from his non-fictional works, he exposed materialism, boredom, lack of spiritual awareness, particularly in their more deceptively innocent forms. All this is regarded by Bernanos as evidence of what he considered to be the dominant contemporary phenomenon: 'the fermentation of a Christianity in decay'. In the same novel, the village priest's comment on his parishioners: 'their serene security appals me', sums up Bernanos's view of his potential readers and indicates the general nature of his attack on them. The novels of Malraux, lacking the religious affirmations of Bernanos, are perhaps even more disturbing with their insistence on the individual's loneliness (a loneliness that is metaphysical in essence) and their preoccupation with death. This view of 'the human condition'—an expression that gained very wide currency after the publication of Malraux's novel, *La Condition humaine*, in 1933—is repeatedly examined by Queneau, Sartre, Beckett, Blanchot, Simone de Beauvoir, Cayrol, and Camus. Sartre reacts with 'nausea' to the superfluity and arbitrariness of the physical world and man's relation to it; Beckett's tramps and Cayrol's outcasts dramatize aspects of the human dilemma; Camus, insisting on the incoherence of experience and the tragic conflict of life and death, described alienated man in his first novel, *L'Étranger* (1942). Whether they accept the fact or not, Sartre is attacking most of his potential readers in his onslaught on bourgeois standards and traditional humanist values in *La Nausée* (1938). A broader and more radical attack, in so far as it is both literary and moral, is present in the novels of Robbe-Grillet. These latter are doubtless the most extreme, as well as the latest, instance of a radical divorce between the modern novelist and his public.

This kind of gulf between reader and writer goes with a highly serious and ambitious conception, by the writer, of his role in modern society. It is a characteristic of many novelists in the twentieth century to make sweeping claims on behalf of their work. A well-known instance setting the general tone is D. H. Lawrence's highly combative remark: 'Being a novelist I consider myself superior to the saint, the scientist, the philosopher and the poet' (in his essay, 'Why the Novel Matters', published posthumously with other essays in 1936 in *Phoenix*). Naturally, seriousness of purpose and ambitious claims take widely differing forms. In the case of Bernanos, for example, they arise from the close connexion he himself established between his role as a novelist and his deep religious feeling. In a letter of 1945 he stated: 'The profession of writing is no longer a profession but an adventure—and primarily a spiritual adventure.' Two years earlier he had given striking expression to his own conception of his function as a novelist by writing to another correspondent: 'As I grow older I understand with increasing clarity that my humble vocation really is a vocation—*vocatus*.' For what may seem more precise, if also more narrow, reasons, Sartre has emphasized the potential power of the novelist and asserted the supremacy, from a certain point of view, of prose over poetry. He argues in *Situations II* (especially pp. 63-64) that the novelist uses words as signs and as instruments, that his concern is with the things to which words point, whereas the poet treats words much more as objects and is primarily interested in them for themselves. This is one of the explanations offered by those who claim, no doubt rightly, that the novel is the most important and influential literary vehicle of modern society. It also lies at the basis of Sartre's theory of a 'committed' literature and prompts him to regard writing as a form of political and moral action. This view has been taken by a number of other novelists; for example, Blaise Cendrars in *Rhum* (1930) and Michel Leiris in *L'Age d'homme* (1939). Cendrars even claims that his *reportage romancé* was written 'to prove . . . that a novel can also be an act'.

A rather different view, asserting that the novel must attempt to encompass the whole metaphysical status of man, has been held by a number of French writers in recent years. Malraux and Blanchot are particularly explicit on this point. In one of the numerous comments which he added to the text of Gaëtan Picon's *Malraux par lui-même* (1953) Malraux says: 'In my view the modern novel is a privileged means of expressing the tragic element in man; it is not an elucidation of the individual' (p. 66). Malraux also describes the novel as 'an instrument of metaphysical consciousness'. Blanchot expressed a similar view, in an article published in *L'Arche* for September 1945, when he claimed that any novel of importance being written today 'offers us an image of our condition in its entirety and is an attempt to show its meaning or its lack of meaning'. This kind of statement, although based on very narrow aesthetic assumptions about what now constitutes an 'important' novel, has led to even broader assertions on behalf of fiction. A number of writers, including Malraux and Camus, see the novel—and indeed all art—as a way of rejecting the created universe by means of rebellion and replacement. In *L'Homme révolté* (1951) Camus argued that the novel can present us with 'an imaginary world created by "correcting" the real world' (p. 325). He added that man can endow himself, in fiction, with the very qualities and conditions he vainly seeks in daily life, so that the novel 'rivals creation and wins a provisional triumph over death' (p. 327).

*   *   *

So far I have emphasized two features, moral uncertainty combined with great ambition, which are common to most novels written at the highest level during this century. This is true to such a degree that reassurance, entertainment, or a direct 'imitation of life' have become increasingly associated, rightly or wrongly, with second-rate fiction. In France, however, exploration and ambition have taken a particular form in the last twenty-five years. Since the late 'thirties, especially, French novelists have attempted on many occasions and in a variety of ways to convey Blanchot's 'image of our condition in its entirety'. The assumption has been that this can be done, and that it should be done. As a result, the whole question of the relationship between philosophy and fiction has been a frequent topic of discussion.

Philosophy, in the strict meaning of the word, is usually regarded as something essentially distinct from art. A literary form, although it may embody the writer's 'philosophy' in the sense of his views about life, has seldom much to do with 'philosophy' as professional philosophers understand the term. Novels have traditionally been concerned with individual characters in relation to specific events. Particularity and action have been essential features of the world the novel discloses. A philosophical treatise, on the other hand, reveals a much more generalized and static world, a world of universality and contemplation. Where the novel emphasizes the world of appearances, the work of philosophy has usually been concerned, above all, with some unchanging reality beyond appearances. The novelist is praised when he captures the spontaneity of lived experience. The philosopher's success lies in a systematic presentation of his intellectual speculations. The novelist presents descriptively. The philosopher argues analytically.

This distinction between the presentation of experience by the novelist and its analysis by the philosopher explains the widespread critical resistance, so often justified, to 'metaphysical' fiction. The novel that really is a novel must contain elements which cannot be replaced, in their essentials, by a philosophical essay. This, I take it, is the meaning of Simone de Beauvoir's claim, in *L'Existentialisme et la sagesse des nations*, that 'the novel is only justified if it is a unique and irreducible means of communication' (p. 105). At the same time, the separation implied by most definitions of fiction and of philosophy has long proved irksome to certain novelists and philosophers alike. Apart from the metaphysical ambitions of various novelists, it is already clear in the nineteenth century that some philosophers, such as Kierkegaard and Nietzsche, were drawn to the creation of a literary vehicle in order to express their ideas adequately. There is increasing agreement now that to discuss Kierkegaard and Nietzsche as less serious philosophers than their contemporaries, or as *littérateurs manqués*, is to miss the point. It seems clear that they wrote as they did because of the nature of their philosophical outlook, because of what they had to say, and because of their discovery that it was impossible to work within the abstract, formalist limits of a thought which showed itself content to observe the laws governing its own exercise, with little or no reference to action or experience.

It is this broad movement away from formalism and abstraction, favoured in particular by certain continental philosophers, which has done much to encourage the steady convergence of literature and philosophy in France in recent years. The ambiguity of experience, and the alien nature of the world in its resistance to rational systematization, were ideas which forced themselves with growing insistence on the attention of writers who thought about the raw material of their novels. At the same time, although academic philosophy often clung to abstraction and seemed indifferent to actual human experience, phenomenology was preaching a return to more concrete thinking with Husserl's slogan: 'We want to get back to things-in-themselves.' One should add, however, that the phenomenologists eventually developed an idealist philosophy out of their realist ambitions, whereas writers such as Sartre, who was deeply influenced by his contact with the German phenomenologists, have done much to emphasize and preserve the original philosophical aim of a return to things as they are.

The consequences of this growing similarity of interests in philosophy and literature, and particularly among phenomenologists and novelists, were set out in 1945 by Maurice Merleau-Ponty in the *avant-propos* to his *Phénoménologie de la perception*. He writes: '... philosophy is not a reflection of some prior truth but is, like art, the direct embodiment of truth ... the only prior Logos being the world itself'. He adds: 'True philosophy is re-learning to look at the world, and in this sense a simple story can present the world to us with as much "depth" and meaning as would a philosophical treatise.' Merleau-Ponty also speaks of phenomenology as representing the will to grasp the meaning of the world directly, as it comes into being for the individual consciousness. This is clearly good sense in so far as experience *of* the world must precede any reliable formulation of thought *about* the world. And such a view governs the emphasis found in existentialist thought, and in the elements from Hegelianism and phenomenology it has chosen to stress, on the subjective, particular, temporal, and dramatic basis essential to an acceptable metaphysical system.

At this stage, of course, the argument has only advanced to a point where the claim is being made that philosophy and fiction have the same subject-matter once the philosopher turns from the contemplation of essences to the scrutiny of existence. The fact still remains that the methods by which the philosopher and the novelist examine existence differ markedly from one another. Nevertheless, these inevitably different methods may still strengthen the relationship between literature and philosophy in two ways. Firstly, the philosopher who rejects intellectual abstraction as his starting-point will find, in the direct expression of human experience which a certain kind of novel achieves, the only really satisfactory formulation, in words, of the initial stages of his own metaphysical thinking. He will tend to write in somewhat analogous terms himself, or at least he will develop his ideas from similar material. In the case of Sartre, who is both a trained philosopher and an imaginative writer, this kind of similarity exists between his philosophical writings and his novels and plays. A comparable degree of identity exists between the philosophy and the plays of Gabriel Marcel. In the first volume of his Gifford Lectures, *The Mystery of Being*, Marcel insists that the drama, as he conceives it, can 'place us at a point of vantage at which truth is made concrete to us, far above any level of abstract definitions' (p. 58). The imaginative dramatist in Marcel has several times offered this 'point of vantage' to Marcel the philosopher. Naturally, if this kind of identity between philosopher and novelist becomes too complete, the novelist ceases to be a novelist. Any literary work which can be replaced, without loss of content or form, by a philosophical essay, is not a work of art. A novel that simple transposes a fully formed ideology into fictional terms—always supposing this to be possible—is superfluous at the same time as it courts artistic death.

This leads to a second point. Although a novel can neither be identical with a work of philosophy nor an adequate substitute for it, it can carry out an imaginative or emotional exploration of a system of thought. It can attempt to see how the system appears to work in a given human situation. It may even be a way of trying to account for difficulties or contradictions that seem to escape rational explanation. This, after all, is what the psychological novel sometimes does. In theory, the psychological novel faces objections similar to those made against metaphysical fiction. It will be severely criticized if it turns out to be a mere illustration or transposition of some psychological system (e.g. the 'Freudian' novel, as distinct from the novel which shows a certain debt to Freud). But where fiction and psychology are concerned, objections are only made in individual cases, and not *a priori*, because psychology is not thought of as a thoroughly abstract idea placed at many removes from direct human experience. On the contrary, all human experience involves psychology in some form. But one may say with equal certainty that metaphysics, as conceived by Sartre, Simone de Beauvoir, Camus, and others, is inseparable from the experiences of human beings. It builds on this basis and can therefore be assimilated by art. And just as the psychological novelist can reveal psychological insights in his fiction, the philosophical novelist, of the kind discussed here, can reveal philosophical insights in his work. To this extent he offers his readers a measure of shared intellectual adventure.

This, I think, is the kind of relationship between metaphysics and fiction that determines the similarity already mentioned between Sartre's philosophical work and his novels and plays. But the similarity, striking though it is, only makes sense because of the difference persisting within it. It has to do with the *exploration* of philosophical ideas by imaginative writing, not their direct *illustration* in fiction. In the essay from *L'Existentialisme et la sagesse des nations* quoted earlier, Simone de Beauvoir makes much the same point. Drawing an analogy with science, which tests hypotheses against concrete realities, she suggests that the metaphysical novelist can conserve the imaginative and emotional elements in art by simply testing his philosophical hypotheses in the particularity of character and situation. The hypotheses may then give rise to problems or implications which the writer had not foreseen. In this way, as his novel develops, the novelist discovers 'truths whose appearance he did not recognize beforehand, questions to which he has no solution'. Consequently, 'he must ask new questions, take decisions, run risks; and thus, when he has completed his novel, he will view it with astonishment and will be unable to translate it into abstract terms since it will have taken on its own meaning and form in one single operation. The novel will then appear as genuine spiritual adventure' (pp. 111–12). This is precisely what the most successful French philosopher-novelists have done. Sartre's novel *La Nausée*, and his collection of short stories, *Le Mur*, are among the most successful examples of this determination to treat the writing of fiction as a cognitive activity.

One obvious result of this particular use of philosophy in fiction, and especially the use of phenomenology or related 'existential' systems of thought, has been to make several French novelists intellectually difficult or disconcerting for the reader. Often, their fundamental philosophical theories are present in their work by implication only. The ideas belong to the works of pure philosophy; certain consequences of these ideas are alone worked out in fictional form. And yet, one cannot really grasp the significance of these consequences without some knowledge of the theories from which they arise. It is here, I think, that we can see a major difference between the modern French metaphysical novelists and certain earlier novelists who presented a 'philosophy of life' in their fiction. In the latter case, the reading of such novels progressively revealed a philosophy which most readers shared and which they could normally understand. But with writers such as Sartre, Simone de Beauvoir, Camus, Blanchot, Beckett, the philosophical ideas which dictate the whole nature of their fiction are often absent from it, or quite alien to the reader, or both. In this way, a striking synthesis is achieved which preserves the strictness of the philosophy while not weakening the art by obtrusive didacticism, but it is a synthesis obtained at the reader's expense. The nature of this recent revolution in fiction was neatly expressed by Joseph Majault, despite his own opposition to it, when he wrote in 1946: 'Formerly, one began with the novel in order to discover the author's philosophy; now it is the philosophy which establishes and explains the characters, and even the very structure of the novel.'[2] No doubt this is one of the reasons why so many French novelists of the last twenty-five years not only receive, but manifestly require, a good deal of elucidation involving philosophical terms. The fact remains, of course, that their achievement as novelists must finally be judged in terms of literature, not metaphysics. But an evaluation of their art must rest, at some point, on a clear understanding of their philosophical ideas.

* * *

The invasion of the novel by metaphysics is no doubt the most striking single feature of French fiction during the last quarter-century. At the same time, however, this invasion has taken a variety of forms and had a number of subsidiary effects. In the case of Sartre and Simone de Beauvoir it has produced the kind of synthesis described above, but in writers such as Cayrol, Beckett, Blanchot, and Robbe-Grillet it has led to very different results. The novels of these four writers are dissimilar on many counts, but they have one characteristic in common. All of them are the novels of writers who, in different ways and to varying degrees, have turned their backs on the traditional procedures of character analysis. All are novels in which the human element is subject to severe pressures and at times almost totally absent. This tendency, already strongly marked in the strange world of the improbable charted by Blanchot, reaches a culminating point in the novels of Robbe-Grillet where a painstaking description of material things has largely ousted characters altogether. It is also a tendency, incidentally, which has its counterpart in much French poetry of the same period. In short, fiction in France since 1935 has turned steadily away from character analysis and turned increasingly towards the scrutiny of inanimate objects. There has been a progressive dehumanization of fiction which has often had complex links with the metaphysical ambitions of certain novelists. This trend has been so vigorous in itself and so varied in its effects that it must rank as a second major feature of French fiction during the period in question.

The rejection of the traditional forms of character analysis, a

[2] J. Majault, *Mauriac et l'art du roman* (Paris, Laffont, 1946), pp. 259–60.

rejection which gradually encouraged the surge of objects into fiction, is something that was already being occasionally discussed immediately after World War I. The feeling grew that the omniscient analysis of their heroes and heroines was a weakness in Balzac and Dickens, in Flaubert and Tolstoy. The great nineteenth-century novelists, with a few exceptions such as Dostoievsky, offered the reader a series of remarkably precise answers to the questions he was likely to ask about their characters. But the objection was increasingly made that we do not experience other people in this way. In daily life we lack an omniscient analyst. In fact, the 'realists' of the nineteenth-century novel were strikingly unrealistic in their assumption that human behaviour is clear-cut in a way that allows of systematic and predominantly rational explanation. About the time that such objections were being made to neatly motivated fictional characters further confirmation became available in the disturbing picture of human behaviour arrived at by analytical psychology. The emphasis was on disintegration and confusion—an emphasis reflected in the pioneering fiction of Joyce and more aggressively expressed in the theory and practice of Surrealism. In the beginning, the result for the novel was not the disappearance of character studies. But a note of uncertainty had entered in. Various aspects of the fictional characters of some writers tended more readily to dissolve into imprecision, or to collapse into unresolved contradictions. It is significant that within ten years of the completed publication of *A la recherche du temps perdu* critics were pointing out this new feature in Proust's characters as he presented them, after revision, in the later volumes of his novel.

Apart from certain psychological theories the widespread weakening of religious conviction, in France as elsewhere, made difficult any easy differentiation between good and evil and, ultimately, any satisfactory definition of human nature in general. This mood was doubtless intensified by the experiences of war and occupation. Shame and fear, heroism and collaboration, deportation and the moral ambiguities of resistance—all these experiences, together with the spectacle of a war spelt out in terms of Rotterdam, Warsaw, Auschwitz, Hiroshima, seemed to bring about a final exposure of traditional humanism. Severe blows were dealt to the French *moraliste* tradition and to assumptions about human perfectibility, the rational nature of man, the inevitability of progress. A new generation was growing up which had little patience with the ageing spokesmen of this tradition: Gide, Duhamel, Martin du Gard, Maurois. Attention turned inevitably to Malraux's query: 'Is there a human nature?' and to Sartre's assertion: 'Man is a useless passion' (however much this latter statement may have been misunderstood). Such a mood, especially among people with literary interests who reached maturity from the mid-'thirties onwards, was bound to prompt dissatisfaction with the assumptions lying behind character portrayal in most novels written before World War II. The attitudes of Bernanos and Malraux to these assumptions, attitudes that were exceptional among novelists already writing in the late 1920s and early 1930s, are among the features which most clearly make them founding fathers of post-Liberation French fiction.

* * *

Such was the prevalent mood, then, when the American novel entered France, close on the heels of the liberating armies, after 1944. For reasons that will shortly be discussed, the great popularity of certain American authors during the next few years was symptomatic of this mood. At the same time, the widespread attempts to write novels in the manner of Hemingway, Steinbeck, Caldwell, and others, or to adapt their fictional techniques in an effort to rejuvenate the French novel, shaped and intensified the mood itself.

Already during the Occupation American novels, in translation, passed with increasing frequency from hand to hand. Copies of *No Orchids for Miss Blandish*, which the French regarded as an American work,[3] appear to have existed in particular abundance. The reading of this book, while being close to a patriotic activity, no doubt also held quite other attractions for many

[3] See T. M. Smith and W. L. Miner, *Transatlantic Migration: the Contemporary American Novel in France* (Durham, North Carolina, Duke University Press, 1955), p. 37.

readers. For five or six years after the war the translation of American fiction, and particularly of works by Faulkner, Hemingway, Caldwell, Steinbeck, and Dos Passos, became a major industry. This is the great period, in French novel-writing, of trial and experiment based on American models. In *L'Étranger*, first published in 1942 but not widely known until 1945, Camus proved a forerunner in the use he made of devices borrowed from Hemingway and James M. Cain. In 1945, also, Sartre put his reading of Dos Passos to considerable effect in *Le Sursis*. Many other novels soon appeared embodying *le style américain* in one sense or other of that very elastic term. Among the most successful later examples were Merle's *Week-end à Zuydcoote* (1949) and Arnaud's *Le Salaire de la peur* (1950).

The discovery of certain American writers seemed to confirm many French intellectuals in the view that their pre-war novel had become artificial and lifeless through excessive refinement and analysis. They admired the absence of intellectual complication in much American fiction, with its directness and roughness. Here were novels in which characters defined themselves, and learned to know themselves, through action rather than thought. Soon similar heroes of active, mindless virility began to appear in many French novels. Georges Arnaud's description of his own fictional characters, in the *avertissement* to *Le Salaire de la peur*, is typical of a widespread attitude:

They refuse to think; they take no interest in their souls. For them, the intelligent man is the man who shoots at the right moment. Sensibility can take its seat behind the steering-wheel of a truck. There is, after all, a lyricism of the prospector's pick and wash-trough. With their feet on the ground, under a tropical sun, they live a virile, trivial existence like figures in a shadow-theatre. They have exposed the naked reality existing beneath what is falsely picturesque. . . .

In this novel the dominant emotions are fear, anger, greed, obstinacy, indifference to human life. But the characters are not articulate about their emotions. They wage a fiercely silent battle against natural obstacles and hazards. The severe restraints placed on analysis are suggested by the author's pithy explanation of one of the characters—an explanation repeated in similar terms about the others—which consists of the simple statement: 'That's how it is. He's like that.'

The main subject of *Le Salaire de la peur* is the driving of two trucks, laden with nitroglycerine, along rough, inadequate tracks through wild and hilly country in Guatemala. The tropical heat, or a heavy jolt due to the unevenness of the terrain, could equally well cause disaster. The first truck does in fact blow up, leaving no trace of itself or its occupants. The only evidence of its passage is a huge crater caused by the explosion. The second truck arrives at the edge of this crater and its two occupants, Gérard and Johnny, get out to survey the scene. Their reaction is characteristically dismissed in fourteen words: ' "Ah well! . . .", said Gérard with a sigh. The time for funeral orations was past.' What we have throughout this novel, in fact, is a behaviourist picture of essentially pragmatic characters. I say 'behaviourist' because action or behaviour, presented as automatic responses to situations, are described to the exclusion of ideas and values. And the characters are 'pragmatic' in the sense that all their attention and energy are focused on the solution of immediate, practical problems. Each is a pragmatist in the sense in which William James defined the term:

A pragmatist . . . turns away from abstraction and insufficiency, from verbal solutions, from bad *a priori* reasons, from fixed principles, closed systems, and pretended absolutes and origins. He turns towards concreteness and adequacy, towards facts, towards action and towards power.[4]

For novelists such as Arnaud and Merle, this approach to character portrayal is prompted more by psychological than by philosophical considerations. Perhaps it was also influenced by literary fashion. But it is clear that such a method of rejecting 'bad *a priori* reasons', 'fixed principles', and 'pretended absolutes' pointed in the same direction as that envisaged by more metaphysically-minded writers. It could provide a useful starting-point in concreteness, and a certain style of action, for their own kind of investigation. One of the clearest examples of such fusion

---

[4] William James, *Pragmatism* (London, Longmans, Green, 1907), p. 51.

between existential philosophical aims and American behaviourist techniques is to be found in Camus's exploration of nihilism, through the character of Meursault, in *L'Étranger*.

The meaninglessness, for Meursault, of many moral and social values is reinforced, for the reader, by Camus's portrayal of him in behaviourist terms. Meursault's actions are simple enough. He attends his mother's funeral; he goes bathing with Marie and takes her to the cinema; he writes a letter for a friend; he shoots an Arab in a moment of panic. But he is unaware, during these actions, of the outrage to moral decency and spiritual values which the public prosecutor will find in each of them. He eventually appreciates, with his mind, the interrelations which the court sees as giving a pattern to his actions, and the interpretations which it employs to expose the guilt of his behaviour. But he himself has experienced no such guilt, has been unaware of ethical imperatives or spiritual absolutes, and their significance for him as an individual remains beyond his moral grasp. The analysis of his 'criminal mentality' by the public prosecutor is entirely alien to his own subjective experience. In short, the claim that events conform to a superior spiritual necessity, or that they can be related to a neatly motivated psychology of character, is presented as a delusion. Individual experience, not abstract principle, is the proper starting-point. This use of behaviourist description to emphasize moral and philosophical scepticism is supported further by the technique Camus uses as his narrative style. Drawing on Hemingway, on his own admission, he simplifies vocabulary and fragmentates syntax in a way that reflects, formally, his unwillingness to accept moral patterns and the conventional view of character analysis.

*   *   *

These behaviourist accounts of character are only one form of the general attack on nineteenth-century methods of portraying heroes in fiction. It should be noted, too, that the humanity of the behaviourist character remains intact even if it receives little emphasis and although we may not easily find a place for such a character within the conventional categories of literary portrayal.

From a different standpoint, however, Maurice Blanchot carries dehumanization much further. He does so in strange, abstract myths which put his work in a class by itself. A novel such as *Thomas l'obscur* (1950), for example, creates its disturbing world of fantasy, in part at least, by a deliberate rejection of most of the elements which the novelist has traditionally held to be essential to his art. And Blanchot's characters, which appear to have the shape of human beings but lack all human substance, are to be explained in philosophical rather than psychological terms. This gives them an intentionally abstract, non-human air—the result of Blanchot's complex literary and philosophical theories.

Raymond Queneau is another unusual writer of the period whose novels, unique and distinctive though they be, not only show the marks of philological and philosophical preoccupation, but have connexions with more general trends in recent French fiction. It would be a mistake, I think, to treat with too much solemnity Queneau's amused contemplation of the absurdity of existence in several of his novels. Nevertheless, in *Pierrot mon ami* (1943), for example, the amusement park in which the novel is set most certainly becomes an image of that frantic nullity which Queneau finds in human life at large. Again, the main character recalls Camus's outsider, Meursault, because of his double alienation both from himself and in the world. But Queneau has also contributed, in certain ways, to the attack on traditional methods of characterization in fiction. He has done so not only by means of satire but by his occasional attempt to convey what might be called a 'primordial vision' of people and objects *before* they have been transformed, by the onlooker's mind or the novelist's pen, into dramas and networks of meaning.

It would be foolish to try to demonstrate more common ground than actually exists between such different writers as Sartre, Camus, Blanchot, Queneau, Arnaud, and Merle. Yet all are, in their way, representatives of what Nathalie Sarraute has called 'the age of suspicion'.[5] That is to say all of them suspect many elements in the traditional picture of human nature and hence

---

[5] See Nathalie Sarraute, *L'Ère du soupçon* (Paris, Gallimard, 1956), esp. pp. 55–77.

they suspect the kind of hero who dominated the prose literature of the nineteenth century. In varying degrees, however, all these writers also show a particular interest in the material objects around them. In their novels such objects often come to the forefront and threaten to displace the characters. Sartre's *La Nausée* is no doubt the most striking example of this tendency. In this novel he not only stresses the alien, contingent nature of a tree-root or a tram-seat in accordance with his philosophical ideas; there are also occasions when he directs the reader's attention to certain objects for their own sake, without any apparent philosophical *parti pris*. A typical example is offered by the remarkable description of paper litter, trampled by feet and soaked by rain, in a public park (*La Nausée*, pp. 22–23). This non-human 'otherness' of the material world (a main feature of Roquentin's experience in *La Nausée*) is also emphasized by Camus. In *Le Mythe de Sisyphe*, as in other essays, Camus speaks of the 'density' and the 'alien nature' of the world. To appraise our situation realistically will be 'to perceive that the world is "opaque", to sense to what extent a stone is alien and irreducible to our understanding and with what intensity nature or a landscape can negate us' (pp. 28, 29). In recent years this 'negation' of human beings by objects has become a major theme of French poetry and fiction alike.

The balance between people and things is sometimes a very precarious one in the novels of Beckett and Cayrol. Both these writers, unlike Sartre and Camus, use many of the resources of literary portraiture precisely to create characters who are distinctly sub-human. Many of their characters live on the very fringe of existence. Beckett and Cayrol have both been haunted by the *clochard*, the tramp, who lives outside the law and outside society. Sometimes their main characters even seem to exist outside life itself. They haunt a kind of limbo which seems to represent the world we know, but after it has collapsed in ruins. In the first volume—*On vous parle* (1947)—of Cayrol's trilogy, *Je vivrai l'amour des autres*, the depersonalized hero of the title is described as follows on the second page:

He finishes the left-overs of your life. He nibbles. . . . He prowls round houses, round cafés, round women; he does so to smell out what he thinks to be life; it's so pleasant to sleep as close to life as possible, by her side, in case she should call. One never knows.

A few pages later various objects begin to make their appearance in the novel and most of them receive careful description by the anonymous narrator: a pair of socks, full of holes and lying on the floor under his bed; a second-hand jacket bought for best wear for 100 francs, &c. The beds, the clothes, the whole physical environment of Beckett's and Cayrol's characters are described in such a way that they contribute much to a feverish, inhuman vision of the world. There are even moments when it is the objects that appear almost human, whereas the human beings are depressed to the status of things.

What I have been saying in the last few pages amounts, then, to this. Since the last war especially, the tradition of literary character analysis has been widely discredited in France. At first this tradition was replaced by the violent, anti-intellectual and consciously non-literary heroes of novels claiming American fiction as their model. These mindless, pragmatic heroes, in their turn, made easier both discussion and acceptance by the reading public of other characters lacking psychological depth but created for much more subtle intellectual purposes. (I am bound to add, in parenthesis, that French writers and critics—characteristically enough—have usually taken their anti-intellectualism very intellectually just as they have often been highly intelligent in their presentation of mindlessness.) In both the 'tough' and the 'metaphysical' novels, however, material objects seem to have occupied the scene more and more as the portrayal of character has become increasingly abstract and non-psychological. The hard, laconic heroes of Arnaud, for example, fulfil themselves by the conquest of material things. These become transformed from obstacles to achievement into objects of achievement. On the other hand, in the case of such writers as Sartre, Camus, Cayrol, and Beckett, the alien, self-sufficient nature of objects is stressed in order to emphasize man's metaphysical predicament in the modern world. In this case material things prevent human fulfilment and act rather as the catalysts of mental anguish or spiritual tragedy.

The reasons for this increasing 'reification' of experience, as it were, are not easy to pin down or define. No doubt different writers have been prompted by different considerations. For some there has been the desire to replace what they regard as an illusory world of meanings by a more solid, verifiable world of material objects. For others, like Sartre, more systematic philosophical reasons are involved—reasons connected with distinctive views about the nature of imagination and of sense-perception. Thirdly, there is little doubt that many novelists have had their vision of the physical world renewed by photography and the cinema, which can reveal in such a striking way aesthetically exciting aspects of familiar objects. With a few writers, too, the aim has been to achieve, in fiction, something roughly equivalent to the revolutionary change from representation to abstraction which has come about in art.

One further reason has been suggested by the novelist Alain Robbe-Grillet. The nineteenth-century novel of Balzac and Flaubert, he says, was built around character and plot because it could still be related to a coherent social order—the commercial, bourgeois society of nineteenth-century France. Robbe-Grillet admits that we continue to live in this kind of society but, he adds, so many things have happened in the last fifty years that we no longer 'believe' in such a society and no longer accept its values. Now if this is so, we can also no longer believe in characters reflecting the nature and standards of such a society. This, says Robbe-Grillet, is why characters in the nineteenth-century sense are disappearing from the work of the more thoughtful and sophisticated novelists of today. Since plot is the outcome of the characters' ideas and reactions, plot also is disappearing rapidly. Therefore, Robbe-Grillet concludes, with that insouciant formalism so typical of a certain kind of French intellectual, with character and plot largely gone we are inevitably left with objects.

*   *   *

With Robbe-Grillet, and to a lesser degree with Michel Butor, material objects dominate the novel with an insistence unequalled by any of the writers mentioned previously. But these objects are also seen in a special way. For Robbe-Grillet, they are neither a challenge to our manliness nor a negation of our humanity; they are simply and solely what one critic has called 'an optical resistance'. As a result they are described, essentially, as they present themselves to our sight. Their surfaces are delineated. Anthropomorphism is (almost always) avoided. What we have is a painstaking topography of things. Furthermore, in accordance with this attitude to material objects, Robbe-Grillet is at pains to avoid analogy and metaphor. The adjectives which he uses are predominantly spatial, visual, and situational. This, of course, is a major way in which he differs from the nineteenth-century realists and naturalists, as well as from contemporary novelists like Sartre and Cayrol. In his work objects do not have personalities. They are not animated, humanized. They are neither indices of status nor symbols of something mysterious and profound that is accessible through them and beyond them. Objects are simply *there*; this is all there is to say about them. They are 'opaque'. They are not mirrors endlessly reflecting man's own image. Objects are *matter* and *form* (a mountain or a seagull) and sometimes *use* (a coffee-pot or the street-plan of a town). But they possess no hidden depths and have no personality of their own. Consequently, the novelist can only represent them properly by a visual description of their surface aspects.

The following passage from *Le Voyeur* (1955) is a typical piece of writing by Robbe-Grillet and contains the features I have just been describing:

The scene is lit by a petrol lamp placed in the middle of a long table made of dark brown wood. In addition, standing on this same table between the lamp and the window, are two white plates placed side by side, just touching, and an unopened litre-size bottle whose dark-tinted glass makes it impossible to discover the colour of the liquid inside it. The remainder of the table is clear except for a few shadows cast on it: that of the bottle, huge and deformed, a crescent-shaped shadow emphasizing the edge of the plate nearest the window, a broad, dark smudge surrounding the base of the lamp.

Behind the table, in the right-hand corner of the room (the furthest corner) the large kitchen stove against the back wall is visible only because of the orange glow from its partly open ash-pan.

Two people stand facing one another: Jean Robin—called Pierre—and the very young, unidentified woman who is much smaller than the man. Both are on the far side of the table (in relation to the window), he on the left—that is to say, in front of the window—she at the opposite end of the table, near the stove.

Between them and the table—occupying the entire length of the latter but hidden from sight by it—is a bench. The whole of the room is thus divided into a network of parallel elements: firstly, the back wall against which we have, to the right, the stove and then some wooden boxes and, to the left, an unimportant piece of furniture in the shadow; secondly, at an indefinite distance from this wall, the sharply demarcated line of the man and the woman; after this, coming forward all the time, the unseen bench, the main axis of the rectangular table—which passes through the petrol lamp and the opaque bottle—and finally the plane of the window itself.

If we re-divide this network by perpendicular lines we meet successively from front to back: the central upright of the window, the crescent-shaped shadow of the second plate, the bottle, the man (Jean Robin, or Pierre), a box placed on its end on the floor; then, one metre to the right, the lit petrol lamp; about one metre further along: the end of the table, the very young woman whose identity is unknown, the left-hand side of the stove (*Le Voyeur*, pp. 223-4).

This passage exemplifies what I have said about Robbe-Grillet's painstaking topography. His description plays over the surface of the objects he sees and emphasizes their form and spatial relationships. It resembles the account a painter might give of the purely compositional qualities of a picture. But Robbe-Grillet also claims to use this descriptive method as a way of refuting tragedy.[6] Tragedy, he says, for writers like Malraux, Sartre, and Camus, lies in a disturbing separation, a cleavage, between man and the world. Camus speaks of 'the primitive (or natural) hostility of the world' (*Le Mythe de Sisyphe*, p. 28) and this same experience fills Sartre's Roquentin with anguish and nausea. For Robbe-Grillet, however, such reactions are simply the result of foolish imagining. There is, in reality, no heart-rending separation between man and the world. There is only distance, a distance which can be measured and which it is self-deluding masochism

---

[6] One of the Robbe-Grillet's clearest accounts of his own intentions is to be found in his article, 'Old "Values" and the New Novel', *London Magazine*, VI, 2 (February 1959), pp. 32-49.

to treat in sentimental or dramatic terms. This means, then, that part of Robbe-Grillet's philosophical intention as a novelist is to refute a conception of tragedy which finds particularly strong expression in existentialist writing. He seems to be saying something which has affinities with the assertion of the poet, Francis Ponge:

> Bien entendu le monde est absurde! Bien entendu la non-signification du monde!
> Mais qu'y-a-t-il là de tragique?
> J'ôterai volontiers à l'absurde son coefficient de tragique.

The novels of Robbe-Grillet represent the most radical experiment made in fiction during the last twenty-five years. By the same token, however, they also seem to demand a thorough revision of the critical standards which we normally invoke when assessing a novelist's work. But do they *merit* this revision which they apparently *demand*? How far can we hope to interpret novels which seem designed to make interpretation superfluous or impossible? Have they really conquered new fields for fiction? Do they represent that genuine response to the ideas and circumstances of our age which Robbe-Grillet has claimed for them? Answers to questions such as these are given in the final essay of this book. I shall do no more, at this point, than end with a brief comment on some difficulties which seem inseparable from Robbe-Grillet's own position.

To begin with, it is unrealistic to claim, where any description in a novel is concerned, that it is entirely detached and has eliminated all 'meaning' from the object described. There must be choice, and therefore a subjective element, in the author's decision to examine one object rather than another, however remote and austere the examination itself may be. Some principle of selection operates even when this decision is not a conscious one. We may well wonder, for example, in the passage quoted above, why a lamp, a bottle, and two plates stand on the table rather than a coffee-pot, a loaf, and a cup and saucer. The question may seem trivial in this particular instance but it should remind us that more important and revealing examples exist. These show some kind of prior bond between the author and the objects which he singles out, among so many possibilities, for detailed description.

Again, it is impossible to write a description that remains strictly confined, from the reader's viewpoint, to the surface of an object. For example, if one were to speak of an 'automat sandwich' this adjective, though in no way anthropomorphic, would immediately set up associations in the reader's mind and these associations would range far beyond the 'topography' of the object. The word 'automat' will suggest to one person the problem of getting a satisfactory meal quickly; to another, the stresses of modern city life; to another, Horn and Hardart automats in New York, and so on. It is true that such associations may have formed no part of the novelist's own intention while writing. But so long as his novels are read these associations will arise unless all his readers suffer from chronic amnesia or have undergone prefrontal leucotomies. Words cannot provide that severely visual medium which Robbe-Grillet's descriptive ambitions require and which can indeed be more readily found in the materials of the sculptor or painter.

Finally, I think there is some substance in the complaint that Robbe-Grillet's novels, in rejecting the established attitudes and methods of fiction, have also turned away from most of the gains made by fiction in the last two hundred years or more. A notable aspect of the history of the novel during this period has been its progressive expansion, into such different areas of experience as morals, psychology, history, sociology, philosophy, &c. In doing so it has fashioned and refined an impressive armoury of weapons; yet Robbe-Grillet, instead of choosing and adapting these weapons to meet the demands of new battles, has thrown his weapons away and gone into the battle unarmed. The result is an interesting impoverishment of literature, but nevertheless an impoverishment. In the end, however, even this action testifies to the liveliness and adaptability of fiction in France. The death of the novel has been confidently proclaimed, over and over again, by the theorists. A glance at French fiction during the last twenty-five years shows this assertion to be as false today as it was in the eighteenth and nineteenth centuries.

PRECURSORS

GEORGES BERNANOS
1888-1948

BY ERNEST BEAUMONT

───────✯───────

IN relation to certain developments in French literature during the last thirty years or so, Bernanos, whose imaginative writing was mainly confined to the decade preceding the outbreak of war, occupies an ambivalent position. The emphasis on the human quandary and on the unsatisfactoriness of the world as we find it; the desire to strip man bare of the false accretions of the past, of traditional values that have become hollow; the need to start metaphysically afresh; all this indeed characterizes the work of Bernanos as it does that of later writers. His contempt for conformity is as savage as one could wish and his sympathy with man's 'revolt' might seem to secure for him a cousinship with Camus, whose ideal of integrity he undoubtedly anticipated. Yet the freshness of vision, the denunciation of mediocrity and of pharisaism, the starkness of expression, all of which relate him quite closely to these later writers, are associated with an ontological view strikingly at variance with that of any other writer of these times. It is fundamentally his revolutionary attitude which links him with later generations; but it is the very dynamic of this revolutionariness which most marks him apart. His revolutionariness is in fact two thousand years old; the centre of his work is the Person of Christ. This is so surprising a fact, particularly to those who do not accept the Incarnation, that the full meaning and force of his work have not always been well understood. Undoubtedly, to some critics in the immediate post-war period Bernanos seemed to have a closer affinity with writers such as Sartre than he would appear in fact to have, now that sufficient time has elapsed for us to ponder his work.

What distinguishes Bernanos as a Christian novelist is his espousal of the consequences of belief. He takes the Gospel seriously. This is always revolutionary, at whatever period it occurs, and that is why, in a study of modern writers of philosophical import, Bernanos, though perhaps ill at ease, is not out of place. No one has stripped man more naked or looked at the world with more childlike eyes, with less spirit of compromise. When he wrote that his idea of justice was that of the humblest peasant taking the sermons he heard at Mass seriously (*Les Enfants humiliés*, pp. 213-14), this was no paradox; and when he spoke of the effeminate fear some people had of the Blood of the Cross,[1] this meant that he had himself drawn the necessary deductions from that shedding of blood. This was the living fact always before him, the life-blood of his books. There is not perhaps any other novelist of whom this can be so confidently affirmed.

As much as for Sartre, freedom is a predominant consideration for Bernanos, though between the Sartrian and Bernanosian conceptions of freedom there is hardly even a point of contact. For Bernanos freedom is essentially liberation from the grip of Satan. At first he seems to have envisaged the writing of novels as an act of liberation for himself, a means of cleansing his mind of his compulsive thoughts. The last words of his short story, 'Madame Dargent' (1922), a ferocious portrayal of the writer's responsibility towards those who model themselves on his fictional characters, inform us that 'more than one murderous image from which the writer frees himself still stirs in a book ten centuries later' (*Dialogues d'ombres*, p. 33). The same idea, with the emphasis on the liberating aspect, recurs in a letter written three years later, in 1925, where Bernanos tells another young writer that the book which will free him will be one where he will slaughter himself without mercy.[2] Yet, though he clearly carried out his own advice, he eventually realized that the writing of books had no effective cathartic value for him. One

---

[1] See *Essais et témoignages réunis par Albert Béguin* (Neuchâtel, La Baconnière, Paris, Seuil, 1949), p. 40.
[2] Quoted in Albert Béguin's *Bernanos par lui-même* (Paris, Seuil, 1954), p. 152.

of the characters through whom he pilloried himself most savagely, Ganse, in *Un mauvais rêve* (written 1935; publ. 1950), confesses that literature frees nobody and that moreover no one can free himself (p. 84). Freedom is to be achieved at much greater cost than the writing of books, exacting and excruciating as this high vocation was for Bernanos himself; it is to be achieved in the issues of life itself, by what means it will presently be seen.

In a newspaper article Bernanos wrote that a real novelist is one who dreams his books or else draws most of his situations and characters out of a fund of subconscious experience, the store of what he called 'the precious, irreplaceable and incommunicable experience of childhood which the crisis of adolescence almost always pushes back into the night . . .'.[3] Elsewhere he affirmed that he wrote in order to justify himself in the eyes of the child that he had been (*Les Enfants humiliés*, p. 195). His work, then, may be seen from one angle as an attempted return to the childhood vision, not through the nostalgic recapitulation of a Proust, but through the confrontation of corrupt adulthood, man in the multifold disguises he adopts, with the purity and simplicity of the childhood vision enduring, by some miracle of Grace, into adult life. Freedom can in fact be achieved only through this confrontation. In almost every work of Bernanos we find the childlike 'saint', be he priest or, as in *La Joie* (1929), a young woman, who 'frees' from their burden of sin his or her enslaved associates. It is not, however, a simple matter of dispersion, but an agonizing process of Exchange and Substitution.

The novels that Bernanos wrote were not the skilful constructions of a craftsman, still less the technical experiments of a juggler with words; nor was he the conscious inventor of new moods and untried perspectives. His novels are purely and simply the objectification of his inner life, the personalization of his hopes and fears, his temptations and aspirations, albeit in a profound transmutation. He did not pose or try to solve problems, for he did not envisage life in terms of problems; it was for him a great mysterious adventure, in which all of his faculties were

---

[3] Quoted by Hans Urs von Balthasar, *Le Chrétien Bernanos* (Paris, Seuil, 1956), p. 365.

engaged, the outcome of which was his eternal destiny. Death, which, like most of us, he greatly feared, was in a sense his guiding thought. We know from a letter that he wrote to one of his teachers at Bourges Seminary that at the time of his First Communion he decided that his aim would be to make, not his life, but his death, happy. Consequently, he considered it logical to live and die for God. In that way, he wrote, he would no longer be afraid of this awful death . . . (*Essais et témoignages*, p. 19). The making of God the centre of his life was his way of facing the fear of death, his preparation for the eventual contingency. This fear is given much prominence in his work. There are no edifying deaths. Abbé Chevance does not want to die and has to be helped by Chantal's gift of her joy (*L'Imposture*, p. 315). When the parish priest of Ambricourt dies, 'thick drops of sweat dripped from his forehead and his cheeks, and his eyes, scarcely visible between his half-closed brows, seemed to express great anguish' (*Journal d'un curé de campagne*, p. 365). Least edifying of all, the death of the old prioress, in *Dialogues des Carmélites* (written 1948; publ. 1949), is a scandal to the community, who do not realize she has assumed Blanche's fear, so enabling the latter in her turn to face the death of the scaffold. Like all else, however, the fear of death only acquires its full meaning and justification in the context of the Agony in the Garden. We are reminded in this same play that, unlike many martyrs and also brigands, Christ was afraid of death (p. 158), and Chantal remembers, in *La Joie*, that Abbé Chevance said of fear that it was the daughter of God, redeemed on the eve of Good Friday (p. 237).

A writer's work, wrote Bernanos in 1939, is his life itself, 'transfigured, made more luminous, reconciled' (*Essais et témoignages*, p. 50). He did not claim to resemble his Country Priest, Abbé Donissan, or Chantal, but at least he asserted that his life did not give the lie to his books; his life, he said, was silent (*Les Enfants humiliés*, p. 208). From his inner life, his life of aspiration and prayer, these fictional characters of his nevertheless draw their sustenance. It is irrelevant to his ability as a writer that he went daily to Mass, weekly to Confession, that he recited the Rosary every day, Compline every evening, but it is not irrelevant to the particular quality that his writing has. It goes without saying that this admirer of the unfashionable Balzac had the power vividly to portray the characters he conjured up from his own spiritual turmoil; otherwise he would not be worth our study. What gives him his importance as a writer, however, is the fidelity with which his fictional universe reflects the life of his spirit, so that, in spite of the occasional melodrama, an atmosphere of almost unbearable authenticity infuses his work. Because it is so faithful a mirror of one man's inner life, we can all see ourselves in it in our potentiality, since we share the same fundamental nature; hence its disturbing impact. The introductory poem to *Les Fleurs du mal*, with its crowning image of Tedium, shedding an involuntary tear as, smoking his hookah, he dreams of executions, a figure in whom Baudelaire expressly invites us to see ourselves, could well stand as epigraph to the darker portrayals of the fictional world of Bernanos. But, unlike the poet, this novelist can reveal the other facet of man's nature in positive fashion, attempt the depiction of the life of Grace with such a degree of plausibility that it cannot lightly be dismissed. His work is all the more disquieting, therefore, to the guilty conscience that we all have, in that it presents this *dual* vision—in which we can measure the full extent of our failure—man in his unforfeited purity and simplicity and man in his various subterfuges and deceits, with his shameful secrets, the fabrications he has woven to cover up his disillusionment, his degradation.

The vision is undoubtedly harsh. How hard was the light that he shed Bernanos did not himself realize till his last years. Writing in *Les Enfants humiliés* (written 1940; publ. 1949) of this interior life that he projected into novels, he affirmed that he could not judge it, as he could not see it from outside. He lived in it like a child in a garden:

But this garden is like all gardens, except that the light is no doubt somewhat harsher than elsewhere, a peculiarity I was not aware of before, but which is clear to me today because, through age and weariness, I have at last come to realize that I have less enjoyed that light than aced it, overcome it, stood up to it (p. 206).

In these later mellower years he came, too, to accept mediocrity, as he came to accept everything else, even claiming in *Les Enfants humiliés* that he could no longer be fully distinguished from the common herd (p. 179), that common herd which, in the earlier novels, is given such short shrift. Indeed, as he wrote in this same work, he had 'dreamed of saints and heroes, neglecting the intermediate forms of our species', and he observed that these intermediate forms hardly existed, that only saints and heroes counted. They would not even deserve a name, did not saints and heroes give them one, their name as men. In short, he concluded, 'it is only through the saints and heroes that I am; they have sated me with dreams, preserved me from illusions' (p. 199). The scorn with which the mediocre are treated is the scorn that the novelist felt for the mediocre in himself. We see ourselves in others and all the objects on which our hatred fixes are the visible manifestations of what is detestable in ourselves. All hatred is self-hatred. All revolt is revolt against the self. The spiritual odyssey, for Bernanos, is the journey towards acceptance, which is fundamentally acceptance of the self.

All the great sinners in the novels of Bernanos are consumed with self-hatred, the consequence of the falsehood in which they are enmeshed, their failure to be themselves, the disillusionment in childhood or adolescence which opened the way to sin and even crime. When Germaine Malorthy declares to her second lover—she has killed the first—that she knows he hates her, she adds: 'Less than I do myself' (*Sous le soleil de Satan*, p. 57). In *L'Imposture* (1927) Guérou tells Pernichon that all goes well till the day when you hate yourself. 'For, my boy, I ask you: to hate your own species in yourself, isn't that hell?' (p. 183.) Whether you hate yourself in others or the whole human race in yourself, the hatred is the same. It is the converse of the Gospel command. Both love and hatred affirm the solidarity of the self with the whole human race, but hatred involves the desire of extinction, of the self in suicide, of others in murder. For Bernanos murder is a form of suicide, the objectification of self-hatred. With that insight which holiness supernaturally confers on Bernanosian 'saints', Chantal de Clergerie tells the Russian chauffeur Fiodor that she knows that he hates his soul and would kill it if he could (*La Joie*, p. 26). What in fact he ultimately does is to kill her, the visible vehicle of Grace, the disturbing witness to God's activity, and then kill himself. In *Un mauvais rêve* Mme Alfieri's murder of the old woman is a crime she commits against herself:

> She herself was the real victim. The secret revolt of her life of failure, the hatred slowly maturing in the course of those ten years of poverty, humiliations, self-doubt, the terrible work of her imagination inflamed by her favourite drug and which Ganse's dark genius skilfully exasperated to the point of hallucination, delirium even, all that had to end in crime, all that was in fact already crime (p. 219).

The criminal act is indeed only a symptom, the symptom of a possession that has long since taken place. It may, however, also be a means of achieving freedom, the last desperate means left when all else fails to free. Thus Mme Alfieri, having committed the murder which expresses the hatred of herself which has invaded her from childhood, filled with euphoria at the actualized deed, is ready to load her guilty secret on to the shoulders of the priest encountered with apparent fortuitousness.

Bernanos portrays, for the most part, only saints and heroes because, in the cosmic issue between God and Satan which is fought out in the souls of men, only they play any part. The mediocre are of no concern to Satan, for they already unconsciously further his interests. Their salvation depends on the freedom that is achieved for them by the merits of the saints. In this desperate struggle, which is how Bernanos envisages the human condition, the focus of attention is necessarily the man or woman whose awareness of the issue is carried to the highest point or whose natural nobility of soul or moral grandeur makes him an object of attraction for the Devil, who seeks to secure only those who are worth enlisting in his revolt, those whose powers are greatest and whose influence is most far-reaching. In each novel we have, therefore, either a saintly or a satanic figure, sometimes both, together with a group of lesser beings on whom their activity is exercised. The activity of the 'saint', however, expressly consists in freeing those who are enclosed in their hatred, in wresting from them the sinful secret on which their pride feeds, in a word, in freeing them from their possession by Satan, a possession which is quite unconscious. For the most part they are victims, the victims of illusions, of falsehoods, of an image of themselves which has no substance, no reality. In possession the person is of no consequence to the Devil, he is only the momentary embodiment of an evil design, the passive agent through whom Satan acts. The saint is also a victim, but in quite a different way. He is a victim, in the sense in which Christ Himself was a victim, in that He sacrificed Himself on behalf of all mankind, assumed their sins, which He expiated by His Passion. To achieve this, Christ Himself had to go against His own human nature, suffering the fear of death in the Garden of Olives and the sense of dereliction on the Cross. He also suffered the temptations of the Devil and betrayal at the hands of Judas. To this divine pattern of human experience the Bernanosian saint finds that his life willy-nilly conforms—with some variation of emphasis from one novel to another. Though it is through Grace that he is enabled to share in the redemptive role, he is called upon to accept the burden placed upon him, to continue to face the challenge, to smother all revolt, not to give in to despair. The role of the saint, therefore, is altogether more active than that of the possessed, the latter term itself suggesting the very passivity of the condition. Indeed, the only real activity is that undertaken by the saint. Thus, rampant as evil is in the novels of Bernanos, especially in such novels as *Un mauvais rêve* and *Monsieur Ouine* (1946), it has no positive force of its own but resembles, to use a favourite metaphor of the author's, a cancerous growth. The charge of Manicheism which has been made against Bernanos can only derive from a misunderstanding of his demonology.

Despite the inroad of Satan in the world of man, human solidarity remains. Indeed, sin itself ensures our solidarity, since no one may escape it. As Chantal says in *La Joie*: 'As for sin, we are all in it, some to enjoy it, others to suffer from it, but in the long run it's the same bread we break by the fountain's edge, swallowing our spittle, the same disgust' (p. 230). She herself, unspoilt by the world, faithful to the childhood vision, recognizes that she is one with the family which has borne her, sharing characteristics with her weak mediocre father and her avid self-deceiving grandmother. In the latter's cheeks she sees the dimples that are in her own and tells her: 'Look, Mamma, I have just discovered something I have known a long time. To be sure, we no more escape from one another than from God. All we have in common is sin' (p. 138). On every sinner the pressure of inherited taints weighs heavily. When Abbé Donissan sees with his supernaturally acquired lucidity the soul of Germaine Malorthy as it is, he sees too that each of her acts is the sign of those from whom she issues, cowards, misers, lechers, and liars. 'It is true', he says to her, 'that I have seen you in them and them in you' (*Sous le soleil de Satan*, p. 208). The father of Abbé Cénabre, through whom Bernanos makes his most probing analysis of diabolical possession, was alcoholic and died young (*L'Imposture*, p. 79). The Evangeline of *Un Crime*, leading the most mendacious of all the false lives fabricated for themselves by Bernanos's heroines, if also the least plausible, is the illegitimate offspring of an ex-nun and probably of a priest, an ancestry which perhaps shows how strongly Bernanos was marked by his reading of Barbey d'Aurevilly. Even the Country Priest has to contend with a constitution handed down to him by alcoholic ancestors, but he knows that, despite his inherited taints, he has sufficient freedom as a human being to give it back to God (*Journal d'un curé de campagne*, p. 327). In the sinners around him, however, he sees the probable victims of a vitiated heredity.

There is a more mystical sense, a more important sense, than the inheritance of degrading propensities, in which human solidarity operates. This is through the Catholic belief in the reversibility of merits, the redemptive value of vicarious suffering. This notion that one person can suffer on behalf of another, expiate the sins committed by others, is of course the extension to the whole Mystical Body of Christ, which is how Catholics view the Church, of the Atonement. As Christ suffered death in expiation of the sins of humanity as a whole, so can the Christian, in voluntary privation and mortification, in self-sacrifice, acquire merits which have a redemptive value for others less spiritually favoured. This belief is in fact the basis of monastic life. In

French literature it has been expounded especially by Joseph de Maistre, Huysmans, and Léon Bloy. It was indeed one of the basic themes of Bloy, who gave this expression to it in one of his last works:

All we can glimpse, in trembling and adoration, is the perpetual miracle of an infallible balance between human merits and demerits, in such a way that the spiritually lacking are helped by the spiritually affluent and the timorous compensated by the daring. Now this happens entirely outside our knowledge, according to the mysteriously hidden economy of the affinity of souls.

A certain impulse of Grace which saves me from a grave peril may have been determined by a certain act of love accomplished this morning or five hundred years ago by a very obscure person whose soul had a mysterious connection with mine and who in this way receives his reward (*Méditations d'un solitaire en 1916*, pp. 57-58).

In English literature, Charles Williams has given currency to the notion under the terms of Exchange and Substitution. Though it is a dominant theme of all his work, one novel in particular, *Descent into Hell*, is devoted to an illustration of its complex working. There, to take the simplest form of its operation, Peter Stanhope assumes the fear that bedevils the life of Pauline Anstruther, who receives from him the joy of her liberation. In return she herself assumes the fear of an ancestor of hers burned at the stake in the reign of Mary. Thus, for Charles Williams, as for Léon Bloy, time is transcended in this spiritual exchange and so even are the confines of the temporal and eternal worlds. This assumption of the trials and difficulties of another person and making them one's own is Charles Williams's interpretation of what is meant by the carrying of one another's burdens, to which we are exhorted in the sixth chapter of St. Paul's Epistle to the Galatians. This Substitution, as illustrated in *Descent into Hell*, seems to be effected in very much the same way as in certain forms of meditation the person at prayer strives to transport himself in imagination to scenes in the life of Christ. Thus Peter Stanhope visualizes Pauline on her way home and imagines the fear that she feels of meeting her *doppelgänger*, effectively experiencing this fear on her behalf.

This kind of Substitution has its place in the conception that

Bernanos formed of the Communion of Saints. The *Dialogues des Carmélites* illustrate how Blanche's fear of death is assumed by the old prioress who dies, not her own death, but, through the fear that she exhibits, Blanche's. As Sœur Constance says: 'We do not die each for ourselves, but each for another, or some even in the place of others' (p. 79). The sub-prioress, Mère Marie de l'Incarnation, also 'pays' for Blanche's fear, a fear not only of death but also of showing fear. Thus, in compensation for Blanche's mounting the scaffold without fear, the old prioress dies in torment and Mère Marie de l'Incarnation is deprived of the martyrdom she desires, a deprivation which humiliates her. Human solidarity thus knows no confines. The form that Substitution usually takes in Bernanos, however, involves a fuller commitment of the victim; it is more sacrificial, in closer conformity with the self-offering of Christ for sinners, though its operation is still limited to those between whom personal contact is established. A confrontation is always necessary before the act is accomplished, a confrontation in which a kind of agonizing duel takes place, the resistance of the sinner, the inert weight of long-formed habit, having to be pierced and broken. If the saintly wrestler is left by these encounters in a state of exhaustion, the sinner by no means emerges from the ordeal unscathed. Indeed, in the extreme cases, he does not survive the removal of the sinful secret which has acquired its dominance over the years and become his reason for living. What matters, however, soteriologically, is not death, but deliverance. The countess, in the *Journal d'un curé de campagne* (1936), dies during the night that follows the tussle between her and the priest, which is in reality a struggle within herself which the priest's very presence brings to its culmination; but, before she dies, she is freed from the state of revolt in which the death of her infant son years before plunged her. The priest, though, has an inkling of the exchange that has taken place: 'The hope that was dying in my heart has reflowered in hers, the spirit of prayer which I thought I had irremediably lost God has given to her and, who knows, perhaps in my name . . .' (p. 221).

It is in the earlier novels that the direst operations of this kind take place, though in every novel Substitution is to be found in some form. In *Sous le soleil de Satan* (1926), in a deliberately disconcerting juxtaposition, the story of Germaine Malorthy's young life serves as prologue to the account of the harassing trials and the supreme temptation of Abbé Donissan. It is left to the reader to make the connexion that between these two people, dissimilar as they are, there is one of those mysterious affinities to which Bloy refers in the passage quoted. Indeed, it is possible to infer that it is on her behalf, in substitution for her, that the priest undergoes his awful torments. The Devil does not need to tempt Germaine, she has given herself to him already. It is in the soul of the priest that the issue is really to be determined and it is there that Satan enters, not as an unsuspected possessor, but as a recognized and unwanted guest who has ever to be opposed and thwarted. The story of Germaine herself is a banal one, echoed in its essentials in many lives, the story of the girl who feels herself first let down by her parents and then by her lover. As in all lives the pristine image is tarnished, but not completely effaced. The crime that she commits, the murder of her lover, is an unpremeditated act, an act that anyone in her circumstances might have performed. In most cases it occurs only in thought, in an unrealized desire, but sometimes it actually happens, and this is an instance:

But those other girls have not committed murder or only perhaps in imagination. They have no secret. They can say: 'How crazy I was!' ... They will never know that, stretching out their young claws, one thundery evening, they might have killed while they were playing (p. 55).

The main emphasis of the novel, however, naturally concerns the priest, whose inner life is polluted by constant skirmishes with the Devil. The *conscious* possession of the girl takes place only after the confrontation between her and the priest, after he has deprived her of her secret, her crime and her pride, showing her the tainted ancestry which lay behind it,

dozens of men and women bound together in the fibres of the same cancer, and the fearful bonds shrinking back, like the cut-off arms of an octopus, right up to the core of the monster itself, the initial fault, hidden to all, in a child's heart (p. 211).

Germaine sees herself as she is, one with the common herd. Back in her room, unable by herself to rise to a new life, having no conception of the divine mercy, she has only one resource, to call upon the master she has served:

He came at once, with no discussion, terribly quiet and reliable. Far as he pushes his resemblance to God, no joy could proceed from him, but, much superior to delights which stir only the emotions, his crowning achievement is a mute solitary frozen peace, comparable to the delectation of nothingness (p. 221).

No doubt, it is a consequence of Abbé Donissan's merits that her suicide is not immediately effective but allows time for the fulfilment of her dying wish to be carried to church.

Having given us in *Sous le soleil de Satan* an ambiguous presentation of saintliness, the portrayal of a man so obsessed by evil that he must constantly fight it, hardly able to distinguish between promptings of the Devil and the inspirations of God and living on the brink of despair a life of unrelenting self-torture, Bernanos chose subsequently to simplify the issue. It is clear that the divine mission that Abbé Donissan undoubtedly exercises is flawed. Though it is to be presumed that Germaine is effectively freed from her possession at the last moment, by a communication of Grace earned for her by the priest, yet it is obvious that he bungles his treatment of her in that he leaves her deprived of her sin and with nothing in its place, utterly empty, so that suicide seems the only course. Similarly, the attempted miracle of the child's resurrection, in the second half of the novel, miscarries. The child's momentary return to life serves only to drive its mother mad and plunge the priest himself into further anguish. One has the impression that in the act of performing the miracle the priest realizes that the order of nature may be reversed by Satan as well as by God. The 'saint' clearly has insufficient confidence in God, insufficient love. In later novels Bernanos modified his attitude to evil. It was no longer to be fought tooth and nail. To fight the Devil is to recognize too positively his dominion. So he should be ignored, overcome by a childlike simplicity and humility, an utter defencelessness. Bernanos did not change his view of the ubiquity of Satan, his presence in the most holy things, his aping of God. Abbé Chevance, in *L'Imposture*, testifies to the potential presence of Satan everywhere:

> The use we make of the most precious things the Lord grants us, bodily and spiritual sufferings, may in the long run corrupt them. Yes! man has defiled even the very substance of the divine heart: sorrow. The blood which flows from the Cross may kill us (p. 62).

But Abbé Chevance and especially his spiritual daughter, Chantal de Clergerie, themselves embody the writer's deepened view, his more Christocentric orientation. The saint was to be less of a hero, in the conventional sense.

Bernanos came to recognize that evil cannot be extirpated. We must in fact live with it, not only the evil in the world, but the evil in ourselves, against which it is, fundamentally, that we rebel. The parish priest of Fenouille, in *Monsieur Ouine*, tells the eponymous 'hero' that he does not rebel against evil. God did not rebel against it, he says, but assumed it. The same priest tells the wife of Arsène, who spends his time ineffectually trying to purify himself with douches of water, that we do not allow evil its place. 'We must fight it according to our strength,' he says, 'and for the rest learn to put up with it in peace' (p. 211). The same point is made in the *Journal d'un curé de campagne*, where the parish priest of Torcy tells his more self-sacrificing colleague from Ambricourt the symbolical story of the secularized nun who was determined to do away with dirt in his church and who spent day and night on her knees with water and scrubbing-brush till she died of heart failure, a martyr to her self-appointed and impossible task. This image of house-cleaning recurs, though to somewhat different purpose, in *Monsieur Ouine*, where the retired teacher of modern languages, describing to Philippe the cleaning of his room, when he first arrived at Néréis, tells how he had to

> clean out the joints, stone by stone, steep them in chloride, like lots of little wounds. Oh! you won't believe me, young man: the mud eaten into by the acid in this way, the mud of a hundred years or two, drawn out of its long dryness, never stopped coming out bit by bit under my fingers, bursting out in big grey bubbles (p. 22).

Evil cannot be washed away, and some methods of cleansing only increase its potency. The image as employed here excellently epitomizes the effect this fat and affable old man, who seems to do nothing but talk, has on the village where he has come to live. The very caricature of the saint, but also his antithesis, symbolically swollen with the absorption of all things into himself, curious of souls, the secret of God, which love alone can know, Ouine frees people of their wretched secrets, thus robbing them of their reason for living, for he leaves them empty, purposeless. He reveals to them their absurdity; he has an ironical indulgence for all things, for all things are to him equally absurd, equally meaningless. A kind of collective despair, reaching its frenzy at the funeral, gathers in the spiritually dead parish. But, in reality, and this is the basis of the portrayal, Ouine is in ourselves: hence the immensity of his power. Philippe himself, Ouine's 'disciple', has an inkling of this truth:

And, in a flash, Philippe glimpses the fact that [Ouine] corresponds in a wonderful manner with what he least knows in himself, a part of himself so secret that he could not yet say whether it were strength or weakness, the principle of life or the principle of death (p. 97).

For Philippe himself we need not fear, since the crippled Guillaume suffers on his behalf, a Substitution which Philippe himself proposes with ironic ferocity. He will go forward in life, vanquishing his obstacles. And you, he says to Guillaume, 'you follow me, but from afar, and we shall see you emerge in your turn, carrying the weight of my sins. Anyway, you are my soul; our salvation, that's your affair . . .' (p. 46). There is no irony, however, in Guillaume's acceptance and in his feeling that his friend's troubles pass through him.

In *Sous le soleil de Satan* it is the same person who is subject to the most violent assaults of the Devil and who at the same time rises to the greatest spiritual heights. In *L'Imposture* and *La Joie*, illustrating the writer's modified attitude to evil, we have the contrasted extremes of diabolical possession, analysed in the most minute detail, and an unspotted holiness, a childlike simplicity which discounts the Devil. Chantal de Clergerie is

too simple, too indifferent to herself, too strongly protected against the first stirring of disappointed self-love to imagine bringing in the dark Angel as a third party in her pitiful adventure. Moreover, she had never bothered much about the Devil and his charms, certain of escaping him through her exceeding smallness, for he whose patience pierces through so many things, the immense gaping stare whose greed knows no bounds, who has brooded in hatred over the very glory of God, has throughout the centuries scrutinized in vain, with all his colossal attention, turned over and over in vain in his fires, like a little unchangeable stone, that most chaste and pure of things, Humility (*La Joie*, pp. 65-66).

This is not to say, however, that Chantal's life follows an untroubled course. On the contrary, she must shoulder the Cross of the burdens of all those around her, in solitude and anguish mount her Calvary, where, betrayed and deserted, she must die an ignominious death.

Essentially, Chantal de Clergerie is the sacrificial victim whose death alone can atone, in conjunction with the divine mercy, for the life of total falsehood, the conscious living of the greatest lie possible, which the unbelieving Abbé Cénabre's priesthood constitutes. For the understanding of the thought of Bernanos it is necessary to follow the soterial action of *L'Imposture* and *La Joie*, which are companion volumes, in some detail. This action is complex. Abbé Chevance, to whom in the shock of discovery Abbé Cénabre confides the secret of his loss of faith, dies without being able to effect any change in the cold tranquillity which follows the possession of the distinguished hagiographer. The humiliating form of his death is no doubt to be associated with his espousal of Abbé Cénabre's secret, but Chantal de Clergerie, whose spiritual development he has nurtured, present at his death, makes it her own, in that mystical exchange through which the divine economy is maintained: 'she innocently received, she made her own, she espoused for eternity the mysterious humiliation of such a death' (*L'Imposture*, p. 318). Unknown to herself, she has assumed the mission of freeing Abbé Cénabre from his unconscious bondage, of delivering him a second time of his secret; but her death alone brings back his faith, albeit at the cost of his reason, for he dies in a mental home.

Chantal's disburdening influence is by no means confined to Abbé Cénabre; it affects all those with whom she has contact. As Fiodor, her eventual murderer, says:

She radiates light without knowing it, she draws our dark souls out of the shadow, and the cruel old sins begin to stir, yawn, stretch themselves, show their yellow claws. . . . Tomorrow, the day after—who knows?—one night, tonight even, they will wake up properly (*La Joie*, p. 156).

The secret of the house which she runs on behalf of her widowed father is, as this lucid server of Satan recognizes, Grace. All are conscious of this disruptive force in their midst, this simple pure girl with whom all falsehood is incompatible; fascinated, rendered unbearably uneasy, desperately refractory to the intolerable image which they have all denied in themselves, they react according to the degree of their enslavement. Basically, no doubt, as Chantal perceives them, 'they drag themselves about, vainly calling to one another in the night, till one of us gathers to himself a single ray of the divine star and reflects it' (*La Joie*, p. 116), but the ray of light, though desired, is greatly feared, and one by one M. de Clergerie's guests take the train. Of those who remain in the house, all save the Russian chauffeur, Fiodor, load their heavy secrets on to Chantal's shoulders; they part with them unasked, unwittingly. Chantal herself, hoping to find solace from her father, finds instead that she frees him of his secret, at the cost of her own peace. Like all the saintly figures Bernanos portrays, Chantal's very presence brings sin to the surface, to the light of day. Though humility hides its significance from him, this drawing power that the holy person unconsciously exercises is vaguely apparent to the parish priest of the *Journal d'un curé de campagne*:

I've had the impression for some time that my presence alone makes sin come out of its lurking-place, brings it as it were to the surface of a being, into his eyes, mouth, voice. . . . You'd say that the enemy disdains to stay hidden when confronted with such a puny adversary, but comes and challenges me to my face, mocks at me (p. 189).

In a similar way, the sermon the parish priest pronounces at the funeral in *Monsieur Ouine* brings the evil which smoulders throughout the village to the point of conflagration, provoking an uproar in which Mme de Néréis is done to death, the unconscious victim of the village's spiritual death. However, the disorder which accompanies the holy person is only the outward manifestation of an ill which in a latent state is always present. The paroxysm in which Satan's power is made visible and in which there is always a victim sacrificed is no doubt, notwithstanding the havoc wrought, basically remedial. Evil is brought to the surface and so, as it were, discharged. It is true that there must be a sacrificial victim, but it is the function of the victim to expiate sin, to discharge evil. In *La Joie* it is through the person of Fiodor that evil gathers its momentum, striking at Chantal, the vehicle of Grace, and spending itself in the suicide of Fiodor himself, whose *raison d'être* has ceased with her death. Though Chantal dies, Cénabre is freed of his possession, and it may be surmised that she continues to live in some degree in the lives of those who have known her.

The Christocentric pattern of Chantal's life and death is emphasized in the vision she has preceding her betrayal and murder, in what is her Garden of Gethsemane. She sees the archetypal sacrifice, Christ offering Himself, in the freshness and vigour of youth, such as she is herself, raising up His Sacred Body in the emblems of bread and wine, before delivering it up to Fear:

And no doubt He offered it to all men, but He thought only of one. The only one to whom this Body truly, humanly, belonged, like a slave to its master, having seized hold of it by cunning, having already disposed of it as of lawful property, by virtue of a bill of sale in due form, correct. Thus the only one who could defy mercy, step right into despair, make despair his dwelling-place, envelop himself in despair, as the first murderer had enveloped himself in night. The only man among all men who really possessed something, who was provided for, having henceforth nothing to receive from anyone, for all eternity (*La Joie*, p. 252).

In this vision Chantal goes towards Judas and offers herself to him:

Simply, as she had offered herself so many times for sinners, with the same movement she went towards this sinner of sinners, her arms outstretched; she offered herself to this impenetrable despair with a mysterious feeling, not entirely horror or compassion, but a kind of holy curiosity (ibid., p. 254).

As she moves entranced, she comes up against Abbé Cénabre

standing before her. The parallel could hardly be clearer. It is to save this Judas that her Christophanic sacrifice is to be accomplished. Bernanos seeks, through the operation of the Communion of Saints, the practice of Substitution by a girl whose compassion and love know no obstacles, the retrieval of despair itself. Dark as is the superficial colouring of his work, it is an attempt, while recognizing the ubiquity of evil, to show how, by total conformity with Christ, man may co-operate in the work of Redemption.

What we may call the betrayal of Chantal is a kind of collective activity. Her father's sudden decision to make a journey is in reality a flight, a shirking of the issue which leaves the way open for the ether-intoxicated Russian to destroy the light which causes him an intolerable hurt. Flight, like all the forms of failure to face reality, day-dreams, drugs, crimes, novel-reading, and even novel-writing, has its place in the work of Bernanos; Olivier Mainville's twenty-mile walk in the night, in *Un mauvais rêve*, is but the extreme example. Even Chantal is tempted to run away, as was St. John Vianney, more than once, from his little parish of Ars, but her distinction is that she stays to face what is in store for her. She meets the death that is to release Abbé Cénabre who, without knowing what has happened, feels the light entering him:

Yes, outside him, out of his power, an event had just taken place—which he did not know of, which perhaps he would never know—yet as real, as certain, as any of those which he had seen with his own eyes (ibid., p. 303).

Of the eternal destiny of Fiodor nothing is hinted; he would seem to be an irredeemable Judas, the lucid and voluntary servant of Satan, unlike Cénabre, who was unaware of his thraldom.

* * *

L'Imposture and *La Joie* are the most ambitious works Bernanos wrote. Nowhere else does he attempt with such probing analysis to get to the heart of saintliness and of its frigid caricature. The first of these companion volumes is intensely disturbing, the second deeply moving. Considered, however, from the aesthetic angle, they share with *Sous le soleil de Satan* a rather imperfect integration of metaphysical substance with literary form, so that the ideas underlying these works are perhaps too easily dissociable from them. Moreover, they are marred at times by melodramatic happenings, by a spiritual staginess. But in his later work Bernanos succeeds in fusing his spiritual vision far more satisfactorily with the literary form; indeed, in the *Nouvelle histoire de Mouchette* (1937) and *Monsieur Ouine* he achieves a felicitous integration of all his powers, spiritual and aesthetic, which places him in the forefront of twentieth-century writers. Since it is a novelist whose ideas are being discussed, it seems appropriate to examine the aesthetic structure of his most accomplished works.

In these later novels, the aesthetic basis itself becomes identified with the spiritual principle which informs the novels. In both the *Journal d'un curé de campagne* and the *Nouvelle histoire de Mouchette* the writer is enabled to sustain his imaginative role with such plausible cogency through the force of his spiritual understanding, fundamentally, we must deduce, through his inner life of prayer, in which the Person of Christ is so central a figure. In each of these novels the vivifying and unifying principle is in fact Christ, though His presence is as it were diffused throughout the text, subtly implied and not blatantly proclaimed. Each of these novels is in a sense based upon a paradox. Transfusing the humble diary of the Country Priest is a parallel life echoed in its essentials. The priest's apparent human failure, his seeming inadequacy, the hostility he arouses in respectable conformists, reflect the earthly vicissitudes of his divine prototype, just as his concordance with the will of God fulfils the same divine pattern. This is, in given circumstances, the living of the life of Christ. Whilst the novel is thus based upon a paradox, a developed contradictoriness, the contrast between the ignominy at the level of human appearances and the greatness in spiritual reality, it receives its dynamism from the implied parallel, the underlying Christophanic significance, the paradox of Christ Himself. The theme of Substitution still dominates the work, for the priest's whole life is one of Substitution since he is living the life of Christ, but there occur even particular instances of its operation in the case of both the countess and her daughter (pp. 167 and 243).

The paradox of the *Nouvelle histoire de Mouchette* is even bolder and the imaginative *tour de force* more brilliant. Based on but one episode, a banal story of rape, the kind of incident that could serve for a sentimental idealization or a 'realist' essay in obscenity, the transfiguring vision of Bernanos lifts it to the highest level of human suffering, makes of it a moving parallel of the great Act of Expiation itself. He not only enters the mind of an unloved and unlovable girl of fourteen, stubborn and ignorant, portraying her from the inside with complete plausibility, but at the same time, purely through the overtones with which he charges his narrative, he succeeds in assessing the spiritual significance of her life and death, presents her in relation to the Incarnation, even though reference to it is avoided. Mouchette is the unconscious victim of the sins of her village. Her rape does not merely add but another humiliation to the many she has already undergone, it deprives her of her supreme expectation, that of love itself, such as she had imagined it; she thus loses her reason for living. The manner in which Bernanos establishes the basic parallel which gives his novel its cogency and its deep meaning is discreet and subtle. It is her harrowing journey on the Sunday morning to the pond where she drowns, a *via dolorosa* in which she is exposed to both solicitude and jeers, but in fundamental solitude and abandonment, that echoes in its poor human fashion the Way of the Cross. The novel is rich in implication. In a village where God has been forgotten, this is the only kind of Calvary that can take place; it is a Calvary adapted to modern conditions, but this is the kind of Calvary that in such a village does take place; it is in the suffering of such as this little girl that the suffering of Christ is nowadays to be encountered. It is the ringing of the bell, as Mouchette crosses the square, for the Mass to which no one now goes, which emphasizes the absence of God in the life of the village and which also draws our attention to this new derivative enactment of the great Sacrifice which is, as it were, taking place outside the church while the sacrifice of the Mass continues unheeded within. The ringing of the bell also points the tragic irony of the journey, for Mouchette is unaware of the Church. This novel is infused with the compassion of Bernanos for those cut off by prejudice and ignorance from the source of their life and health. Though her death is self-inflicted, an unpremeditated act to end the intolerable humiliation she feels, the external fulfilment of the emptiness within her, yet she is most truly the victim of the whole village's turning away from God. She is what she has been made by the force of circumstances, by those other lives which have failed to inspire in her any other attitude than revolt. The godless village drives her, unintentionally, unconsciously, to the pond where she herself did not even know she was going.

The success of the *Nouvelle histoire de Mouchette* is due to the intense religious feeling of the author which allows him to bring into an acceptable relationship, an implied parallel, two such incongruously dissimilar elements, the rape and suicide of a girl of fourteen and the Passion and Death of Christ. To achieve this, the author must have been able to draw on great depths of human compassion and deep spirituality alike. In a way, this novel extends the idea of Substitution to embrace those unaware of the redemptive value of their suffering, the large numbers of those who have never even heard of the Mystical Body.

It may seem superficially that the literary genesis of *Monsieur Ouine* differs from that of the *Journal d'un curé de campagne* and the *Nouvelle histoire de Mouchette*, owing as they do their profound unity, their richness of substance and suggestion, to the latent presence of Christ. That unifying figure is absent from this novel which, as a consequence, is incoherent. It is fraught with dark, mysterious happenings, hints of perverted relationships never fully brought into the open, unsolved crimes, senseless murders. The connexion between Ouine, the quiet, withdrawn thinker of evil thoughts, and the village of Fenouille, in which they are actualized, is never made entirely clear; the extent of the priest's spiritual activity is equally shrouded in obscurity.

Bernanos succeeds brilliantly in creating the mystery which invests life itself, with its unclarified issues, with evil rampant, with a seemingly ineffective parish priest dealing quite inadequately with his hopeless task. Yet, although this novel may be said to possess no unity, to have a deliberate lack of unity, or only a tenuous one supplied by the person of the eponymous 'hero', 'a unity of mirrored reflections' as Mme Magny so admirably calls it,[4] the unity of himself with the happenings in the village which reflect him, in a deeper sense the Person of Christ still provides the basic unity of the novel; His absence from it is most eloquent. The world without Him is chaotic, meaningless; nothing holds together. The novel itself is only held together by this pervading sense of His absence, the darkness without Him, the mystery embracing all things.

Monsieur Ouine possesses that multifold possibility of interpretation which ensures undying life for a work of art. It presents us with a 'slice of life' undreamt of by the realists, an example of apparent impenetrability, especially in the corrupt text originally published, which must be the envy of every seeker after the hermetic. Yet this technical virtuosity, by an author for whom questions of technique had no importance, is in a sense accidental; Bernanos has merely striven with all his integrity, with all the accuracy of which he was capable, to embody in terms of village life his vision of the world as it is, with God forgotten and despised, with disorder consequently manifest, confusion everywhere, tedium breaking into violence. The absence of connecting links between the juxtaposed episodes and between them and the conversations of Ouine and Philippe echoes the world as it appears to man today, as it in fact appears to a number of later French novelists, such as Beckett and Robbe-Grillet. It is mainly through this novel that the most fruitful association may be established between Bernanos and the younger generation, but even this work takes its full meaning only from an *arrière-pensée* that most of them could not acknowledge.

* * *

[4] Claude-Edmonde Magny, 'The Devil in Contemporary Literature', a chapter in *Satan* (London, Sheed & Ward, 1951), p. 448.

In each of his books is embodied Bernanos's own experience of life; his novels are never illustrations of an abstract system of thought. The whole man is fully committed in all that he wrote; the phrase which he used of *Sous le soleil de Satan*: 'I have there wholly given myself',[5] applies to all his major works. The vision he sets before us is strangely compelling; in spite of ourselves we are lifted into it. The issues that he faces unflinchingly are fundamental: death, evil, our function as human beings, our relations with one another, our destiny. The fact that he was a Catholic dominates of necessity the whole vision. The cohesive force of it is the figure of Christ, the unifying instrument the Mystical Body. Evil is not shirked; on the contrary, many may feel that it receives exaggerated emphasis, ever the French tendency in English eyes. The terrifying alternatives with which Bernanos seems to present us are possession by the Devil or the carrying of the crushing burden of other people's sins, the following of Christ to Calvary, alternatives clearly incompatible with complacency or comfort. The notion of diabolical possession is not a cheering thought to entertain on our own behalf. Bernanos does not even allow us the loophole of a crude implausibility through which we might escape the inferences for ourselves in which his works abound. Where a certain coarseness in the conception might be alleged, in *Sous le soleil de Satan*, the materialization of Satan is not affirmed categorically; the possibility is left open that the priest, in that state of tension in which his whole life passes, may have charged a purely human encounter with an ingratiating little horse-dealer with his own obsessive preoccupations, mingling the events of the external world and his inner life. Far from abolishing the complex workings of the human mind in favour of an arbitrary satanic intervention, Bernanos is at pains to indicate by what gradual processes, compounded of inherited propensities and the experience of others and the self, the soul becomes enslaved to the enemy of God. There is no brusque seizure, but a patient and relentless wearing down from the start, from childhood, the whole operation being of course unconscious. It is, in fact, God whose action may be

[5] Bernanos, *Le Crépuscule des vieux* (Paris, Gallimard, 1956), p. 66.

instantaneous, fulminant. To be fully, irremediably, effective the power of Satan requires human consent:

> It is from ourselves that he must draw supreme consent and he will not receive it before God has spoken in His turn. For however long he believes he may delay divine Grace, it must gush forth, and he awaits in immense terror the necessary inescapable outflow; for his patient work may be destroyed in one moment. Where will the thunder strike? He doesn't know (*L'Imposture*, pp. 103-4).

Thus, though the decision is man's alone, the last word, as it were, rests with God.

The world of Bernanos is a battleground of opposing forces, positive luminous energy and opaque inert resistance, but it is a warfare in which the effective combatants, far from inflicting suffering, take it upon themselves. Moreover, through the incalculable operation of spiritual Exchange and Substitution, we are all, without exception, closely related, inextricably and immeasurably involved one with another. No sin, no evil, is a private matter. Human solidarity, what Charles Williams called the Coinherence, ensures that all sin, as well as all suffering, implicates the whole human race. The one is in any case the reverse face of the other; saint and sinner share the same experience, the one in freedom, the other in enslavement. There is between them the most intimate soterial relationship. Gide's view of the Church as the Barque of St. Peter, in which the faithful are all comfortably ensconced while the rest of humanity is left to flounder helplessly in the sea, reveals itself as a facile simplification. There are other ways of identifying oneself with humanity as a whole than the one chosen by the advocate of availability.

Bernanos remains unique, a visionary with a gripping power of evocation, owing little to any predecessors, though at the impressionable age he was attracted by Hello and devoured Balzac. Neither has he in the strict sense had any successors; a visionary does not found schools. His keen awareness of man's predicament, his deep compassionate concern and his contempt for facile remedies unite him to some extent to some post-war writers, but this affinity must not be allowed to overlay the important distinctions. 'I have never been a restless soul', he wrote from Brazil in 1940, 'and . . . I feel, in all the grossness of my nature, grossly at ease in obedience and discipline. . . .'[6] These words could hardly be echoed by Sartre or Camus. Though the reading of Bernanos is a profound and disturbing experience, the upset it provokes is fully positive. The compulsive intensity of his vision leads us, for the time being, at least, to look more deeply into ourselves, to face those issues we tend to postpone to an ever-receding date. That he himself faced them, not only his books but accounts of his death reveal. It is no surprise to learn that the work which his death forestalled was a life of Christ; all that he had written leads to this central figure, the prototype of self-sacrifice, the essential Victim.

Novels by Bernanos:

Sous le soleil de Satan, Paris, Plon, 1926.
    Star of Satan (trs. Pamela Morris), London, Lane, 1940; New York, Macmillan, 1940.
    Under the Sun of Satan (trs. H. L. Binsse), New York, Pantheon Books, 1949.

L'Imposture, Paris, Plon, 1927.

La Joie, Paris, Plon, 1929.
    Joy (trs. Louise Varèse), London, Lane, 1948; New York, Pantheon Books, 1946.

Un Crime, Paris, Plon, 1934.
    The Crime (trs. Anne Green), London, Museum Press, 1947; New York, Dutton, 1946.

Journal d'un curé de campagne, Paris, Plon, 1936.
    The Diary of a Country Priest (trs. Pamela Morris), London, Collins (Fontana Books), 1956; New York & Toronto, Doubleday (Image Books), 1954.

Nouvelle histoire de Mouchette, Paris, Plon, 1937.

Un mauvais rêve, Paris, Plon, 1950 (written 1935).
    Night is Darkest (trs. W. J. Strachan), London, Lane, 1953.

Monsieur Ouine, Paris, Club des Libraires de France, 1955 (the Plon edition of 1946 is defective).
    The Open Mind (trs. Geoffrey Dunlop), London, Lane, 1945.

Collected short stories:

Dialogues d'ombres, Paris, Plon, 1955.

[6] Quoted in *Bernanos par lui-même*, p. 179.

ANDRÉ MALRAUX
b. 1901
BY CECIL JENKINS
──────────☆──────────

THE nature of Malraux's reputation—his latest incarnation is as Minister of State in charge of Cultural Affairs in de Gaulle's Fifth Republic—forces us, even in a brief study, to view him as a total phenomenon. For the ascendancy over several generations of Frenchmen of this novelist, art critic, and man of action derives from an amalgam of a legendary and almost uniquely privileged kind.

Privileged, because the novels seemed to carry not only the authority of spectacular experience but the weight of history itself. *La Voie Royale* (1930) reflected a bush expedition in search of valuable sculpture in the ruined Buddhist temples that had once lined the old Royal Road in Cambodia—as a result of which Malraux, at the age of twenty-two, was condemned to three years' imprisonment (never served) by a Pnompenh court. *Les Conquérants* (1928) and *La Condition humaine* (1933) were assumed to be a faithful rendering of the spirit of the Chinese Revolution, in which Malraux was known to have been engaged as a propagandist—Léon Blum concluded a political meeting in the suburbs by sending his audience off to read *La Condition humaine*. *Le Temps du mépris* (1935) was the offering of the man who went with Gide to Berlin to appeal for the liberation of Dimitrov. *L'Espoir* (1937) was read as a front-line report from the man who, at the outbreak of the Civil War, had gone to Spain to organize the *Escadre España* and who had himself flown on sixty-five missions as a cockpit-gunner. *Les Noyers de l'Altenburg* (1943) gave us the Malraux taken prisoner in 1940 and, transposed as the adventure of Vincent Berger, a meditation on his whole career. Even *Les Voix du silence* (1951) was necessarily received as the higher speculation, in the field of the plastic arts, of the propaganda chief of the *Rassemblement du Peuple Français* and grey eminence to de Gaulle. Malraux, for several generations, has been the Knight Errant, the 'helmeted angel', the Absolute Witness, the very prototype of the committed writer, the man who privately assumed the public tragedies which constitute the fatality of an age. And all this bathed in the Malraux legend. . . .

The mass of apocrypha surrounding this extraordinary man would make a volume in itself. Among many wonderful (if untrue) stories there is, for example, that of an exasperated Malraux urging a hesitant de Gaulle to seize power in the late 'forties: 'Here we are at last, on the bank of the Rubicon. And you, *mon général*, what do *you* do? You sit and fish!' There are sober printed sources committed to the startling statement that Malraux speaks seventeen languages (he lays claim only to 'some slight acquaintance with the dead languages, a little Chinese and a few words of English'), just as there are still those who contrive to find that his handwriting—a very ordinary, industrious, rather boyish script—'looks curiously like hieroglyphic incisions in stone'. To the twofold extra-literary authenticity conferred by the assimilation of the work to the life on the one hand and to the force of history itself on the other, there has been added something of the invulnerability of myth.

Now the objection to this picture is not simply that it is too colourful—Malraux is indeed a colourful, an attractive and, in many ways, an admirable man—but rather that it conflicts with the concrete reality of the work and that, since its implications are ultimately false, it tends to betray Malraux's artistic purpose. It offers us a conquering legend—whereas it is perhaps more important to remember that the legend began as the protective, mythical self-projection of a brilliant but nervously intense, claustrophobic, and vulnerable young man whose central awareness seems to have been a haunting sense of estrangement. It creates a curious contrast between Malraux the revolutionary novelist and the Malraux who later elaborated an anti-mimetic view of art—whereas, as he himself will say in conversation, '*Les*

Voix du silence and *La Condition humaine* are one and the same thing'. It obscures the real continuity in his thinking by overstressing the importance, in this particular context, of the incompatibility of Chinese Communism or Spanish Republicanism with French Gaullism. It presents us with a man dedicated to historical action—whereas a cold look at Malraux's career reveals that the part of his life devoted to his selective, spectacular, discontinuous activity has been small, that his political options have tended to be negative rather than positive, that dangerous commitment is not necessarily total commitment, that like the Garine of *Les Conquérants* he is less a man of action than 'a man capable of action—on occasion' (p. 23), and that he is, in the end, essentially a writer. It suggests the journalistic or even the propagandist novelist tied to realism—whereas Malraux was largely using contemporary history as pliable fictional material, the 'Revolution' as formal symbolism and realism as an idiom of persuasion in the service of a fundamentally anti-historical vision. It presents us, in fact, with a Malraux whose contradictions are to be reduced, in external terms, only to 'betrayal' or to be resolved, as so often happens in criticism of his work, only at the level of the elegant, transcendent paradox.

The truth, however, is surely that Malraux has been one of the great Romantics of his generation. That his vision as a writer is not dependent upon his career as Witness is confirmed by a glance at the early phantasy *Royaume farfelu*, drafted mainly in 1920. For his basic story of man's tragic defeat is already presented in exotic ellipsis—the cosmic tone, the exalted strangeness, the pessimism, the warring armies, the massacres, the tortures, the central image of blindness, the insects, the scorpions, the obsessional fear of the meaningless human ceremony, the irony and the immanence of death: all are here. Malraux, indeed, classes himself by implication with Faulkner and Lawrence as a 'dominated novelist' and sees the novelist as starting, not at all from the desire to render the relative world, but from obsession—reviewing Gide's *Nouvelles nourritures* in the *Nouvelle Revue Française* of December 1935, he speaks of the world as being for the writer merely 'the means of expression of a private drama'

(p. 935). The novelist involves the world in his obsession in order to objectivize and justify the obsessional vision—the world itself is merely instrumental, since his aim, and his achievement, is the creation of an autonomous world. It is indeed the consistency of the autonomous world which provides the 'density', the 'tone', and the 'mystery' which Malraux looks for as signs of quality in the work of his contemporaries. Now Malraux himself begins with private estrangement and solitude and, in his novels, we see him seeking to valorize this limited and exceptional experience of life in external terms—as the plight of man crushed by the blind fatality of history in a violent age, but also, and more profoundly, as the hopeless estrangement of man in the post-Christian world. For the real tragedy in Malraux is the death of God and the death of man which, for him, derives directly from it—'for you', says Ling in *La Tentation de l'Occident* (1926), 'the absolute reality was first God, then man; but man too, like God, has died' (p. 166); and in the Pleyel speech of 1948 we find Malraux repeating: 'the drama of the Europe of today is the death of man'. And it is striking to see the fundamental pessimism of the young Malraux with regard to the humanist values of the age paralleled by the mature Malraux of *Les Voix du silence* where, expressing once again his scepticism as to 'progress, science, reason and democracy', he insists that 'reason alone cannot explain or justify man' (p. 538). Man, for Malraux, is dead because he has clearly failed to take the place of God, because the loss of the soul means the loss of identity, because, like Heidegger's *Sein-zum-Tode*, he is now forced to define himself 'vertically' in terms of the only totality that remains: death.

And in his pathetic vision of a violent post-Christian night of death and despair, illusion and non-cognition, solitude and suffering, Malraux gives us contemporary man as a kind of absurd glow-worm. Glow-worm, because he somehow secretes his own light in this blackness and, by a tragic mystery, appears to deny the very principle of the night in which he moves. But absurd, because this mystery remains unsanctioned and unresolved, because the glimmer of consciousness appears to reflect nothing beyond, because he is ultimately the plaything of every contingency that an indifferently hostile universe throws up as fatality. In the absence of some transcendence to turn the darkness into light, man is absurd and the human lot intolerable. 'The modern world', wrote Malraux in the N.R.F. of June 1927 in a review of a work by Massis, 'carries within itself, like a cancer, its lack of a soul. It will not free itself from this absence, implied by its own law. And it will continue thus until men are convulsed by a collective call to the soul' (p. 818); 'Europe', he said very simply in conversation in 1952, 'needs a transcendence'; 'the next century's task', he tells an interviewer from *Time*, in its issue of 18 July 1955, 'will be to rediscover its gods' (p. 26). At bottom, Malraux has consistently felt this absurdity of man, within the terms of contemporary humanism, to be irretrievable and our time to be a dark, unreal interlude between Christianity and the next universal religion. Far from being the privileged voice of the historical world, he has been the herald of a new fundamental age, the Romantic millenarian, the voice of the anti-history which he calls Destiny.

His own aesthetic of the 'novel of destiny'—even if the reality of the historical world drove him beyond it towards epic in *L'Espoir*—makes this clear. Like Greek tragedy which, as he constantly argues, was a 'questioning of man's destiny'—and an 'anti-destiny' in that the very representing of destiny constituted a moral victory over destiny—the novel, as the representative art form of contemporary man 'who does not know where he is going', is properly the tragic poem of Man and his Destiny. Which at once devalues the story of men in their history. 'The modern novel', he writes in the margin of Picon's *Malraux par lui-même*, 'is in my view a privileged means of expressing the tragedy of man, and not an elucidation of the individual' (p. 66) —we move away from the novel of characters, implying a belief in the opaque reality of the human world, towards the novel of situation. Since the elliptical idea of destiny must somehow be concretized within the terms of the relative world, we move necessarily towards the extreme situation—self-assertion against savage tribes, insurrection, war—which not only makes possible but confers some historical status upon the supreme moment in which the human act, affirming itself against the world, can assume its full metaphysical significance. Malraux insists that he does not 'compose' his novels and indeed, even in the midst of revolution, plot and external conflict, expressive of the world's continuity, are devalued—his scenes tend to be separate, vertical moments of time juxtaposed as by a cinematic *montage* technique. Even in the heat of action, the real conflict for his hero is internal —between himself and the world, between his will to destiny and his finitude. The staccato style of *Les Conquérants* (which Grasset advertised as a 'new conception of the novel') treats external reality as a shifting kaleidoscope of visual fragments, to be incorporated at will into the intensity of the character, but having no necessity of its own—even in *L'Espoir* the character's verticality predominates. And there are everywhere compelling images and verbal tricks—'Spain was this twisted machine-gun . . .', 'France was this old woman . . .'—suggestive of an almost ideographical expression of the relative world. Through the world, Malraux's 'metapracticians', as Mounier has called them, are living that denial of the world which is their destiny—the world itself is allegory.

Except, of course, that this allegory *is* the world itself—and the momentous world of the Chinese Revolution or the Spanish Civil War which, independently of Malraux's vision, the reader necessarily assumes. It is significant that in the three novels which he privately regards as unsuccessful—*La Voie Royale, Le Temps du mépris,* and *Les Noyers de l'Altenburg*—Malraux was operating without the prestige, the pressure, and the urgency of time of the revolutionary situation. For, by a curious and ironical paradox, the anti-historical vision depends for its force upon the force of history, as the anti-time of the vertical moment of destiny depends upon time. It is this essential ambiguity which gives his novels their 'bite' and their peculiar fascination.

*   *   *

That the 'man of action' starts, tragically, from a fundamental disbelief in action emerges starkly from the very remarkable post-war essays *La Tentation de l'Occident* (1926) and *D'une jeunesse européenne* (1927). Man, who replaced God, is now dead in his turn—science, progress, humanism, individualism, and liberal democracy have manifestly failed. He finds himself alone with his suffering and his death, alone with an irrelevant psychic structure deriving from Christianity. For the Christian imperatives remain as the form of our sensibility, the prism through which we see the world: we are absurd, soulless Christians, we are unreal. The Freudian and Surrealist attack on the unity of the personality means for Malraux that man, unable to construct his own reality, is bent upon destroying it. And yet the old order of existence—change, time, suffering, death—remains; the old fatalities cry out for a new idea of man that might incorporate them. Such an idea, however, is impossible, for it is clear that it could only be based on man himself and it is also clear that man himself is absurd, that no human reality exists. Now that he has dethroned the God who reconciled all contradictions, man is separated from his own meaning, he is unknowable and unknowing, a prisoner of a stylized ego which is a cunning machine of mirrors reflecting only inwards towards chaos. He is torn by an inner conflict—Malraux maintains this dichotomy throughout his work—between his subjective reality and his objective reality, between his self-awareness as an irrelative 'intensity' and his mind which is the unreal derivative of a dead civilization. He cannot know himself objectively, since self-analysis discovers only the absurdity of the particular, since he is a monster of wish-fulfilment whose very memory is biased. Nor can he know others, as the human relationship *par excellence*, love, eloquently demonstrates. The irony of the lover's situation is that his feeling depends upon two distinct orders of sensation: his own and those that he *ascribes* to the other. In fact, however, he can never meet the reality of the other, only his own expectation, only himself—knowledge is onanistic. If the only answer to this total absurdity is a new soul, a new religion, it is clear that this answer must come from without—the essays end in paralysis. And the Malraux of *La Tentation de l'Occident*, feeling only a 'sad irony' before the cold statues called 'fatherland, justice, greatness and truth' (p. 204), knows in advance the vanity of action.

And yet, for the young man who feels estranged from his civilization at every level, who is all nerves and intelligence and suffering, action is an organic necessity. He at least possesses his intensity, his brute awareness of his own uniqueness. If hardly a value, it can be made into one, used as a lever—his very youth and sexual vigour can be willed into an idiom. Since he has nothing to lose, he can reject a life that is a mere fiction, opt for the austere reality of the haunting knowledge of death and live life as a savage Nietzschean experiment. And certain temptations—war, or killing—remain as potentially cognitive experiences. Can he, by disrupting the appearance of the world, get beyond the old complex of responsibility, guilt, and remorse and smash through the glass towards a more real perspective? Perhaps not, but he will at least, by living passionately at the limit of his nerves, have tried to score some mark of personal identity upon the metal walls of the human prison, he will at least have tried to actualize his metaphysical absurdity, to possess as in a violent embrace his tragic destiny. Which leads us to the heroes of *La Voie Royale* and *Les Conquérants*—and to the underlying experience of Malraux himself in the East.

The ascertainable facts about these years are briefly as follows. For various technical reasons, the harsh three-year sentence imposed by the Pnompenh tribunal in 1924 was not carried out. Malraux, however, was humiliated by the smug ironies of the Saigon and Paris papers, as well as by his own naïveté in making rather wild claims about himself which were easily disproved and ridiculed. He returned to France, only to go back to Saigon in January 1925, intent on revenge. For the brief period of its existence (17 June–14 August) before it was choked by the authorities, he was co-editor of a revolutionary newspaper *L'Indochine* which, if farcical enough, compared very favourably with its more official contemporaries. He spent the next fifteen months or so shuttling between Saigon and Canton, being connected with the Young Annam League and with propaganda in Canton. He was not a Communist, nor was he in any sense a 'leader' of the revolution, nor did he identify himself with it philosophically—Marxism had no answer to individual death. He was sailing before the wind of destiny—China was something of a metaphysical playground and he liked the climate of insurrection, which he somewhat quaintly called 'the science of urbanism'. *La Voie Royale*, in its essentials, is an invention, with the hero Perken being a 'phantasy character'. He was almost certainly neither in Canton for the events portrayed in *Les Conquérants* (although he arrived shortly afterwards) nor in Shanghai for those described in *La Condition humaine*. His achievement in these three novels becomes the more real when it is made clear that they are not reportage but courageous works of imagination.

La Voie Royale and *Les Conquérants* are parallel projections of the exploration of a certain Nietzschean impasse. Perken, in *La Voie Royale*, asserts himself against the jungle in order to make enough money to set up a private domain of kingship and eroticism, walled off from the world by a screen of machine-guns, which will enable him defiantly to realize his estrangement and to leave a scar on the map—yet the shadow of impotence has already fallen across his life. Garine, in *Les Conquérants*, is a virtuoso of action organizing a general strike in Canton—yet he knows that his action is a drug, that he cannot believe even in its results since he cannot believe in any form of social organization; he knows that his very victory will be his defeat since the revolution will discard the non-believer, he knows that by remaining in the East in his worsening state of health he is in fact committing suicide. Garine's jungle is the Chinese revolution—in the relative world, destiny can be enacted only as total, if grandiose, defeat. The adventurer's sense of complete estrangement is partly organic, partly the result of humiliation and self-hatred—as late as 1937, in New York, if with some little coquetry perhaps, Malraux himself was giving as his reason for fighting in Spain the fact that 'he did not like his life'. The adventurer, however, has elected to will his estrangement 'lucidly' as his destiny, to live beyond good and evil and dissolving pity as a heroic gambler, as a deliberate tragic outlaw. His formal values are only the pitifully restrictive ones of courage and loyalty to other outlaws and in fact, through his *Herrenmoral*, he is seeking his revenge against the universe in terms of power, suffering, eroticism and—under pressure—killing. Yet he is merely organizing his own estrangement into a machine which mangles him. His real destiny would seem to be his very 'lucidity', his own false, separatist notion of Destiny—and this real destiny is implacable. At bottom, beyond the cat-and-mouse game with death, he is secretly conniving at his death, trying to assume it as the only defining agent, trying to live it as the ultimate meaning—Perken's final concern with 'achieving' his death is of an almost artistic kind. But one final discovery remains to be made: that one cannot achieve death, since death is not an entity, that one can only die. Within the terms of these two novels, there is no way out of the impasse. Malraux himself, however, attempts in *La Condition humaine* the painful possession of the world—if only, in the end, to involve it in his own despair.

He takes as his situation the attempted *coup d'état* in Shanghai in the spring of 1927. Chiang Kai-shek, the leader of the nationalist Kuomintang, is waiting to enter the city with his army. Meanwhile, the left wing of the movement, led by the tiny Communist fringe, takes over the city as a forcing move. The British and French interests, like the Chinese bankers, become alarmed at this development and combine, through the French Consul, to buy off Chiang Kai-shek on condition that the Communists be eliminated. This is performed most efficiently by a swoop at dawn, three thousand of the insurrectionists being killed and the leaders burnt alive in the boilers of locomotives. Malraux transposes the French Consul as the big industrialist Ferral and gives the leading role played by Chou En-lai to Kyo. *La Condition humaine*, however, is not really a political novel. Malraux refines a confused and bloody tragi-comedy into pure tragedy, increases the violence, loads the dice ironically against the characters, places the emphasis on problems that no collective movement can solve and, rather against the historical facts and at the price of internal contradictions in the novel, makes Moscow the remote God of Destiny. Nor is it to be seen as a heroic novel centred around Kyo and Katow, since its formal structure excludes this interpretation. Gisors, Clappique, and Valérie, for example, are clearly too highly developed to be merely subsidiary characters and, above all, there is the Epilogue which devalues the heroism. In the first scene of the Epilogue, Ferral discovers that, since the effete French government will not give him sufficient backing, the events in Shanghai have been historically meaningless: 'total nonsense' (p. 392). In the second and final scene, Gisors, having retreated into opium in order to escape the reality of the grief caused him by the death of his son Kyo, refuses to go to Moscow, rejects his own teaching and, in fact, denies the terms in which his son had lived and died. The novel, for Malraux, preoccupied at this time with Greek tragedy and with the problem of treating each character as a destiny, has rather ten major characters—as befits the immensely ambitious story of a species on a planet, the bold attempt at a modern Everyman that he very explicitly called *La Condition humaine*.

The title reflects Pascal's famous 'image of the human condition' as a host of condemned men in chains, seeing some of their number selected and butchered each day and awaiting their own turn. In the great scene in which the heroes lie waiting to be burnt alive, Malraux translates this appalling ellipsis of life in literal terms. Indeed, it is the powerful infrastructure of the whole world. All men, in the end, are equal before death in this dark and airless world where political definitions and formal moral attitudes are curiously irrelevant. Good and evil are ultimately external to a world where all men are victims, where all are constantly living their death, where all are watching and waiting. And each, in a pathetic effort to cheat this waiting, has his useless, elected idiom, his Pascalian *divertissement*—Kyo his revolutionary heroism and his tragic will to dignity, Ferral his will to power and his sadism, Clappique his denial of the world through mythomania, Tchen his erotico-religious killing, Gisors his opium and his contemplation of the world's vanity. . . . And each *divertissement* is merely a prison within prison, an anti-destiny which itself hardens into a destiny—for there is no escape. With the symbol of the record from which Kyo cannot recognize his own voice—Malraux later emphasizes its central importance to the novel in *Les Voix du silence*—we are back to the black absurdity and loneliness, to the old dichotomy which for Malraux is insoluble. The world is unreal and the individual man, separated from the world by a chasm and from himself by another, is a mere madman—'every man', says Gisors, 'is mad' (p. 400). There is no relief for the 'incomparable monster' (p. 68) of the irrelative intensity; cognition, love, and human relationships are impossible; a man is an island of suffering surrounded by blackness. In this intolerable situation, he gropes instinctively towards some absolute, towards one or other of the three forms of completeness that are apprehended and established in depth throughout the novel: death, communion, and godhead—'every man', says Gisors again, 'dreams of being God' (p. 272). But godhead is attainable only as glory—and glory, like communion, only in death. Kyo, whose heroic, moth-like death is a kind of moral masterpiece, buys a little meaning from the world at the cost of annihilation, but the structure of the novel imprisons even this despairingly negative fraternity and glory in irony. If Gabriel Marcel was right to see in this powerful X-ray of the world a 'metaphysical pessimism which makes Schopenhauer look like milk-and-water',[1] it is because the only completeness, the only valorizing term of reference, the only reality of *La Condition humaine* is death. Malraux, having exhausted the illusory hope of the earlier hero, has involved one of the most significant movements of the contemporary world in his despair.

And yet the revolution, even if its philosophy is nonsense and its organizers unacceptable, remains perhaps as a possible climate. And values have at least been formulated—if only as the opposite of suffering and of Kyo's 'immutable solitude' (p. 67), we have dignity and the will to fraternity.

*　　　*　　　*

After celebrating his Goncourt Prize by undertaking a one-day flight over the Yemen desert in search of the legendary capital of the Queen of Sheba—and creating something of an academic scandal by publishing seven articles and some rather imprecise aerial photographs in *L'Intransigeant*—Malraux emerged gradually

---

[1] See Marcel's review of *La Condition humaine* in *L'Europe Nouvelle*, no. 799 (3 June 1933), p. 517.

as one of France's leading anti-Fascist writers, giving frequent addresses on art at the *Maison de la Culture*, speaking in Moscow, Madrid, London, and New York and, finally, fighting on the Republican side in Spain. He was not a Communist or Marxist but an anti-Fascist—and he was not, by temperament, a non-interventionist. He believed that the choice between democracy and Communism had been superseded for the intellectual by the threat of Fascism—in the altered historical context, he must now choose broadly, like it or not, between Communism and Fascism. Malraux, who is fond of saying that in politics it is important to choose one's enemy, did not opt *for* Communism—he opted *against* Fascism. And, in fact, underlying his speeches at this time, there is a hesitant idealism centred upon two words: fraternity and quality. Even if man, with the collapse of religion, has lost his soul, he must try to achieve some equivalent awareness of his dignity or quality. This, for Malraux, implies an acceptance of the idea of universal brotherhood, a climate of fraternity. He steered his own path quite firmly through these demanding years in terms of a tentative secular religion.

If *Le Temps du mépris* is a relative failure, it is not because it is propaganda. In fact, with Kassner alone in his prison cell and struggling in the face of suffering and death with his destiny, Malraux had his essential situation. But, without the pressure of the revolutionary situation, he was forced to invent and he could not invent a Kassner. His theme was fraternity and he asserts it movingly, but a mere glance at such a work as Fučík's *Notes from the Gallows*[2]—if direct comparison would be unfair—makes the reason for his failure cruelly clear: he did not as yet possess the human experience necessary to represent communion among men. Yet the ideal of fraternity which he had set up against the haunting solitude became real in Spain—if momentarily, for he saw only the heroic early stages of the struggle. The war changed him. Paradoxically, in this climate of action in the midst of fratricidal war, he achieves a certain relaxed simplicity —this time he really was the Witness, this time the legend had come true. And *L'Espoir* reflects all this. If he still retains great

[2] Julius Fučík, *Notes from the Gallows* (London, Lawrence & Wishart, 1948).

thematic control over his material, we move away from stylized tragedy towards epic, from the vertical, claustrophic, black-and-white world of *La Condition humaine* towards panorama, from literary conceptions such as Hero and Man of Action towards the representation of men in situation. If Malraux is right in his view that this work is his highest achievement, it is because it was the product of a unique balance between his instinctive vision and a fully resistant, because fully apprehended world. And, indeed, we have an orchestration, a range of colour, a humanity, an intelligence, a density, a profound architecture, a sheer talent which make this book—tossed off in eight months—one of the important novels of our time.

It has been said, on the strength of Malraux's opposition: *être et faire*, that he himself loses in the conflict between fraternity and the exigencies of organization, that the novel is propaganda, that we are offered the choice: Communism or nothing. But this conflict is the very subject of the novel and the moral and political quality of the book depends upon the counterpoint of four basic attitudes, not two. There are the Anarchists, who represent for Malraux the noblest element in revolution but whose semi-Christian, self-sacrificing heroism cannot win the war—wars are won with armies rather than with ideals. Then there are the Communists. They may well be able to win the war, but, it is everywhere asked, will not their political realism and their brutal discipline destroy the idealism which for Malraux was the very meaning of the war? In fact, the centre of gravity of *L'Espoir* lies outside this opposition between Anarchists and Communists. If the Communist Manuel might seem to be the formal hero, he is convincing only as a tormented and inconsistent Communist, who feels that he is 'becoming a little less human each day' (p. 290) and who is 'saved' by Malraux from the Party on the very last page. In the end, he gravitates towards the group of characters—Garcia, Magnin, Scali, Guernico, and Ximénès—who represent the third and central attitude in the novel. These men—non-Communists and intellectuals, some of them Catholics—are concerned with Malraux's own hope of establishing quality within fraternity. It is because of this hope that they have consented to act. They reject the choice between Communism and nothing as a false dilemma, they are attempting to live *être et faire* correlatively. The war, says Garcia in effect, is a hard fact. They must either fight Fascism and take the risk of the Communists winning and replacing economic slavery by political slavery—or do nothing. To do nothing is immoral—and futile, since their only hope of maintaining their viewpoint is by participating, by remaining a factor. He rides over the dilemma. And yet, like Magnin, he is constantly and painfully aware that all this is uncertain and provisional, that all historical action is 'unjust', that the great hope and fraternity of the 'Apocalypse' are being remorselessly inflected by the reality of war. Which brings us to the final and inevitable attitude in the novel, latent in the new and relaxed cosmic tone informing the style itself.

The fact is perhaps that the world came one day to look like a Malraux novel and that Malraux went to see—but found the world different. Malraux, on the ground, feels, realizes, and represents fraternity at last. Malraux, in his aeroplane, discovers the serenity and the beauty of the world, the sheer size of the sky—and the absurdity of the little human adventure beneath. The very discovery of fraternity reduces fraternity to inadequacy. If the universe is no longer felt as the oppressive weight of blackness, it is felt in the end as something more terrible still—as the ultimate indifference of daylight. In the thick of battle, we get a sentence like this printed as a complete paragraph: 'The sun shone brightly upon the line of bodies and upon the blood' (p. 25). And, if the title is established by a subtle counterpoint between the opposing attitudes, it is ultimately the old art-historian Alvear, half outside this novel of civil war, who gives it its hard edge of despair. For it is he who knows that the Revolution, in the wider sense, is merely another form of the old illusion of eternal life—'the blind man's song of hope' (p. 234).

Spain was perhaps also a private tragedy for Malraux. He left when the idealism was settling down into murderous civil war, when the birth of an army had already signalled for him the death of the hope of quality in fraternity. On the one hand, he has established himself within the world—when the time comes to fight again, he will fight magnificently. On the other hand, he has moved beyond the world—for the fraternity itself, if real, depended upon the exceptional situation of civil war, and even civil war could not sustain it. Back in Paris in 1938, with Spain and his novel already far behind and with the Faubourg St. Honoré running a new line in fetishes—'Munich-toi de ton petit parapluie'—he went back to art, to Spengler, to fundamentals. Between Malraux and his 'starry skies' the world no longer constitutes a powerful barrier: his great period of novel-writing is over. The stage is set for *Les Noyers de l'Altenburg*, *Les Voix du silence* and, indeed, for the adventure of Gaullism.

* * *

Les Noyers de l'Altenburg—his latest and in all probability, he thinks, his last novel—introduces Malraux's search for 'fundamental man'. Writing at the darkest moment of the war, he deliberately opts out of historical meanings by giving us the parallel destinies of a father on the German side in the first war and a son on the French side in the second. If the work is fragmentary and lacking in passion as a novel, it achieves its unity as a meditation and, indeed, a debate on man.

The case against man is presented as formidable. There is Berger's discovery, after his Eastern adventure, that action is vain. There is his idea that Western psychology, in that it is based on introspection, is based on illusion—with its clear implication that human nature is an arbitrary Western concept deriving from Christianity, that there is no fundamental man. Above all, there is Möllberg's Spenglerian-type discovery that history is only an absurd phantasmagoria of irreducible, watertight civilizations, separate from one another and having no continuity, no progression, no developing meaning. The vanity of action, the illusion of human nature, the mirage of history, man alone with no guide at all in the vast mathematical emptiness. . . . If Malraux's answer to this is rudimentary and irrational, it nevertheless constitutes the force of the book. There is the apprehension of the unity of destiny of the Bergers of Reichbach; there are the prisoners-of-war, with the gloss of society rubbed off them, reverting to the statuesque simplicity of medieval men; there is the confident irony of the old woman waiting patiently for life to run its hard course; there is the transcendent purity of the song of the mad Nietzsche in the darkened railway-carriage; there are the German soldiers protesting instinctively against the defilement of man by bringing their gassed victims back to their own trenches. Surely this implies an awareness of man's dignity, of his fundamental nature; surely the mystery of life itself cannot simply be explained away? Berger, at the colloquy, is presented with the symbolical alternative which leads Malraux towards his title: either these statues have meaning for us as they had for their medieval makers or they are merely pieces of wood. If he has no answer at the discursive level, he nevertheless has the feeling that art, if only as response, is somehow eternal and this confidence is mysteriously strengthened, as he walks alone at night, by his discovery of the tenacious, intermediate reality of the living walnut trees of the Altenburg. Malraux emerges from his exhaustion with a 'secret', a 'gift', a glimpse of a possible Being and of a possible eternity of art. But history intervenes again: the war, the Resistance, the Provisional Government in which he is Minister for Information, the collapse, the confusion of the Cold War, the *Rassemblement du Peuple Français*—and Malraux becomes perhaps the greatest Gaullist of them all.

Essentially because he was defending art. On the immediate level, he believed that Stalinist Russia threatened the world not only with political tyranny but with cultural barbarism, that in this situation political liberalism was too weak to preserve the freedom of culture, that France needed a strong government—a variant of the hard Cold War line of the period. But Malraux also believed that modern culture was dead, that reason and the sciences had failed, that parliaments were obsolete, that political programmes and parties were irrelevant, that France now had a universalist mission, that from Gaullism there might emerge a new human type, a 'Liberal Hero' on the lines of Lawrence of Arabia—that the world must be saved and saved in the terms of his own despair. And this stark fundamentalism was really a way of keeping politics at arm's length. On the immediate issues: practically nothing; look in the speeches for concrete proposals and there appear to be two—the suppression of the Communist Party and the setting up of cultural centres in the larger towns. But all this—for Malraux, struggling with Spengler, is drowned in Spenglerism—bathed in the frenzied light of Doom, Destiny, the Death of Empires, the Death of Man. When the world has been destroyed by atomic bombs, we are told in effect, art will rise again from the ruins, if only for a new species. Man becomes the Artist, the history of humanity the history of Art, the Cold War a strange struggle for 'the plastic heritage of the world'. Malraux's Gaullism, in fact, was an anti-politics, as Destiny is an anti-history. Now his private anguish was certainly real, but the Cold War was real and the political problems of France were real. Had de Gaulle come to power at this critical time, Malraux would after all have become an important political figure in Western Europe. Within this necessary perspective, his utter solemnity begins to resemble the frivolity of the *enfant terrible*. And, indeed, that this 'tragic humanism', this hollow Romantic catastrophism clothed in luridly quintessential language, should have been regarded by many as a noble expression of the Western ideal in the Cold War period is a curious reflection upon the uncertainty of the time.

He perhaps also emerges, for similar reasons, as something of an *enfant terrible* in the sphere of art. *Les Voix du silence* and the other writings in this field are impassioned, immensely suggestive works which contain some brilliant formal analyses, particularly of the development of individual and collective styles. In the end, however, Malraux is hardly convincing in his attempt to set up art as a 'fraternity of masterpieces' constituting an 'anti-destiny' and indeed—paradoxically and in deep opposition to contemporary rationalist thought—as a kind of transcendence establishing 'the first universal humanism'. If he appears to be partially successful in asserting the 'consciousness' of the artist and his freedom from historical and psychological determinisms, he scarcely thereby strengthens his answer to Spengler—in 1952, after the publication of *Les Voix du silence*, he was still saying in conversation: 'In the end, the only serious one among them is Spengler.' Essentially, having separated art from history, he puts up the 'Imaginary Museum' itself: the fact that we now through reproduction possess the cultural heritage of the planet, that from the rich confrontation of old and new fresh values emerge, that the Museum is alive with the constant, evolving dialogue of these 'voices of silence', that this transcendent, dialectical metamorphosis is an eternity of a kind. Yet his Romantic subjectivism surely plays him false. Is not this eternity of flux an historical betrayal of the 'conscious artist', even at the level of specifically artistic intention? And, if Malraux wrests from their cultural context all the works of the past in the name of the anti-historical autonomy of art, he is in fact, and explicitly, evaluating them selectively in terms of response to our own agnostic 'culture of interrogation'—which is not an artistic, but an historical phenomenon. Ironically, his anti-historical aesthetic would seem to be based on a narrow historical instrumentalism and the artist's 'conquest' would seem to emerge as an almost Spenglerian fatality. The world and history, once again, cannot so easily be put in parenthesis.

* * *

If the Malraux who again became a government minister in 1958 appeared to lapse once more, in introducing a structural reform of the National Theatre, into the old language of cultural Messianism, it must be said that there is also, in Malraux, the realist who knows that the essential task of the 'provisional consular régime' has been to end the war in Algeria, and that the creation of cultural centres necessarily comes second. In the end, however, it would seem to be clear that his true importance does not lie in the field of action or, indeed, in the field of formal thought. The antithesis between mind and the irrelative 'intensity', if obviously real, cannot in hard psychological terms be equated simply with the opposition between the individual and the world—the individual-in-the-world is more complex than this. The sleight of hand involved in the Heideggerian attempt to turn the external contingency of death into the internally defining structure of finitude has been dismantled very thoroughly by

Sartre in *L'Être et le néant*, while the impossible attempt in the earlier novels to live the inversion of life that is destiny leads demonstrably only to visceral certainties, to moral hysteria and to failure. The private struggle with Spengler seems somewhat marginal, while the 'tragic humanism', as so far presented, is essentially an antithetical, a Romantic and literary conception. To say this, however, is perhaps only to bring out the real importance of Malraux—which is that of the novelist. For, if the thinker sometimes gives strange answers, the novelist has certainly posed the questions. And, if destiny is illusion, it is an illusion which can inform a confrontation with the world of great poetic intensity.

'The only way', writes Malraux in 'N'Était-ce donc que cela?',[3] his essay on T. E. Lawrence, 'in which the mind can escape the absurd, is to give it form and expression by involving the whole world in it' (p. 17). This—with great courage, great talent, and a certain moving will to humanity—Malraux has done. He has lived out his own drama with an intensity that is rare in the extreme and, in projecting it upon the world, he has contrived compellingly to confront several generations with some of the major moral and psychological choices of the time. He necessarily remains an important term of reference.

Novels by Malraux:

Les Conquérants, Paris, Grasset, 1928.
    The Conquerors (trs. W. S. Whale), London, Cape, 1929; New York, Harcourt, Brace, 1929.
    (Two paperback editions of this translation appeared in 1956 (London, Mayflower, and New York, Beacon Press) with a *postface* by Malraux himself, translated by Jacques Le Clerq.)

La Voie Royale, Paris, Grasset, 1930.
    The Royal Way (trs. Stuart Gilbert), London, Methuen, 1935; New York, Smith & Haas, 1935.

La Condition humaine, Paris, Gallimard, 1933.
    Storm in Shanghai (trs. Alistair Macdonald), London, Methuen, 1934. (This same translation, entitled *Man's Estate*, was reissued by Methuen, 1948, and Penguin Books, 1961.)

[3] Printed in *Saisons*, no. 3 (Winter 1946–7), pp. 9–24.

Man's Fate (trs. H. M. Chevalier), New York, Random House, 1934.
Le Temps du mépris, Paris, Gallimard, 1935.
Days of Contempt (trs. H. M. Chevalier), London, Gollancz, 1936. (This same translation was issued as *Days of Wrath*, New York, Random House, 1936.)
L'Espoir, Paris, Gallimard, 1937.
Days of Hope (trs. Stuart Gilbert and Alistair Macdonald), London, Routledge, 1938. (This same translation was issued as *Man's Hope*, New York, Random House, 1938.)
Les Noyers de l'Altenburg, Lausanne, Éd. du Haut-Pays, 1943, and Paris, Gallimard, 1948.
The Walnut Trees of Altenburg (trs. A. W. Fielding), London, Lehmann, 1952; Toronto, Longmans, 1952.

(*The Royal Way*, *Man's Fate* and *Man's Hope* are also published in New York by Modern Library.)

SUCCESSORS

RAYMOND QUENEAU
b. 1903
BY MARTIN ESSLIN

———————☆———————

'"Everything foreigners think French novels ought to be—improper, without exceeding the bounds of decency." . . .' That the English publishers of the translation of *Zazie dans le Métro* should have thought it fitting, or necessary, to advertise the book in these terms is a measure of the incomprehension of one of France's major poet-novelists in the English-speaking world. It also indicates how totally unknown a writer, whose fame and importance have been solidly established in France since the 'thirties, still remained here in 1960.

Admittedly Queneau is not a writer readily to be recognized by the critics and reviewers who act as intermediaries between French culture and the culture-conscious readers of quality papers or week-end reviews. His work lacks the easily recognizable signposts of importance. It is funny, free from portentousness, highly allusive and distinguished by a virtuosity of language that is not readily accessible to an ear not quite attuned to French colloquial speech. Nor is Queneau one of those novelist-philosophers who are prepared to go to great lengths to explain themselves in treatises and manifestoes. He is an original thinker, nevertheless, and of particular importance in that his thought represents a point of intersection between French existentialism on the one hand and Anglo-Saxon linguistic philosophy on the other.

Queneau is that rarest of rare phenomena in an age of specialists and watertight compartments of culture: a truly universal, encyclopaedic mind, a poet who is also a philosopher, mathematician, and scientist, the editor of the brilliantly conceived (though not always equally brilliantly executed) attempt at presenting a complete synthesis of twentieth-century culture, the *Encyclopédie de la Pléiade*.

The son of a Le Havre draper, Queneau read philosophy at the Sorbonne, devoted himself to mathematical studies and became a member of the surrealist group. After military service as a *zouave* in North Africa, he returned to Paris and continued to be involved in the stormy internal dissensions of the surrealists till he broke with André Breton in 1929. In the same year, during a stay at the Portuguese seaside resort of Azanhas do Mar, he read Joyce's *Ulysses*, a work which became a decisive influence on his development as a writer.

Ulysses helped Queneau to crystallize his thought on a question that had preoccupied him since his student days: the question of the divergence between the written language and that spoken by people in their daily lives, or rather: the problem of how one could write in a language as it was actually spoken instead of employing an idiom fixed and fossilized by grammarians long since dead and fettered by rules of spelling that made language something *seen* rather than heard.

Queneau himself has described how he first became aware of this problem while reading popular papers like *L'Épatant* with its racy reproduction of the vernacular, or the works of the mid-nineteenth-century caricaturist and social satirist Henri Monnier, creator of that petty-bourgeois prototype, Joseph Prudhomme, and the poems of Jehan Rictus. In studying English Queneau had encountered the same problem in discussions of English and American slang. But above all, he had been deeply impressed by his discovery of Vendryes's great book on the living French language, *Le Langage* (written 1920), which revealed to him the immense distance between the grammatical structure of French as fixed by sixteenth-century grammarians and seventeenth-century writers and as it is spoken today. Vendryes pointed out, for example, that the supposedly still Latin syntax of spoken French showed affinities with such out-of-the-way languages as Chinook, spoken by American Indians of the North-Western United States. In Chinook the indication of the grammatical relationships contained in a sentence is separated from the concrete concepts used, so that a phrase like 'the man killed the wife with a knife' would appear in a form rather like: he her did with / man wife knife kill. Yet in spoken French, Vendryes showed, exactly the same syntactic structure, separating the algebraic indication of the abstract framework of thought, the *morphème*, from the concrete data, the *semantème*, was quite frequently to be found—in phrases like: 'Elle n'y a encore pas / voyagé, ta cousine, en Afrique'. Thus, Vendryes argued, the daily speech of the common people differs from the written language not only in vocabulary, but also in syntax and morphology: the *passé défini*, the *imparfait* of the subjunctive are no longer used in normal speech; the complex rules for maintaining a logical relationship in the use of tenses have long been abandoned, if they were ever really used outside the printed page.

What impressed Queneau in *Ulysses* was the freedom with which Joyce handled the vernacular, his boldness in the variation between a number of different prose-styles used parodistically and the intricate formal pattern of correspondences between the modern novel and its Homeric counterpart.

In the summer of 1932 Queneau went to Greece.

On the boat I began to study modern Greek and to talk with Greeks about the struggle between the *Kathareuousa* and the *Demotiki*, between the language that strives to differ as little as possible from the ancient Greek and that which is actually spoken. . . . It was then that the elements listed above crystallized and that it became clear to me that the modern French language would at last have to break loose from the conventions by which it is still hemmed in when written (conventions of style and spelling as much as of vocabulary). . . . It also struck me that the best way of establishing this new language would not be by writing about some event among ordinary people (for this might make one's intentions misunderstood) but by taking the example of those men of the sixteenth century who used modern vernaculars in writing about theology or philosophy, and putting into spoken French some philosophical text: and as I had the *Discours de la Méthode* with me, I decided to translate it into spoken French . . . (*Bâtons, chiffres et lettres*, pp. 13–14).

The book which grew out of this idea was Queneau's first, and according to some critics still his most important, novel: *Le*

Chiendent (1933). This is an intricately patterned narrative exploring the nature of being and non-being in bold and varied vernacular language.

The structure of the novel itself betrays the mathematical education of its author. It is, as he himself has pointed out, composed of ninety-one sections (seven chapters, each made up of thirteen sections) because 91 is the sum of the numbers from 1 to 13, the ultimate sum of its own digits being again 1. Each of the ninety-one sections of *Le Chiendent* in turn observes its own inner unity, each adhering to the three unities of time, place, and action, but also strictly confined to one single genre of narration: narration proper, narration with reported speech, pure dialogue, *monologue intérieur*, reported monologue in *oratio obliqua*, letters, newspaper reports, and dreams.

This rigid inner structure of *Le Chiendent*, clearly modelled on that of *Ulysses*, its foundation on the principle of *number*, represents Queneau's desire to achieve a *poetic* novel: numbers after all are the basis of poetic structure and 'if the *ballade* or the *rondeau* have perished, it seems to me that as against that disaster a new strictness ought to show itself in the practice of prose (ibid., p. 23). And if it were objected that the imposition of such purely arbitrary patterns must needs produce an extremely arbitrary picture of reality, Queneau's answer would undoubtedly be that this indeed is the poet's and the artist's task: the world itself is arbitrary and absurd; only the thinking individual can give it a pattern, however arbitrary. Things have meaning only in so far as they exist in a mind, so the mind is free to impose its pattern on being. This indeed is the theme of *Le Chiendent* which boldly attempts to present a set of variations on Descartes's philosophy: *cogito ergo sum*. (Descartes himself is mentioned in the book in typically cryptic terms. Saturnin, the philosophical concierge, asks himself why it is that card-players in the cafés always tend to call the waiters Descartes, loudly calling out to them—Descartes! des cartes!)

The hero of the book, Étienne Marcel, a bank clerk, who has been leading a completely routine life, wholly unthinking and unconscious, and who therefore has not been in existence, comes into being at the moment when, in passing a shop-window, he notices a waterproof hat which has been filled with water, to demonstrate its quality, so that two little rubber ducks float inside it. From that moment on the hitherto two-dimensional lifeless shadow that used to be Étienne Marcel gradually swells into three-dimensional being and is immediately involved in a series of adventures. But Étienne comes into being also through becoming an object of observation: somebody who has noticed his routine movements between his bank and the railway terminus from which he commutes, becomes interested in him and begins to observe his mode of life. Thus Étienne acquires, at one and the same moment, not only subjective being but also an objective existence in the eyes of an observer—or in Sartrean terms (and *Le Chiendent* appeared ten years before *L'Être et le néant*) Being-for-Itself as well as Being-for-Others.

Le Chiendent is a novel rich in bizarre characters and intricately patterned plots. At its core stands a further elaborate exploration of the relationship between thinking and being (or non-being), consciousness and reality. A chance remark, spoken by someone while visiting the shack of a poor old rag-and-bone merchant, le père Taupe, to the effect that such old men are sometimes found to have been misers and millionaires, is misunderstood and sets off a whole series of elaborate attempts to secure the supposed fortune. As a consequence a young waitress is persuaded to consent to marry the old man and is poisoned on her wedding day: a set of concepts to which nothing had corresponded in reality, which solely existed in the mind of a foolish old woman who misunderstood a remark reported to her, have changed reality, have given rise to elaborate movements of things and human beings (the family coming together from the four corners of the earth to attend the wedding), and have finally blotted out a young and vital human being. As Queneau puts it in another novel, *Le Dimanche de la vie*, false or falsely understood words set up *zones of error* which can become *zones of trouble* and can ruin a human life.

The mistaken belief, the idea that old Taupe is a rich man, when he is not, concerns something which is not and therefore falls into the category of non-being. And yet that which *is not* has concrete effects on the reality that *is*. Thus non-being can be more real than being. That is the subject of the profound meditation by Saturnin which, on pages 256–8 of *Le Chiendent*, forms the philosophical kernel of the book. The affinity between Queneau's thought and Sartre's existentialism, which was formulated at a much later date, is certainly striking. What Sartre calls the nothingness at the centre of Being-for-Itself, the pure potentiality at the core of human consciousness which is *nothing* but freedom, the realization that man perceives himself in his ability to choose between modes of being, is very much akin to Queneau's conception that in the absurdity of the universe reality is a product of chance, choice, and the curious by-products of consciousness, the perception of true and false ideas.

As the story of *Le Chiendent* proceeds it becomes more and more fantasticated. The characters are engulfed in a vast war between the French and the Etruscans, led by a queen called Miss Aulini; the war lasts for decades until in the end a small band of the characters of the novel are all that remains of the forces of Gaul, as France then is again called. The war ends in complete exhaustion. The characters disperse and before we know where we are they are back in the situation from which the novel started. The last sentences of the book are identical with the opening passage. What we have witnessed was the unfolding of potentialities, which may, or may not, be realized. We thought we were reading a story about people, but we have merely been following the arbitrary constructions of a writer. For as Étienne, or Queneau, said earlier in the book:

'People think they are doing one thing, and then they do another. They think they are making a pair of scissors, but they have made something quite different. Of course, it is a pair of scissors, it is made to cut and it cuts, but it is also something quite different . . . [or take] a house. It is a house because one lives in it, but it is also something else. . . .'

'It would be interesting if one could say what that is, that "something else".'

'No doubt. But that is not possible. That depends on the circumstances, or it cannot be expressed. Words too are manufactured objects.

One can look at them quite independently from their sense. . . . Apart from their meaning they may express something entirely different. Thus the word teapot describes *this* object, but I can also consider it outside that meaning, in the same way in which I can look at the teapot itself quite apart from its practical use, disregarding that it is supposed to be used for making tea or even that it is a simple receptacle. . . .'

'. . . Do you think that the birds and the pebbles and the stars and the shellfish and the clouds have a meaning? That they have been made to fulfil some purpose?'

'I don't think so,' replied Étienne . . . 'anything in nature can acquire meaning; when human beings give it a meaning. . . . That is what's so strange . . . one thinks one is doing one thing and one is doing another. One thinks one is seeing one thing and one is seeing another. You are told one thing, you understand something else, and what you should have understood is a third thing again. . . .'

'For me,' said Pierre, 'the things, the world, do not have the meaning they are pretending to have. The world is not what it purports to be; but I don't believe it has another meaning. It has none.' (*Le Chiendent*, pp. 126-7).

It is precisely because the world has no meaning that imposes itself that the creative artist is free to construct his own patterns according to his own private numbers and rhythms. In the face of the vast chaos that confronts us we can create small areas of order and symmetry like children building sand-castles on a beach lapped by the endless and formless ocean.

And it is because our own thought is the principle of order in the amorphous nothingness of the universe, because our lives are formed by our thought, and because thought is conditioned by language, that there is so close a link between modes of being and habits, and the destruction of ossified habits, of language. It is in poetry that we can give meaning and measured order to the formless universe—and poetry depends on language, whose true music can only come from a return to its true rhythms in the living vernacular.

Queneau's rich and varied *œuvre* as poet and novelist is devoted to the destruction of ossified forms and the dazzling of the eye by phonetic spelling and authentic Chinook-type syntax. Even a casual glance at his books will show numerous examples of this kind of alienation effect: 'spa' for 'n'est-ce pas',

'Polocilacru' for 'Paul aussi l'a cru', 'Moua chsui dpari' for 'Moi, je suis de Paris', 'Doukipudonktan' for 'D'où qu'il pue donc tant', to give but a few samples of the surprising aspect of what Queneau calls the new, or third, French language. How can there be poetry, he argues, when the numbers of the verse are ruled by the mute *e*, which is not pronounced, only seen, and thus confines poetry to the printed page? How can such poetry still be understood by the people?

It is significant that some of Queneau's own verse has in fact achieved real popular currency in the form of *chansons* that have become best-sellers, above all the song 'C'est bien connu' that was made famous by Juliette Gréco:

>Si tu t'imagines
>Si tu t'imagines
>fillette fillette
>si tu t'imagines
>xa va xa va xa
>va durer toujours
>la saison des za
>la saison des za
>saison des amours
>ce que tu te goures
>fillette fillette
>ce que tu te goures ...
>
>*L'Instant fatal* (Paris, Gallimard, 1948, p. 24).

These verses give a good idea of the combination of unusual spelling and simple language with judicious use of argot terms ('se gourer') that is characteristic of Queneau's approach. Not all his verse, however, is as simple: even in his later poems the influence of surrealism is at times strong and produces bold imagery and opaque free association.

For Queneau there is no sharp dividing line between prose and poetry. Many of his novels contain passages in verse; even in seemingly dry wastes of prose he manages, cunningly, to insert an occasional Alexandrine. His second novel, *Gueule de Pierre* (1934), the first part of a trilogy that later appeared in one volume as *St. Glinglin*, is rigidly constructed in three movements, the last of which is in verse. Its sequel and companion novel, *Les Temps mêlés* (1941), opens with a sequence of poems, which is followed by a monologue, while the third part is in dialogue and constitutes, in effect, a play in five acts. This ambitious trilogy which was completed by the appearance of *St. Glinglin* (1948) —a rewritten version of the first two parts, eliminating some of the verse and dialogue and adding a new third section—is an attempt at retelling the myth of the sons' killing of the father which Queneau had found in Freud's *Totem and Taboo*. Its composition coincides with Queneau's psychoanalytic treatment which he underwent from 1933 to 1939 and which is also the theme of his autobiographical essay in verse, *Chêne et chien* (1937).[1] The oak and the dog are, in Queneau's view, the two possible etymologies of his name, and represent the dual nature of his personality, its preoccupation with the mud and excrement of existence on the one hand, and its idealism, the upward striving of the noble oak, on the other.

This period of the exploration of his own self also produced Queneau's two autobiographical novels: *Les derniers jours* (1936), which he now repudiates, and *Odile* (1937). In the first of these books we see the young philosophy student from Le Havre, somewhat forlorn in Paris and vainly searching for sexual experience, involved with a crowd of more or less savoury fellow-students from his home town as well as with an elderly swindler sporting a number of aliases (the multiple personality is a favourite character in Queneau's novels). There is also an old geography professor from the lycée at Le Havre who suddenly realizes in his old age that all his teaching has been a fraud as he had never been to any of the countries he described in his lessons. In the centre of this merry-go-round of characters there stands Alfred, the wise waiter in a favourite student café, who sees the group come and go. Alfred has second sight (another recurring theme in Queneau's work) and is thus a symbol of destiny, the fixed point outside time from which history can be recorded.

Odile tells the story of Queneau's breach with the surrealists.

[1] Later included in collected poems for 1920-51 under the general title, *Si tu t'imagines* (Paris, Gallimard, 1952).

It contains a savage portrait of André Breton in the vain and pretentious character of Anglarès. The narrator, Roland Travy, is a young man, recently returned from military service in North Africa, who spends his time in endless mathematical researches and is taken up by the surrealists because Anglarès has misunderstood some of his theories about mathematics and thinks that Travy's views fit in with his own. The latter, however, prefers the company of a circle of prostitutes, pimps, and racing touts among whom he finds his love, Odile.

Queneau, who had married in 1928 and become the father of a son in 1934, had left his employment in a bank for journalism and was at one time in charge of a daily column entitled 'Connaissez-vous Paris?' in *L'Intransigeant* (the column plays a certain part in his novel *Le Dimanche de la vie*). From 1930 onwards he had been working at the Bibliothèque Nationale on a vast enterprise: he wanted to write a comprehensive survey of all the *fous littéraires*, the literary cranks, of French literature. This vast body of research never appeared in the form he had originally intended. But much of it was used in the novel *Les Enfants du Limon* (1938)—another ambitious attempt to create a novel on a wholly symmetrical pattern. But the quotations from the vast work on the literary cranks, inventors of fantastic cosmogonies, squarers of the circle and mad social reformers, never blend entirely with the ups and downs of a large and eccentric family around which the plot of the book is built. Yet the literary cranks are a fascinating illustration of Queneau's philosophy because they represent so many new patterns of the universe in a world that can be made to assume a different guiding principle according to the thinking of each differently oriented, or distorted, brain. Our normal universe is only one possible case in an infinity of others, just as Euclidean geometry only represents one possible case in an infinity of potential systems.

In *Un rude hiver* (1939) Queneau returns to his native Le Havre and to memories of his youth. Here again it is the effect of a *zone of error* that is explored, only the error is a deliberate one: the negative tendencies in a man's mind lead to the killing of many human beings. The time is the First World War. Lehameau, a man in his thirties who has been wounded in the initial phases of the fighting and now works in the port administration, falls in love with an English WAAC. Lehameau is a non-conformist, he is disgusted by official anti-German propaganda and hates Jews and Freemasons, so that he secretly wishes for a German victory. He meets a mysterious Swiss businessman who, when he learns about his pro-German opinions, begins to ask him questions about the movement of ships. Lehameau guesses that the man is a spy and yet he does not hesitate to give away a certain amount of information in a casual way. When his affair with the English girl auxiliary comes to light the girl is sent back to England. Lehameau mentions the sailing of the ship to the Swiss businessman. The ship is torpedoed and the girl he loves is killed. He denounces the Swiss and has him shot. On Sundays Lehameau, who is a widower, has been taking out two children, a boy and a girl. Their grown-up sister is a prostitute. The children themselves first drew him into conversation in the street. Lehameau has become fond of the little girl. Now that he is about to leave for the front—his wounded leg having healed—he realizes that he loves her.

Un rude hiver is as carefully and as ironically constructed as all Queneau's novels. Lehameau has lost his first wife and his mother in a fire which burnt down a cinema. He now loses his second love by drowning. He loves the English girl, Helena, but never succeeds in making love to her. He is aware of his suppressed desire for the little girl, Annette. But the only time he makes love to anyone in the course of the book is when, slightly drunk, he comes to see Annette, learns that she is not at home, and is induced to spend the night with her sister, the prostitute. When he leaves for the front at the end of the book we feel that he will never return, so that his love for Annette will remain as unconsummated as that for Helena. It is a strange, dry, astringent book. It can be fully understood, however, only in the light of a passage in *Chêne et chien* from which we learn that Queneau's father preferred, during the First World War, 'the pointed helmet over there to the socialists' and that he subscribed, like Lehameau, to the Swiss papers in order to be able to read the German communiqués. So that Lehameau is, in some ways, a portrait of Queneau's father.

After a brief period of military service Queneau became, in 1941, secretary-general of the important French publishing house of Gallimard, the publishers of the *Nouvelle Revue Française*, who launched an impressive number of great writers, Proust and Gide among them.

At the age of thirty-seven he had thus reached a position of real influence in the literary world and had achieved the maturity and self-assurance necessary to produce some of his finest work.

The novel *Pierrot mon ami* (1942) must certainly be counted among his finest achievements. It is perhaps the most perfect of all. The first impression of a slight, tender, humorous novel is a deceptive one, for this is a book with a serious philosophy behind it. It is only the effortless simplicity of the telling of the story that hides the delicacy of its construction and the depth of its thought. *Pierrot mon ami* is a poem on chance and destiny, on the relationship between what should have happened and what actually does happen. The book thus has two plots—a potential one and an actual one. And the potentialities always fail to come to fruition by a hair's breadth. Pierrot, employed in a fairground, the Uni-Park, falls in love with the big boss's daughter and almost, but never quite, achieves his aim. He meets the guardian of a mysterious mausoleum in which the remains of a Balkan prince who died on that spot on the fringes of the Uni-Park, are being maintained in solemn and well-endowed state. The old man takes a liking to Pierrot and wants to make him his heir and adopted son. But Pierrot is too casual to turn up at the right moment and so this potential manifest destiny also remains un-realized. The Uni-Park burns down and Pierrot almost plays an important part in solving the mystery surrounding the man who is destined to rebuild the fairground as a zoo. But just as he is about to reveal the identity of the man in question to the lady who has been searching for him, he himself turns up and steals his thunder. And so in the end Pierrot, who might have played a part in all these exciting and romantic events, has only drifted through them.

It was one of the most rounded, most complete, most autonomous episodes of his life, and when he thought of it with all the concentration required (which incidentally happened only rarely) he saw quite well how the elements that made it up could have linked together in an adventure that could have developed on the level of mystery to be resolved in due course like a problem of algebra, in which there are as many equations as there are unknowns, and how it had not happened like that—he saw the novel that this could have made, a detective story with a crime, a guilty party and a detective . . . and he saw the novel that it had become, a novel so lacking in artifice that it was impossible to know whether there was a riddle in it to be solved or not . . . (p. 211).

Pierrot represents one of the main types of the Queneau hero: the simpleton who is a natural poet and who passes through the world without understanding it, without seeking to understand it. In an absurd and meaningless universe this is the most rational and least foolish of all possible attitudes: the taking of life as it comes, without thought of the morrow, and with the resulting freedom to enjoy its simple pleasures. It is precisely because Pierrot is not troubled by the unrealized possibilities of his adventure, by that which is not though it could have been, because therefore he remains in the realm of being and moves forward without any strong desires or predetermined plans, that he avoids disappointment and remains wholly free. He drifts from one job to another: when he loses his work in the Palace of Fun (where the fun consists of making the ladies walk over a jet of air that blows up their skirts) he has no fear of his future and, indeed, without much effort, he drifts into another job, assistant to a fakir. When he loses that too after the fairground has burned down, he is hired to drive some animals back to the country, and undertakes that work with the same gravity and unconcern with which he executed his previous weird employments. It is characteristic of Queneau's method that in describing Pierrot's journey to the country he introduces his two passengers, Mésange and Pistolet, without further details; he merely notes their reactions at meals, their moods of gaiety and depression. Only much later, and by the way, he discloses that Mésange is an ape and Pistolet a wild boar. To Pierrot they have been personalities like any human being, and so they are to Queneau.

Loin de Rueil (1944) has the same lightness of touch, the same mellow, thoughtful gaiety, that gives *Pierrot mon ami* its charm. Yet the hero of this book is Pierrot's opposite in that he is a dreamer who still indulges in the potentialities of being: a French Walter Mitty, Jacques L'Aumône, constantly sees himself in the role of the romantic hero in an endless series of possible situations. But then, like Pierrot, Jacques is never too serious. He too accepts what life brings. Having abandoned his job, his wife and son, for the sake of a music-hall singer, he loses his ambitions and practises humility. After a series of incredible adventures he lands in Hollywood and becomes a film star under the name of James Charity. And so the book closes in a circle: earlier we have been present when young Jacques went to the cinema and saw a cowboy film of which, of course, Jacques L'Aumône himself was the hero. Now, at the close of the story, Jacques's parents and his little boy go to the cinema: they see a cowboy film of which James Charity *is* in fact the hero. His ex-wife is puzzled. The film star reminds her of someone. It is as though she had seen him before. But then, one often imagines the most incredible things. Suzanne, Jacques's ex-wife, is now the mistress of des Cigales, an elderly poet who used to know the young man. Jacques's wife, and co-star in Hollywood now, is Lulu Doumer who once was a maid in des Cigales's house. Here too, then, we have the ironic symmetry of a world in which, in Queneau's phrase, characters and situations are made to rhyme, like the patterns of lines in a poem.

Des Cigales, the poet, suffers from a disease which he calls *ontalgie*—the pain of being, an existential sickness, which resembles asthma 'but is more distinguished'. It is asthma from which Queneau himself suffered in his youth, the sickness that made him aware of the problems of being and non-being and gave him the desire for the freedom, ease, and gaiety that his writings express.

Le Dimanche de la vie (1951) completes the trilogy of Queneau's happiest novels. Here too we meet a saint-like simpleton, Valentin Brû, who drifts through life with gay unconcern. Like Pierrot, Valentin is potentially a poet and a thinker, but too unambitious and lazy to take up serious work. And so when, during his military service, he pleases the tastes of an ageing shop-keeper, Julia (a draper like Queneau's parents), he marries her; his charm earns him the inheritance of his mother-in-law's shop in Paris; so he moves to Paris and runs a shop devoted to the sale of frames for pictures and photographs. Julia, who fancies that she has divinatory powers, secretly starts an establishment as a clairvoyante; when she suffers a stroke Valentin disguises himself as a veiled lady and practises the same trade—with astonishing success. When the war of 1939 breaks out he is called up, but survives to be reunited with his wife. Again, the simple story of simple people conceals a philosophical theme: Valentin is something of a saint and a mystic, he spends his time trying to observe the flow of time:

'... I think of passing time, and as time is identical with itself, I think always of the same thing, that is, in the end I think of nothing ...'
The other one looked at him, surprised. Valentin added amiably:
'It elevates the soul' (p. 286).

In contrast to Valentin, the stable character who meditates on time and eternity and is thus true to himself, stands Paul, his brother-in-law, a civil servant who later becomes an armaments manufacturer and profiteer. He is so unstable that even his family name is in constant flux, being different, though similar, every time it is mentioned: Bulocra, Brelugat, Brolugat, Brédéga, Botugat, Botegat, Bodrugat, Botucla, Bodéga, Bradoga, &c., &c. At one point he even loses the identity of his first name and appears briefly as Jules Bodrugat.

Valentin's only intellectual passion concerns the battle of Jena. His greatest ambition is to see the battlefield where Napoleon destroyed the Prussian Army. He fulfils that ambition just before the outbreak of the war, just before he becomes part of an army that is to be destroyed by the Germans.

The last glimpse we get of Valentin (after the fall of France) is on the station-platform in Toulouse. Julia, who is looking for him, notices him in the crowd that is trying to storm an empty train. Three young girls in slacks are trying to climb into the train through the window. Julia sees Valentin approaching to help them. Is this, however, an act of Christian charity on the

part of the philosopher, saint, clairvoyant, and simpleton?—
'Julia shook with laughter: it was to get his hands on their
backsides' (p. 306).

In *Pierrot mon ami, Loin de Rueil,* and *Le Dimanche de la vie*
Queneau had reached the full mastery of his own type of poetic
novel, written in his own demotic language, and making use of the
full range of narrative techniques that he had employed, much
more self-consciously, in *Le Chiendent* and *St. Glinglin.* It was the
desire to exercise his virtuosity that led him to produce what is
perhaps his best-known work in the English-speaking countries,
Exercices de style (1947), an astonishing *tour de force* of pure technique of language and narration. Here a simple incident (a
passenger has an angry exchange in a bus, and is seen two hours
later at the Gare St. Lazare talking to a friend who is overheard
telling him that there is a button missing on his overcoat) is told
in ninety-nine different styles of narration, covering the entire
gamut of possible styles, approaches, figures of speech, literary
genres. The same story is told metaphorically, subjectively,
objectively, as an ode, in Alexandrines, as a Japanese Haiku, in
coded permutations of groups of letters, in apocopes and syncopes,
in noble and vulgar, interrogatory and negative style. Not all of
these exercises are equally successful, not all are equally witty. But
they all illustrate Queneau's basic assumption: the primacy of
language and thought over reality. The same incident can appear
in ninety-nine different moods, and mean ninety-nine different
things, in ninety-nine different modes of language. It can assume
a political, philosophical, or, for that matter, a medical or
botanical aspect. The incident, itself arbitrary in its nature, and
arbitrarily singled out as an incident (for in reality it is not even
that, there being no connexion between the two chance appearances of the same shady character), can be made the material for
wholly arbitrary treatment. In the end we are left with ninety-nine more or less pleasing, more or less skilful, arbitrary exercises
of language which not only have nothing in common, but which
are ultimately related to nothing. The exercises in style remain
real: but the pretext from which they arose has itself no reality to
speak of. In other words, fiction, in Queneau's opinion, is not

concerned with the transcription of reality but with the creation of meaningful or beautiful patterns from the meaningless jumble of random happenings that only become real when perceived in an ordered pattern.

Exercices de style had a great success with the public: it was immediately appreciated as a *jeu d'esprit*, performed by the famous Frères Jacques and issued as a long-playing record.

Its popular success in France was exceeded only by that of Queneau's latest novel, *Zazie dans le Métro* (1959), in which his handling of demotic language fired the public imagination for the first time and aroused general laughter and amusement. Here the simpleton hero is not a young man but a little girl, Zazie, who is taken to Paris by her mother and parked with her Uncle Gabriel while the mother is occupied with her lover. Zazie is wholly innocent, but uses the foul language she has picked up in the *demi-monde* milieu in which her mother moves, and this is the source of a series of broadly comic effects. Moreover, Zazie's uncle, a female impersonator who performs a suggestive dance in a night-club, is surrounded by a weird cast of low-life characters who are hurled into a wild whirl of mad incidents by Zazie's irrepressible zest for life. Zazie wants, above all, to ride on the métro. But the métro is on strike, and her wish cannot be fulfilled. Only after a night of wildly farcical incidents at the night-club, when the métro runs again, is Zazie finally put on a train. But now she is too tired to be aware of her ride. And in the end, when her mother asks her whether she has seen the métro, Zazie laconically remarks: No.

Zazie is certainly Queneau's most easily accessible book, but it also seems his most laboured work, the one in which he openly aims at broadly farcical effects. No wonder that English critics did not notice the brilliant philosopher-poet behind the clowning. Yet the intention of showing the mad rat-race and corruption of urban life against a figure of innocent humanity is clearly present in the book. Zazie is drawn into a world of homosexuals, swindlers, sex-maniacs, mindless pleasure-seekers: they can be seen as picturesque characters introduced for the sake of picturesqueness, or again as monsters introduced in gruesome colours by a moralist. Louis Malle, the young *avant-garde* film director who turned *Zazie* into a hilarious film, certainly saw the book in this light. He declared that his film was built on the pattern of those Westerns where a long-legged character arrives in a wide-open town which he leaves behind him all cleaned up when he departs again.

With *Zazie* Queneau, in many ways the most refined and esoteric of French writers, became a best-seller. If, in reaching this consummation, he did not aim at, or achieve, his own highest standards, the success of the book was nevertheless a great vindication: for, if he was right in campaigning for a literature in the language actually spoken by the common man, he had to demonstrate the common man's response to hearing—and above all *reading*—his own everyday speech. In *Zazie* as in some of his *chansons* Queneau has triumphantly bridged that most dangerous gulf of our culture, the gulf between the artist, the intellectual, the highbrow on the one hand and the common man on the other. Queneau, a real poet, has written a song like 'Si tu t'imagines'. Queneau, a novelist imbued with the traditions and craftsmanship of Proust and Joyce, has figured in the best-seller lists with *Zazie*.

Curiously enough, an earlier attempt at achieving a broad popular success in a deliberately unintellectual type of fiction had failed: in 1947 Queneau had written a book, obviously intended for the readers of the tough, fast-moving adventure thriller, somewhere between Simenon and the author of *No Orchids for Miss Blandish*. It was issued by a popular publisher in covers less distinguished than those of the *série blanche* of Queneau's own firm, Gallimard. Moreover, it was published as a translation from the original English with a fictitious author on the title page: a lady called Sally Mara. The book, *On est toujours trop bon avec les femmes*, tells an episode of the Irish Easter Rising of 1916. One of the girl clerks remains behind in the General Post Office and is thus drawn into the siege of the building: gradually she yields to the advances of each member of a group of rebels. But when the rebels surrender and the victorious British forces, led by an officer who is her fiancé, relieve the building, she has the rebels shot because, she alleges, they had made some mildly improper suggestion to her. In writing this book Queneau followed the example of his friend Boris Vian, who had published an equally daring semi-pornographic novel, *J'irai cracher sur vos tombes* (1946), with the same publisher and also under an Anglo-Saxon pseudonym. But Queneau's appearance as Sally Mara was more than just an excursion into the tough fringe of literature. It was an attempt at following in the footsteps of his great model, James Joyce, by emulating him and by entering into his Irish world. Sally Mara's novel was followed, in 1950, by the publication of her diaries, her *Journal intime*. It seems as though these two books were to form part of a much larger design: the creation of an imaginary writer and her works. But it appears that this intriguing plan has been abandoned.

Queneau's excursions into the field of popular literature are balanced by his continued and steady output of poetry, some of it light, but much of it ambitiously 'avant-gardist'. Apart from the autobiographical poem *Chêne et chien*, Queneau's most sustained poetic effort is the charming *Petite cosmogonie portative* (1950), a didactic poem in the eighteenth-century tradition, a retelling in rhymed couplets of the whole history of evolution. It is characteristic of Queneau that human history rates only a single couplet in this long scientific poem:

> The ape, with ease, became man bit by bit.
> who, in due course of time, the atom split (p. 121),

after which the rest of the sixth and last canto is devoted to the genesis and development of machines down to calculating machines capable of superseding man.

An intellectual who can reach the best-seller list, a poet who can write a song to figure in the hit parade, Raymond Queneau is one of the truly universal men of his time: an encyclopaedic mind equally at home with higher mathematics or Hegel (he has edited a book of lectures on that philosopher), he has also translated George du Maurier's *Peter Ibbetson*, Sinclair Lewis's *It Can't Happen Here*, and Amos Tutuola's *The Palm Wine Drinkard*. Queneau has worked as a film-script writer on René Clément's *Monsieur Ripois* (English title: *Knave of Hearts*), on a film for Bunuel and one of those of the *nouvelle vague* (*Un Couple* directed by J.-P. Mocky). He has appeared in a short film himself, giving a lecture on mathematics (*Arithmétique*, directed by Pierre Kast). Queneau has even held a one-man show of his own paintings. And—as one of the leading brains in France's leading publishing house—he exercises a very considerable influence on French writers, readers, and reading habits. He is a member of the Académie Goncourt and a Transcendent Satrap of the College of Pataphysics.

It is the last of these positions that, however, best characterizes the essential Raymond Queneau, the poet-novelist who started out as a surrealist but discovered his true literary and philosophical ancestry in Alfred Jarry, the creator of *Ubu Roi* and *Faustroll*, the patron saint of the science of pataphysics which is defined as 'the science of imaginary solutions, which symbolically attributes to the outward aspect of objects the properties implied by their virtuality', or, in other words, the vision of the world by which the artist can make objects *mean* and *be* what he wishes them to mean and to be, by virtue of the freedom of his imagination. Pataphysics is a gay science: like its sister philosophy, existentialism, it sees the universe as absurd; unlike existentialism, though, it does not take that knowledge as tragic but, on the contrary, as a matter for laughter. It regards the lack of real conclusions and real solutions as a form of freedom, the freedom to indulge in imaginary solutions. Queneau, in one of three prefaces he wrote at various times for one of his favourite books, Flaubert's *Bouvard et Pécuchet* (whom incidentally he does not regard as dunces, but as seekers after truth), approvingly quotes Flaubert himself, who once remarked (in a letter to Bouilhet, 4 September 1850): 'The stupidity consists in wanting to arrive at conclusions . . .'.

Hence the true heroes of Queneau's novels are those wise simpletons who reject the quest for the absolute and confine themselves to the simple pleasures of here and now. In some sense therefore they, and Queneau himself, are existentialists. For them, existence certainly comes before essence, although they shrink from commitment to causes, which tend to be absolutes and categorical imperatives. They remain free because they are in a perpetual state of potentiality, always on the threshold of a new choice.

For Queneau, the author of the *Petite cosmogonie portative*, a strictly accurate, if poetically light-hearted, account of current scientific thought on evolution, there is no real contradiction between being a scientist and a pataphysician. For the true scientific method is based on the constant readiness to reject any hypothesis in the light of new experimental evidence. Science itself therefore can never claim to represent an absolute: it remains a body of hypotheses, i.e. imaginary solutions. If there is no absolute, knowable reality we are relieved from the necessity, or the stupid pretension, of knowing any absolute conclusions and solutions. And the poet is free to construct his universe by weaving intricate patterns of symmetrical characters, delicately balanced against each other, by constructing his stories according to cabbalistic numerological principles and by inventing new concepts and syntactical structures.

It is this freedom from the burden of knowable absolutes, the rejection of rigid systems, which makes language so important. If ultimate reality is absurd, or for ever beyond our ken (which, in practice, means the same thing), and if we are therefore free in constructing our own limited world as a private game or diversion, the form of our thought, the mould from which it springs, becomes the shaping, creative element that will determine the world we move in. And that mould is language.

That is why all of Queneau's effort centres on his endeavour to renew the fossilized, dead mould of contemporary literary French by going back to the real speech of real people.

I don't want to say that literature, that poetry should be reduced to a mere shorthand copy of what one contemptuously calls the language of *concierges* which, after all, is merely that of the academicians with a few minor mistakes added. The task is . . . to give style to the spoken language. In this way we might witness the birth of a new literature. I believe that a dead syntax is such a damper that when we have got rid of it, there will not only arise a new literature but also a new philosophy ('Conversation avec Ribemont-Dessaignes', *Bâtons, chiffres et lettres*, pp. 32–33).

Yet, and this is very important to remember in order to avoid misunderstandings, Queneau does not believe that language *is* reality, or that a belief in the free play of the imagination eliminates such concepts as truth and the need to be just right in finding the words to fit what is to be described or defined. It is merely that this is an *inner* consistency, a test of reality and fitness within a strictly delimited field:

One does not eat the word bread, one does not drink the word wine, but, well said, they have their importance nevertheless. I do not believe in language if it takes itself for what it is not; I do not believe in a poetry that is a lie. It is exactness which gives even the least obvious metaphors their value. An Emperor changed the way of life of the Chinese by changing their language. It is this which seems to me quite possible. There is a power in language, but one must know how to use it; there are different kinds of levers and a block of stone cannot be moved with a nutcracker (ibid., p. 37).

Novels by Queneau:

Le Chiendent, Paris, Gallimard, 1933.

Gueule de Pierre, Paris, Gallimard, 1934.

Les derniers jours, Paris, Gallimard, 1936.

Odile, Paris, Gallimard, 1937.

Les Enfants du Limon, Paris, Gallimard, 1938.

Un rude hiver, Paris, Gallimard, 1939.
    A Hard Winter (trs. Betty Askwith), London, Lehmann, 1948.

Les Temps mêlés (*Gueule de Pierre*, Vol. II), Paris, Gallimard, 1941.

Pierrot mon ami, Paris, Gallimard, 1942.
    Pierrot (trs. J. Maclaren-Ross), London, Lehmann, 1950; Toronto, Longmans, 1950.

Loin de Rueil, Paris, Gallimard, 1944.
    The Skin of Dreams (trs. H. J. Kaplan, Norfolk Conn., New Directions, 1948.

(*Sally Mara*), *On est toujours trop bon avec les femmes*, Paris, Éd. du Scorpion, 1947.

St. Glinglin (*précédé d'une nouvelle version de 'Gueule de Pierre' et des 'Temps mêlés'*), Paris, Gallimard, 1948.

(*Sally Mara*), *Journal intime*, Paris, Éd. du Scorpion, 1950.

Le Dimanche de la vie, Paris, Gallimard, 1951.

Zazie dans le Métro, Paris, Gallimard, 1959.
    Zazie (trs. Barbara Wright), London, Bodley Head, 1960; New York, Harper, 1960.

Short stories, &c.:

Exercices de style, Paris, Gallimard, 1947.
    Exercises in style (trs. Barbara Wright), London, Gaberbocchus Press, 1958.

Une Trouille verte, Paris, Éd. de Minuit, 1947.

A la limite de la forêt, Paris, Fontaine, 1947 (limited edition).
(This is the first chapter of an unfinished novel.)

Le Cheval troyen, Paris, Visat, 1948 (limited edition).

(Last two items translated by Barbara Wright as *The Trojan Horse* and *At the Edge of the Forest*, London, Gaberbocchus Press, 1954.)

JEAN-PAUL SARTRE
b. 1905

BY JOHN WEIGHTMAN

———————✯———————

ALL Sartre's fiction deals with the themes of his philosophy. It shows the human consciousness caught in an alien, ultimately incomprehensible world, of which the first manifestation is the body in which that consciousness finds itself. There is no God and, therefore, no universal, objective system of values. Nor can there be any 'given' system of secular morality, such as humanist thinkers are fond of imagining. Each individual is perpetually faced with freedom of choice and is aware of his freedom and his contingency as an anguish. Instead of assuming the responsibility of freedom, he tends to conceal his situation from himself by accepting conventional social values as absolutes. The extreme example of guilty benightedness is the bourgeois reactionary (*le salaud*, the swine) and, generally speaking, sin takes the form of that wilful unconsciousness or semi-consciousness which Sartre calls *la mauvaise foi*. This may lead to a deliberate limitation of other people's freedom. Living is a perpetual quest for self-coincidence, but since a consciousness cannot easily grasp itself, it looks for confirmation of its being in other consciousnesses. We tend to urge other people into certain roles so that we can use them as stable reflectors of ourselves; sometimes we wish to dominate, sometimes to be dominated, but in either case we are escaping from freedom into an ossification based on *mauvaise foi*. Virtue consists in exercising our freedom in such a way that we respect the freedom of everyone else.

I cannot attempt a general appraisal of the philosophy thus rapidly summarized and which Sartre elaborates so ingeniously and at such enormous length. My task is the rather different one of inquiring into his use of philosophy for the purpose of his novels. Not many professional philosophers have written novels, and of those that have, Sartre is by far the most eminent. In his case, then, the question arises very clearly; is it advisable for a novelist to have an explicit philosophy? The same question can be put in an alternative form: why should a philosopher want to write novels? At first sight, the two activities of philosophy and novel-writing seem quite distinct. The philosopher attempts to give an account of life in terms of ideas; these are independent of individuals, although of course they depend on individual minds for their realization at any particular moment. The novelist, on the other hand, presents human behaviour in descriptive chunks; he may indulge in an intellectual conclusion from time to time, but his peculiar talent is for the handling of character and plot in such a way that the reader willingly assents to the description without trying to reduce it to its intellectual analysis. Those people who prefer literature to philosophy—that is, who believe that literature achieves a more subtle account of reality—would argue further that if an episode in a novel can be readily elucidated, this is a proof of poor writing. When the intellectual framework of a novel is too visible, the work belongs to the inferior genre of the moral lesson or *roman à thèse*. The function of the novel proper, they would say, is to achieve a rightness, a uniqueness of detailed notation which is at the opposite extreme from intellectual schematization. In this sense the novel is ultimately irrational, whereas philosophy is rational.

Now Sartre has been criticized on the ground that his three fictional works, *Le Mur* (a collection of five short stories), *La Nausée*, and *Les Chemins de la liberté* are merely illustrations of his philosophical ideas. (The same charge can, of course, be brought against his plays, with which we are not here concerned.) But a preliminary answer to this criticism might be, in respect of the novels, that Sartre is not the kind of philosopher whose work is diametrically opposed to novel-writing. He does not aim at devising a system of abstractions tangential to, or remote from, ordinary living. He does not meditate timelessly on Truth and

Beauty, nor does he go in for circumscribed linguistic analysis. As a phenomenologist, his concern is to grasp situations in their concrete completeness. As an existentialist, he is compelled by his philosophy of consciousness to think of particular people in terms of their awareness of themselves and of others. His thought is technical, no doubt, but it also constitutes a 'philosophy of life' in the old-fashioned sense. When a philosophy tries to adhere in this way to the whole surface of existence, it is clearly not far removed from a literary approach. Indeed, we may ask whether the philosophers of the post-Kierkegaardian tradition should not be more properly termed philosophical literary men. As a philosopher Sartre has, of course, been exposed to the complementary charge of basing his thought on obsessions and convictions that are proclaimed dogmatically, without being justified by argument. However, he himself might answer that instead of using his novels to illustrate his philosophical ideas, he deduced his philosophical ideas from the grasp of reality he obtained through writing his novels; or, alternatively, that there is no rigid dividing line between the two forms of activity, since a perfect novel would also be, from his point of view, a perfect piece of existentialist philosophy.

When we look at the dates of his writings in order to follow his development, we see that *Le Mur* (1937-9) and *La Nausée* (1938) came out before the major philosophical statement, *L'Être et le néant* (1943), although two works on limited aspects of his thought should be mentioned: *L'Imagination* (1936) and *L'Imaginaire* (1940). It is true that Sartre was trained as a philosopher before he produced any literary work, but the official philosophy or philosophies he was taught had little in common with the one he finally evolved for himself. The three volumes of *Les Chemins de la liberté* were published after *L'Être et le néant*, the first two in 1945 and the third in 1949. Since 1949, Sartre has devoted himself to critical, polemical, and dramatic writing, and has failed to produce the promised fourth volume of *Les Chemins de la liberté*. While further elaborating his philosophical ideas during the last ten years, he has given no hint of wishing to return to the novel form. In view of these facts, it seems reasonable to suppose that he is more of a philosopher than a novelist. My opinion is that novel-writing was only a phase in his career, but a very important phase, precisely because of the kind of philosopher he is. It can be maintained that he needed to write *La Nausée* in order to make his philosophy clear to himself. The book is about a philosopher becoming aware of his own philosophy; actually, the character is presented as an ex-adventurer turned historian, but this does not make him any the less a philosopher. And if I may anticipate a judgement I shall develop later, I should say that *La Nausée* is impressively unique because of its fusion of philosophy and literature. There is perhaps no other work in which the philosophic temperament (of a certain kind, at least) is given such a complete literary description. The book can be called either an autobiographical *roman d'apprentissage* of a very specialized kind or a twentieth-century *Discours de la méthode* cast in fictional form. After *La Nausée* and *L'Être et le néant*, Sartre was in full possession of his philosophy as a system of ideas of a fairly rigid nature, in spite of its being open, as it were, on one side, through its insistence on the perpetual newness of freedom. Although this system leads back to life, or more accurately is not meant to be separate from life, it is nevertheless an intellectual construction and not a collection of immediate perceptions. I shall argue that, from this point onwards, Sartre tends to write more mechanically. *Les Chemins de la liberté* is without the organic necessity of the earlier fictional work. It is a comparative failure, partly because Sartre is now apprehending reality to some extent in terms of already formed assumptions, and partly because the philosophy he has evolved is defective. It raises a central problem of action for which he can find no solution.

* * *

The two pre-war volumes, *La Nausée* and *Le Mur*, have obviously to be taken together, but there is some uncertainty about the order in which they were written. Two of the short stories included in *Le Mur* were published before *La Nausée*, and the other three afterwards. Mr. Philip Thody, in his interesting and useful study of Sartre,[1] deals with *La Nausée* first, because he considers it less satisfactory than the collection of short stories. I cannot agree with this order of importance. Four of the short stories seem to me to be incidental works which, on internal evidence, one would guess to have come before *La Nausée*. The fifth, 'L'Enfance d'un chef', was completed afterwards, but it is almost like a shorter, alternative version of *La Nausée*, in which Sartre is using up childhood memories that he had not managed to put into *La Nausée*. However, the actual dates of composition are not very important. Both volumes belong to the period when *L'Être et le néant* was being written, or about to be written. The question is: are they simply translations into fictional form of Sartre's philosophy? Mr. Thody appears to think they are, since he writes of *Le Mur*:

> There are five stories in the volume, each of which illustrates one of Sartre's favourite philosophical ideas. The title story, 'The Wall', refutes Heidegger's idea that man can live towards his own death and thus humanize it. The second, 'The Room', illustrates the impossibility for the sane mind to enter deliberately into the world of madness. The third, 'Herostratus', explores the extreme confines of anti-humanism; the fourth, 'Intimacy', is a study of the idea of bad faith; and the fifth, 'The Childhood of a Leader', exposes the way in which the human mind can escape from the feeling of its own superfluousness into the comforting world of Rights (op. cit., p. 23).

He adds a little later, after saying that *La Nausée* is long-winded:

> Each one of the stories . . . has a conciseness which comes from being written to illustrate a particular philosophical point (op. cit., p. 37).

Each story is undoubtedly connected with the point Mr. Thody mentions, but they all have an intense emotional vibration which is not easy to fathom. Would they have this vibration if Sartre had simply set out to illustrate something that was already clear in his mind? I should say rather that Sartre is grasping parts of his philosophy emotionally, or perhaps using the fictional form because he senses contradictions that he cannot account for rationally. I should add that the stories are not uniformly successful.

[1] Philip Thody, *Jean-Paul Sartre: a Literary and Political Study* (London, Hamish Hamilton, 1960).

'Le Mur' is set in Spain during the Civil War. It is told in the first person by one of three Republican prisoners who are spending the night in the same cell before execution in the morning. The 'wall' of the title seems to be both the literal wall against which they will be lined up and the wall of inevitability which is the nearness of death. Each of the three prisoners exhibits pathological symptoms of fear, but the narrator, Pablo, is not afraid internally. Although he sweats profusely, his will remains free, which is in accordance with Sartre's staunch Cartesian belief, explicitly affirmed on many occasions later, in the separateness of mind and body. The major change in Pablo is that the proximity of death obliterates his sense of values. He wants to die 'decently' (*mourir proprement*) and he refuses to betray the whereabouts of his important friend, Ramon Gris, but he has no reasons for these two 'good' impulses:

> I knew that he was more useful to the Spanish cause than I was, but I didn't care a damn for Spain or the Anarchist Movement: nothing had any importance any more. And yet there I was, I could save my skin by handing over Gris and I wouldn't do it. This seemed rather comic to me. Sheer obstinacy. 'Pig-headed, that's what I am' I thought, and I felt a strange uprush of cheerfulness (*Le Mur*, p. 34).

Finally, through his sense of the sheer absurdity of the situation, Pablo decides to play a trick on his captors. He gives them false information about Ramon's hideout. But it so happens that Ramon has moved to that very place, and so is shot. Pablo is reprieved and we leave him laughing hysterically at the quirks of fate.

This I feel to be the least convincing of the stories, for two reasons. The physical symptoms of fear are described too systematically—Pablo sweats, Tom urinates, and Juan trembles. I have been told that Sartre got the idea of the story from an article on the effects of fear in a technical journal. Rather strangely, he puts into the cell a Belgian Red Cross doctor who braves the cold to observe the prisoners with a mixture of sadism and scientific interest; perhaps the doctor is merely the imagined author of the article. More important is the unlikelihood of someone who took part in a civil war for political reasons losing all sense of value at the approach of death, when the possibility of death must always have been part of his calculations. What Sartre is saying is that human mortality makes nonsense of human values. If this is so, even the apparent tragic irony at the end is pointless; Ramon is mortal, therefore where and when he dies is of no significance. But human mortality does not make nonsense of values, if normally we believe in them, because they remain valid for the survivors, and this is why ordinary individuals are prepared to risk their lives for social reasons. Sartre is putting forward the purest, the most general form of despair about death, under the disguise of Spanish local colour. Why does he do this? If I had to make a long shot, I should say that he himself did not take part in the Spanish Civil War because, at that point, he was convinced of the futility of all action. But he felt guilty, as we can see from the first volume of *Les Chemins de la liberté*, and a way of relieving the feeling was to project himself into a condemned Republican and show how this Republican would see the futility of action, while still remaining irrationally decent. If this guess is near the truth, the story was a way of making himself suffer fear in imagination, while at the same time expressing both his intellectual conviction of futility and his 'decent' instincts.

The second story, 'La Chambre', produces a similar sensation of ambiguity. Eve, the heroine, is married to Pierre, who is suffering from some unspecified form of mental degeneration and will be completely imbecilic in a year or two. They live together in one darkened room and Eve tries to enter into Pierre's nightmarish hallucinations. Her father, a well-preserved, commonsensical bourgeois, urges her in vain to put Pierre into a mental home. At the end, Pierre shows the first sign of passing beyond hallucinations into drooling vacancy, and Eve decides that she will kill him when he is about to sink into pure animality.

The emotional suggestion of the story is that Eve is right to cling to Pierre, because his madness is a more genuine attitude than the bourgeois father's banal convictions. Actually, this madness, a feature of which is a mistrust of material objects, is akin to the sense of alienation of the existentialist hero, as we shall see him developed in the character of Roquentin in *La Nausée*. One implication of the story is 'Better be mad than bourgeois'. Yet the scales are not unduly weighted against the bourgeois father. This is a better work than 'Le Mur' because the tragedy of the situation is felt in the round, as it were, and with intense compassion. But the claustrophobic theme is not an idea; it is an obsession, which reappears in two of the plays, *Huis Clos* and *Les Séquestrés d'Altona*.[2]

'Érostrate', the third story, takes the form of a monologue by a pathological killer and sadist, Hilbert, who has given up his sober office-job to make his name immortal by a supreme gesture against mankind. He proposes to go out with his revolver and shoot five people, then run home and kill himself with the sixth and last bullet when his pursuers are about to burst in on him. Actually, he runs in the wrong direction, gets confused and seeks refuge in the lavatory of a café. He discovers that he is unable to take his own life and surrenders. But why is he unable to kill himself? This is another unexplained impulse, like Pablo's 'decency'. It cannot be accounted for simply by the external, technical reason that, had he killed himself, he would not be alive to tell the tale. We probably have to understand (although it is not clear whether this is a deliberate intention on Sartre's part or not) that having made his gesture, having wakened up society from its slumber by shooting some of its members, Hilbert is relieved; his pathological tension has snapped. The first part of the story had shown him getting sexual relief by sitting fully clothed with a revolver in his hand, while a naked prostitute adopted undignified postures in front of him. The gun is presented very obviously as a symbol of sex, or alternatively the phallus is a gun, firing at a distance. Hilbert cannot

---

[2] Since the above was written, Simone de Beauvoir has revealed in the second volume of her autobiography, *La Force de l'âge*, that Sartre himself suffered from the sort of hallucination and obsession he describes in 'La Chambre' and in other parts of his work. This had been denied by Sartre's former secretary, Francis Jeanson, in his *Sartre par lui-même* (1955), which now turns out to have been an unreliable source of information. Simone de Beauvoir also mentions many characters and incidents that Sartre obviously adapted for the purposes of his fiction.

use sex to enter into communion with a woman, because the idea of physical contact revolts him. He does not want to be 'eaten up' by the Other. His pleasure comes from humiliating the Other by treating her as an object. His victory is to bring a blush to the cheek of a prostitute. He has a fantasy about puncturing the prostitute with bullets as he punctures the crowd. In both his private relations with the prostitute and his public relations with society, he shows himself to be an alienated consciousness only able to establish negative contact with humanity through shock. In this, the most powerful of the stories and one which rings true in every detail, the existentialist feeling that the mass of mankind lives in an unbearable twilight of *mauvaise foi* finds hysterical expression. Here the implication is: 'Better be a pathological killer than remain unaware of the human situation.'

'Intimité' presents characters who are on a rather lower intellectual plane than those in the three previous stories. The chief example of bad faith is Lulu, a young woman who is married to an impotent husband, Henri, and is having an affair with a very virile lover, Pierre. The lover is urging her to leave her husband and to come away with him. He is being helped in the attempt by Lulu's best friend, Rirette, who likes to think that she is managing Lulu. However, Lulu is of two minds. She enjoys the impression of having big, harmless Henri under her thumb; he is a sort of grown-up baby. She also has a sneaking liking for sex with Pierre, although at the same time she is resentful about it and tells herself at length how disgusting it is. (Her remarks about men are exactly complementary to those of Hilbert about women.) After a tiff, she leaves Henri and prepares to go off with Pierre. But by a number of semi-conscious moves she eventually works her way back to Henri and to the *status quo ante*. Pierre accepts the situation because the new form of life was, in any case, going to be difficult to organize. Rirette is disappointed, because her efforts to manage Lulu have come to nothing.

This is a puzzling story, unlike the others in that it contains no emotional hostility to anyone. But for the occasional reference to existentialist themes, it could almost have been written by Colette. Lulu is not a simple case of *mauvaise foi*: she is a complicated amalgam of shallowness, cruelty, sentimentality, exhibitionism, lesbianism, narcissism, heterosexuality, and puritanism. It is the last characteristic which makes her most recognizable as a Sartrian character. She is absorbed and repelled by her body as a sort of embarrassing appendage to her consciousness, and she dreams of pure, platonic communion. I am not sure that she quite comes together as a convincing creation. Would she both show her nakedness to her young brother and feel polluted by her lover? In any case, is frigidity not very rare in this type of Frenchwoman? Sartre seems to have attributed his ambiguous disgust with the flesh to the sort of human being who is usually least troubled by it. Some of Lulu's characteristics appear to come from a real woman mentioned in Simone de Beauvoir's autobiography, but this woman was predominantly lesbian.

Lastly, 'L'Enfance d'un chef' tells of a young bourgeois, Lucien, whom we follow from the dawn of consciousness in childhood to the point in early adult life where he identifies himself with some of the traditional values of his class. The narrative has a Flaubertian ring, which is curious when we remember in what harsh terms Sartre usually refers to Flaubert. 'L'Enfance d'un chef' is really a small-scale *Éducation sentimentale* in which so many contemporary young Frenchmen have recognized something of themselves that it has become the most famous of Sartre's stories. The hero, from his earliest years, is obsessed with the problem of self-coincidence, although he does not recognize it as such. When he is a toddler, his mother allows his hair to grow long, as used to be the habit in French bourgeois families, and he wonders whether he is a boy or a girl. Later, he tries hard to be a dutiful son who loves his mother, but he can neither fully sense his identity in relationship to hers nor be sure that he loves her completely. Only when he sees his father behaving with paternalist authority to the workers in his factory does the world take on a fixed and appreciable order. Adolescence is a confused slumber from which Lucien awakes suddenly with the question: 'Who am I?' He becomes friendly with a young anarchist who introduces him to a Surrealist homosexual, and for a while he carries uncertainty to the point of inversion. Then he is saved by meeting a bone-headed, anti-Semitic member of the *Action Française*. He discovers that if he declares himself anti-Semitic, his prejudice is respected by the people around him. He takes a lower-class mistress and becomes a reactionary rowdy. He has found relief at last by adopting a crude system of aggressive values. In the final sentence, he decides to grow a moustache to make his appearance fit his persona.

In this superbly written story many of the details sound so true and yet so unusual that they seem to have been transcribed from actual experience. This is particularly the case in the homosexual episode, which consists of purely realistic description, with little or no admixture of the existentialist vocabulary. If the story has a weakness, it lies in the tendency to caricature. One wonders if so sensitive a child and adolescent would accept such a crude escape from the anguish of non-coincidence with the self. Perhaps the subtle parts represent Sartre's own experience while the conclusion is a more external attack on his usual *bête noire*, the bourgeois *salaud*.

*   *   *

Whereas 'L'Enfance d'un chef' gives an existentialist life-story from childhood to the acceptance of *mauvaise foi* in early manhood, *La Nausée* shows a character, Antoine Roquentin, experiencing the existentialist revelation as a crisis at about the age of thirty. We are to understand that, until then, he has led an active, adventurous life as an archaeologist-historian in various parts of the world. When the story opens, he has been living for some time in the seaside town of Bouville (modelled on Le Havre) where, with the help of documents deposited in the municipal library, he is writing the life of a minor eighteenth-century figure, M. de Rollebon. The book takes the form of a diary which he starts keeping in order to try to elucidate certain strange experiences that have recently bothered him. He is all alone in the town, apart from casual acquaintances he has made in cafés and in the library. He is, in fact, all alone in the world; the person nearest to him is his ex-mistress Anny, from whom he has been separated for four years. He is, therefore, an isolated consciousness all ready to become aware of its contingency, and this indeed is what has happened to him. His curious experiences are attacks of contingency-sickness, that are going to multiply and reach a paroxysm in the course of the book.

We can distinguish three main aspects of this existentialist awareness, which occur as alternating themes and are sometimes orchestrated: (*a*) the irreducible strangeness of all objects; (*b*) the despicable, comic or tragic *mauvaise foi* of the mass of society which has either not experienced, or has suppressed, its nausea; (*c*) the impossibility of grasping the immediate reality of time. They had all been present in the short stories: objects are treated as alien in 'Le Mur', 'La Chambre', and 'L'Enfance d'un chef'; the bourgeoisie is held up to ridicule in 'Érostrate', 'La Chambre', and 'L'Enfance d'un chef', and the difficulty of self-coincidence in the last-named story is a manifestation of the problem of time. But in *La Nausée* they are restated with a quite unique brilliance and copiousness of development.

The initial symptom of Roquentin's new state is the disgust he experiences when he picks up a pebble to throw it into the sea. This disgust cannot at first be analysed, and it is not until a similar sensation occurs when he touches a door-knob or shakes somebody by the hand or watches a café-proprietor's braces hesitating between various shades of purple that he realizes what is happening. The external world, which includes his own body, has ceased to be recognizable, has no necessary relationship with his consciousness, is a vast excrescence proliferating in various ways independently of anything he may think about it. The climax comes when Roquentin perceives, with the intensity of near-madness, that a tree-root in the municipal park just is, and that however much he may bombard it mentally with words, it remains densely unintelligible. Shortly before, he had been sitting on a seat in a bus and had been struck by the fact that the word 'seat' was ridiculously unrelated to the object to which it was supposed to apply. As he says: 'Things have broken loose from words.' By this, I think, we have to understand that human language is a kind of futile gesturing in the face of an impenetrable universe. Roquentin not only makes the statement intellectually; the conviction runs through all his descriptions and produces a constant displacement of attribution; people, or parts of people, are seen as things, things are seen as animate beings, abstractions become concrete, solid realities melt into vapours. This, of course, is what happens normally in all metaphorical writing, but its continuous recurrence in *La Nausée* is part of the existentialist vertigo. When Roquentin, on looking out of a window, sees an old woman scurrying across a courtyard and, without comparing her to an insect, describes her in insect terms, the reader realizes the unintelligibility of the world with the same poetic shock as is produced by Eliot's lines in 'Prufrock':

>I should have been a pair of ragged claws
>Scuttling across the floors of silent seas.

The prose of *La Nausée* is at times admirably poetic, and all the more so through being consistently intelligent and astringent. There are no finer set-pieces in modern French literature than the description of Sunday at Bouville, or the café scenes or the meditation on the tree-root in the park, and their vividness is due, paradoxically, to the repeated suggestion of a discrepancy between language and the world and a constant confusion of different orders of reality.

The reference to Eliot is not an idle one, because *La Nausée* might be termed Sartre's *Waste Land*. Just as, in Eliot's poem, there is an uneasy consciousness which cannot make sense of the world and is therefore especially interested in human types such as the Cockney women or the young man carbuncular, who seem to coincide with their being, so Roquentin, in his isolation and peculiarity, is acutely aware of the bourgeois solidity of Bouville society set hard in its *mauvaise foi*, and of the humble reality of charwomen, waitresses, and other subordinate individuals, who have identified themselves with their social function or their individual fate. Here I must refer again to the ritual of the Sunday morning walk during which the various levels of middle-class society go through a process of display as stereotyped as an animal behaviour pattern and a perfect illustration of Being-for-others. Sartre also gives his satirical talent full rein in the brilliant portrait scene in the museum, where Roquentin analyses in turn the careers of the civic worthies who made an absolute of their class assumptions and so earned a place in this swine's gallery. He has an unerring sense of the little gestures which reveal the triviality of social reflexes or the automatism resulting from the renunciation of inner freedom. The proprietress of 'Le Rendez-vous des cheminots' and the proprietor of the Café Mably make only fleeting appearances, yet they are quite unforgettable.

Only three characters, besides Roquentin himself, are outside the social pattern: the anonymous exhibitionist in the park; M. Achille, the semi-imbecile who comes into the café; and the Autodidact, the Socialist humanist who is reading all the books in the library in alphabetical order. The exhibitionist hardly counts; he is wrapt in his trance of vice, which is, presumably, little more than an extreme form of Being-for-others. M. Achille collapses when his doctor appears, and obsequiously accepts his role as a semi-imbecile. There remains the Autodidact, who is treated at considerable length and with affectionate cruelty, because he is a foil to Roquentin. He believes in all the things that Roquentin no longer accepts; the nobility of man, the value of writing, the excitingness of life, the existence of truth in books. Rather unfairly, perhaps, he is brought to complete disaster through a slight homosexual misdemeanour. The episode is marvellously realistic, and although intellectually biased as a judgement on humanists, artistically right since it removes the one person Roquentin could talk to and so rounds off the story.

By now he has, in any case, been reduced to a vaguely conscious transparency through the working of his third neurosis, the obsession with time. This has taken various forms. The first sign of it was his sudden disillusionment with active life, which led to his return from the Far East and his temporary retirement to Bouville. He eventually comes to see that he has given up adventurous travelling, because an 'adventure' is a fictitious construct in time (perhaps Sartre is here criticizing by implication Malraux's novels of adventure, *La Voie Royale*, *Les Conquérants* and *La Condition humaine*). While you are engaged on an adventure, all you are aware of is grains of time succeeding each other, and each one is ordinary, since no given moment of consciousness can be exciting to itself. An adventure can be anticipated or looked back upon; it cannot, without dishonest theatricality, be apprehended as such in the act of living. People have different methods of making time falsely significant. For instance, Roquentin's mistress, Anny, would give a tragic intensity to the last hour of each of their meetings by behaving badly at first, so that the imminence of parting would weigh heavily on each of the happy moments of reconciliation. She had a longing for 'perfect moments', a longing which might be considered as the female counterpart of the masculine thirst for adventure.

The renunciation of adventure has, however, been succeeded by another illusion. After writing a good part of his book in the studious vacancy of his hotel bedroom or the public library, Roquentin gradually comes to realize that he has given up living himself in order to live by proxy through M. de Rollebon. Or, to put it the other way round, he is lending his being to a dead man, in order that this dead man may recapture a semblance of life. At first, Roquentin had supposed that he had only to study M. de Rollebon's papers carefully to discover the secret of his life. Then he begins to doubt both the validity of the evidence and the interest of M. de Rollebon's exploits, even when they can be elucidated; perhaps they are no more real than Roquentin's own. Finally, it comes upon him in a flash that M. de Rollebon is irretrievably dead; the past does not exist; it is never more than an idea in the present and a very uncertain one at that. History is a retrospective construct, a more or less gratuitous creation of the historian's present. M. de Rollebon's life and Roquentin's own early adventures are equally remote, since they are all dead and gone.

Roquentin has only one more step to make in order to understand that consciousness, in its purest form, is the sensation of the present falling continuously and inexplicably into the past.

The fact of living in time is the most subtle and the most piercing feature of contingency. The tragedy of life is not simply that we live and then die; it is rather that we are dying at each moment. We yearn for coincidence with our being, but such coincidence is by definition ruled out, since we are always, as it were, on the moving psychological platform of time. No other novelist or philosopher that I have read gives such a delicate analysis of the anguish of time as Sartre in *La Nausée*. He may bring it in during a lull in the narrative; Roquentin looks out of his window and sees an old woman hobbling along the street; as he watches, she concentrates upon herself all the exasperation he feels at the unintelligible fact that now she is here and, in a little while, will have turned the corner; future, present, and past jostle each other in an unhappy act of consciousness. Or the anguish may underlie a major episode, such as the description of Sunday, where it reinforces the strangeness of the animate and the inanimate world. In either case, Sartre manages, with great originality, to introduce the sensation of the passing of time into the texture of his writing.

After describing the various aspects of the existentialist revelation so admirably, Sartre is left with the problem of deciding what to do with his hero. Roquentin is far more intelligent than Lucien in 'L'Enfance d'un chef' and, in any case, a good part of his meditation has been about the *mauvaise foi* of bourgeois society. It follows that he cannot adopt Lucien's solution of the flight into simple aggressiveness. Sartre very cleverly staves off the final decision for a while by making him receive an unexpected letter from Anny just at the point when he is losing faith in M. de Rollebon. Anny asks him to come and see her in Paris. This gives him a 'project'; he may be able to explain his experience to his former mistress and re-enter society through establishing some new form of communion with her. However, when the meeting takes place, she turns out to be as disillusioned as he is. She has lost her belief in 'perfect moments' and has given up all hope of psychological satisfaction. She continues to travel with her new lover, a rich Egyptian, but her movements are as pointless as Roquentin's immobility. The conversation between them is beautifully done and Anny comes alive as a difficult, half-intellectual woman, yet this is the one part of the book which may seem rather contrived in its suspicious symmetry. Perhaps Anny's irritable disillusion is meant to be a caricature of Roquentin's more genuine and fundamental revelation. Certainly, in spite of her intellectual explanations, Anny irrupts into the last part of the book as a very human and irrational figure. It may be that the reader's uneasiness is due to the fact that she is too powerful a presence to be introduced at so late a stage. She takes over from Roquentin's consciousness for the duration of the episode and browbeats him in a tragi-comic way, which rather diminishes his intellectual stature. Whether or not her forcefulness warps the aesthetic pattern of the book, the point is that when Roquentin sees her get into the boat-train for London, he knows that his last link with his old identity is broken. He has no public or private life, no purpose in existing and no external need to do anything, since he can survive on his small but adequate income.

It is here that Sartre takes his one and only leap into art for art's sake. Roquentin has noticed that during his crises in the 'Rendez-vous des cheminots' he experiences great relief on hearing a gramophone record of an American negress singing a popular song, 'Some of these days'. Although only this particular piece of music has the power to affect him in this way, it does not do so by appealing to his emotions as a human song about a human situation. Its virtue is that, while the record is playing, Roquentin feels he has moved, as it were, out of contingent time into absolute time, where sounds follow each other with perfect necessity. It seems impossible not to understand his relief as an escape from the relativity of living into a Platonic heaven of art. At any rate, during his last hours at Bouville, he hears the record again and it occurs to him that he could perhaps try to write a book—not a history book, but some work in a genre he is not yet able to specify—that would have an absolute quality, comparable to that of the negress's song. He imagines the song as having been written by an exhausted, middle-aged Jew in the sweltering heat of a New York summer; the Jew was a lump of suffering, contingent flesh; the song is free and pure. It is not definitely stated that Roquentin will achieve his aim. The book ends at the point where he is about to take the train back to Paris, but the implication seems to be that the diary we have been reading is, in itself, his escape into the absolute, or that he will recast it to make it so.

In so far as Sartre is Roquentin, *La Nausée* is obviously Sartre's temporary escape. But what is the intellectual validity of such a solution? Iris Murdoch, in her excellent book on Sartre,[3] argues that the aesthetic conclusion is just sketched in and that Sartre does not really believe in it. If none of Roquentin's present thoughts can confer necessary form upon his past, says Miss Murdoch, then neither can a partial image of that past, worked up into the wholeness of a work of art, confer necessity. But is the 'necessity' of a work of art not different from philosophical necessity? For me, *La Nausée* has a kind of necessity, because it is a masterpiece which provides me with a satisfaction parallel to that found by Roquentin in 'Some of these days'. It gave Sartre himself no more than passing relief. The artist is, by definition, a person who is condemned to see the necessity of his work only in flashes, at the moment of creating it in the external, social medium. He can never really enjoy it from outside as contemplated necessity, in the way his readers can. But, objectively, *La Nausée* is an absolute, in the sense that it is precisely a valid, linguistic expression of the impossibility of finding an absolute. Language, fortunately, allows such paradoxes. It is true that Sartre does not go deeply into the question and even confuses it slightly by indulging in a typical, anti-bourgeois flourish. Roquentin declares that, of course, he is not to be compared to an aunt of his who had once said to him: 'Chopin's *Preludes* were such a help to me at the time of your poor uncle's death.' One of the limitations of Sartre's savagely anti-bourgeois mind is that he cannot admit that a middle-class aunt may have had an inkling of the absolute while listening to Chopin during the temporary sincerity of grief. His prejudice is such that awareness of

---

[3] Iris Murdoch, *Sartre, Romantic Rationalist* (Cambridge, Bowes and Bowes, 1953).

the absolute has to come to a *déclassé* intellectual listening to a non-highbrow song written by a Jew and sung by a negress.

*   *   *

The three volumes of *Les Chemins de la liberté* are undoubtedly a great disappointment after *La Nausée*. It is as if Sartre's talent had become coarser and he were deliberately ignoring subtleties that he had been fully aware of in his earlier work. The chief weakness is that the central plot or theme of *Les Chemins* is developed with an uneasy mixture of dogmatism and uncertainty, which eventually leads to a break at the end of volume three. The published fragment of volume four, *La Dernière chance*, although brilliantly written, confirms that the book had run into an impasse. If, as now seems likely, Sartre never completes it, it will remain as an uneven document on Sartre himself and on our time.

There is no reason to suspect the title of being ironical. Between the end of *La Nausée* and the beginning of *Les Chemins*, perhaps under the impact of the Munich crisis, Sartre had obviously switched from the idea of looking for an absolute in art to a belief in the necessity of action. Since the distinguishing feature of man is the exercise of his freedom, Sartre seems to be setting out to show how, in the context of contemporary France, different characters use or abuse their freedom. At first sight, this is a step forward from *La Nausée*. It might be argued that Roquentin, in spite of his acuteness, was not aware of his true position. As a *rentier*, however modest, he was living as a parasite on society and was thus involved in the guilt of the capitalist system, and was even, in his own way, an example of *mauvaise foi*. Sartre has never tired of emphasizing in his later writings that, by the very act of living, we are committed; the refusal to take part in politics is itself a political attitude. But if you decide to 'assume your freedom', how exactly should you act? This is a problem that Sartre has never been able to solve. On the one hand, he seems to be urging the reader on to action, as if the essential duties were obvious; on the other, he offers no definite policy. He does not always appear to realize, either in his theoretical writings or in his novels, that anti-bourgeoisism, far from being a programme, may degenerate into a sterile emotional release. Whereas *La Nausée* is, on the whole, acceptably anti-bourgeois, because it is a contemplative work, written from the point of view of someone who is trying to record a certain momentary vision of the world, *Les Chemins* is unsatisfactory through being to some extent programmatic yet charged with a negative emotion which is much stronger than any of its positive recommendations. In *La Nausée* Sartre had poured scorn on the blind exercise of freedom. The Autodidact tells Roquentin that he has read a book by an American on the theme: Is life worth living?

'Life has a meaning if you are prepared to give it one. You must begin by acting, by throwing yourself into some undertaking. You may reflect later, but by then the die has been cast, you are committed. I don't know what you think about that, Mr. Roquentin?'

'Nothing,' I answered. Or rather, I was thinking that it was precisely the sort of lie that the commercial traveller, the young couple and the white-haired old gentleman must be constantly repeating to themselves (p. 144).

[The people listed are unredeemed social or human types.]

Sartre's later philosophy has as one of its tenets: 'Life has the meaning we are prepared to give it', and this is only a hair's breadth from the American's reviled principle, especially since Sartre has never supplied an adequate ethical test by which to judge the various meanings one can give to life. Some of his simpler writings, such as *L'Existentialisme est un humanisme*, could almost have been written by the Autodidact.

In place of the single hero of *La Nausée*, *Les Chemins* has three main characters: Mathieu, a teacher of philosophy in a Parisian secondary school, and his two friends, or erstwhile friends, Daniel, a homosexual, who seems to have no occupation other than being homosexual, and Brunet, an active Communist. There is also a host of secondary characters, some of them very vividly depicted. Mathieu, like Roquentin, has some of the features of Sartre. Judging by the details supplied in the second volume of Simone de Beauvoir's autobiography, Daniel is modelled on a French

Algerian, also a teacher and a friend of Sartre and Simone de Beauvoir. Brunet may be an idealized version of Paul Nizan, Sartre's contemporary who broke with the Communists at the time of the Hitler-Stalin Pact and was killed at the beginning of the war. Many of the minor characters and episodes are directly transposed from life.

A defect immediately visible in the first volume is that the three main characters are too symmetrically compared and contrasted. Mathieu is a decent, intelligent man, permanently afflicted with a mild form of Roquentin's anguish, unable to decide what to do with his life and naturally incapable of achieving self-coincidence. He envies Brunet who, having opted for Communist action and identified himself sturdily and intelligently with the Party Line, is thus relieved of the burden of finding an individual 'project'. Daniel exhibits the problem of self-coincidence in a still simpler form; he knows he is homosexual, yet cannot fully realize the fact. He therefore inflicts various forms of self-torture on himself, in the endeavour to achieve objective awareness. If Sartre borrowed elements from the model suggested by Simone de Beauvoir, he certainly systematized them too much. The character has a melodramatic sharpness and forecasts Sartre's later interest in Jean Genet as a subject for existentialist psychoanalysis, but is hardly convincing within the context of the book.

The action of the first volume, *L'Age de raison* (1945), is chiefly concerned with Mathieu's attempts to obtain enough money to enable his pregnant mistress, Marcelle, to have an abortion. It does not occur to him to marry her, in the first place because he is tired of her and secondly because an intellectual of his sort does not marry and found a family. While he is engaged on the humiliating quest for money, he has a nagging worry about not fighting in the Spanish Civil War. Another burden is his obsession with a young girl of Russian extraction, Ivich, who petulantly leads him something of a dance. Although Mathieu has a social function as a teacher, and even some admiring pupils, he lives outside the orthodox framework. His brother Jacques is the exact opposite, a successful bourgeois 'stinker'. We are clearly meant to prefer Mathieu, and even to like him, but for my part I find him rather tedious. He is really Roquentin, put into a slight social context but deprived of Roquentin's subtlety of vision and reflection. My suspicion is that Sartre had used up all the good material for the character in *La Nausée* and did not want to repeat himself. If Mathieu had been presented firmly in some ironical perspective—the most highly evolved type of French intellectual absorbed in begging money for an abortion at a time of international crisis—his predicament would have been more interesting. But in this large-scale work, Sartre's touch has become unsure. For no apparent reason, Marcelle, the pregnant mistress, is treated very harshly, as if Sartre were working off on her his hatred of the contingency of the flesh. It was quite in keeping for Roquentin, an extra-social character suffering from existentialist vertigo, to speak about 'the extreme stupidity of begetting children'. Mathieu, who is instinctively on the Republican side in the Civil War and therefore in favour of life and progress, and who in any case is a teacher, that is, a member of a profession which depends on people producing children, cannot have this simple Bohemian approach without being immature. He behaves as if, by finding money for the abortion, he will have done his duty. His character hangs together to some extent; teaching without believing in teaching, fornicating without believing in love or fertility, being obsessed with a child-woman, taking anti-bourgeois reflexes as a form of political virtue. Sartre shows us all this, but he seems to have failed to get the material quite into perspective, although sometimes he writes too openly in terms of his explicit ideas. His admiration for Brunet, the staunch Communist, has a touch of *naïveté* about it, like his indulgence towards Mathieu. The volume ends by Daniel marrying Marcelle in order to punish himself. Mathieu, rather solemnly, envies Daniel his ability to exercise his freedom; it never seems to occur to him that there is a moral problem in allowing the child to be born into the rather weird ménage that Daniel and Marcelle will form.

The second volume, *Le Sursis* (1945), is a panorama of Europe at the time of the Munich crisis. The same group of Parisian characters recur, with the addition of many others, including Neville Chamberlain, Sir Horace Wilson, and Beneš. In order to convey the simultaneity of events, Sartre has taken over from Dos Passos the technique of juxtaposing short fragments of narration in a mosaic. A little of his existentialist approach survives in that he shows some characters, oblivious of the general political situation, struggling pathetically or nastily to achieve self-coincidence. On the whole, however, the book owes very little to existentialism. It has the simplicity and high colouring of a Zolaesque novel. Sartre displays enormous talent in giving us glimpses of dozens of human situations, many of which he could, no doubt, have worked up into short stories, but the total effect is one of gratuitousness and monotony. Why these particular scenes and not others? In some cases, he is writing out of his experience. Elsewhere, to round off the picture, he is inventing, and not particularly well. His references to Chamberlain, for instance, are quite unconvincing, because—with an unconscious political dilettantism worthy of Mathieu—he misses out the whole political context of Chamberlain's behaviour. Chamberlain, like the other political characters, is just a few personal mannerisms, a meaningless old man in a committee-room. Not having a politically realistic mind, Sartre does not see that although Europe may appear to be absolutely chaotic in detail, it is governed by certain fluctuating political structures. He writes authoritatively, as if he were explaining the complex relationships in an immense human pattern, yet he has surprisingly little interest in, or grasp of, the pattern. *Le Sursis* is marred by a curious, insistent obtuseness, characteristic of Sartre in certain moods.

With the third volume, *La Mort dans l'âme* (1949), we return to close-ups of the three principal characters at the time of the French defeat. Mathieu and Brunet are with the army. Daniel, a non-combatant, is in Paris at the time of the arrival of the German troops. Each runs true to form. Mathieu drifts along with events, and when the Germans are finally sweeping all before them he is in a little village with other French soldiers who have lost their officers. A handful of privates and a sergeant, inspired by simple French patriotism, decide to try to hold up the German advance, for a few minutes at least. They establish themselves in a belfry overlooking the main road and Mathieu, again conforming to someone else's act of will, takes up his position with them. The Germans arrive and the heroic, suicidal little group of Frenchmen succeed in stopping the advance for a short time. Mathieu, in a sudden frenzy, fires shot after shot, with the feeling that he is revenging himself for all his past hesitations. We assume that he dies at the end of his hysterical outburst but Sartre refrains from making this clear, perhaps because he wished to reserve the possibility of reviving the character (the one closest to himself) at some later stage. However, whether Mathieu dies or not, his outburst, as he is firing on the Germans, is not at all admirable. It is an echo of Hilbert's violence in 'Érostate': killing is being used as a way of establishing a relationship with the world, and this time Sartre's attitude towards his character is seriously ambiguous. Daniel, too, re-echoes one of the short stories. In the confusion of occupied Paris he picks up a young *révolté*, Philippe, and—having left the pregnant Marcelle in the provinces—is free to devote himself to the pleasure of corrupting Philippe. The episode is related with garish brilliance but does not ring nearly so true as the parallel seduction in 'L'Enfance d'un chef'. By now, Sartre seems to be writing with dangerous facility.

Mathieu having disappeared, Brunet takes over as the main character. The last hundred pages of the volume contain a magnificent description, obviously a first-hand account, of the rounding-up of the French prisoners and their transference to Germany. Sartre's existentialist vision stands him in good stead here, because captivity consists in the removal of the possibility of the main 'project' and the falling back on subsidiary 'projects' to prevent the character from disintegrating. Brunet, being a puritanical Communist, immediately sets about discovering like-minded people among his fellow-prisoners in order to impose on them and himself a discipline that will prepare them for the day of liberation. His story is continued in the published fragment of volume four, *La Dernière chance*, where, with an unexpected return to subtlety, Sartre shows Brunet's impersonal resolution gradually being undermined. His closest friend in the prison-camp is a disillusioned ex-Communist, Schneider, whose affectionate irony troubles him. Brunet begins to have doubts about the infallibility of the Party Line. He and Schneider try to escape and Schneider is shot dead. We leave Brunet at the point where his impersonal support has broken and his one valid personal affection has been destroyed. This is the end of the book as it now stands.

In spite of the unfinished, shapeless, panoramic nature of *Les Chemins*, it is clear that the same psychological pattern is repeating itself in the case of the three main characters. They are as defeated by life as Roquentin was. Therefore, the confident title of the book is unjustified; the 'roads to freedom' lead, in fact, to a tragic impasse. My suspicion is that Sartre did not expect this to happen. The general tone of his post-Liberation writing suggests that, having rejected the aesthetic solution adopted at the end of *La Nausée*, he set out to show how the existentialist consciousness could effect a return to society. He has never ceased to preach commitment and action, but his most successful artistic products, such as *Les Mains sales* and *Les Séquestrés d'Altona*, belie the vigour of his hortatory declarations by being, like *Les Chemins de la liberté*, tragedies on the subject of the impossibility of meaningful action. There is a gap in his thought between the masterly, negative (yet strangely bracing) analysis of consciousness in *La Nausée* and his plunge into commitment. The ferocity with which he lambasts bourgeois 'stinkers' in *Les Chemins de la liberté* and continues to attack them elsewhere must be partly due to the fact that he is working off on them his exasperation at being unable to achieve, in his own thought, a genuine transition from negative to positive.

Novels by Sartre:
La Nausée, Paris, Gallimard, 1938.
    The Diary of Antoine Roquentin (trs. L. Alexander), London, Lehmann, 1949.
    (This same translation was issued as *Nausea*, Norfolk, Conn., New Directions, 1949.)

Les Chemins de la liberté, Paris, Gallimard, 1945-9:
  i. *L'Age de raison*, 1945.
     The Age of Reason (trs. Eric Sutton), London, Hamish Hamilton, 1947, and Penguin Books, 1961; New York, Knopf, 1947.
  ii. *Le Sursis*, 1945.
      The Reprieve (trs. Eric Sutton), London, Hamish Hamilton, 1948; New York, Knopf, 1947.
  iii. *La Mort dans l'âme*, 1949.
       Iron in the Soul (trs. Gerard Hopkins), London, Hamish Hamilton, 1950.
       (This same translation was issued as *Troubled Sleep*, New York, Knopf, 1951.)
  iv. *La Dernière chance* (fragments published under the title, 'Drôle d'amitié', in *Les Temps Modernes*, nos. 49 (Nov. 1949) and 50 (Dec. 1949)).

Collected short stories;

Le Mur, Paris, Gallimard, 1939.
  Intimacy, and other Stories (trs. L. Alexander), London, Peter Nevill, 1949; Norfolk, Conn., New Directions, 1952.
  (This same translation was issued in a limited edition as *The Wall . . . and other Stories*, New Directions, 1948.)

SAMUEL BECKETT
b. 1906

BY MARTIN ESSLIN

———————☆———————

IF the novel is defined as a pleasant tale, spun for the amusement of the reader by craftsmen of narrative technique, adept in the invention of interesting characters and the construction of intricately patterned plots, then Samuel Beckett could not be called a novelist at all, at least as far as the books he has written in French are concerned. But if, on the other hand, it were permissible to define the novel as a work in prose in which an imaginative artist may explore, with uncompromising honesty, ruthless integrity, and utter frankness, the human condition in all its naked absurdity, then prose poets like Franz Kafka or James Joyce can be called great novelists. Then too Samuel Beckett can take his place among them as one of the most profound and most significant novelists of our time. For Beckett, like Kafka, does not write for the amusement of readers. It is doubtful if, in writing his books, he ever even thinks of readers. Beckett writes because he has to write, because he is under a compulsion to search for the nature of his own self, and thus to explore the depths of being, the nature of the predicament of man and his existence.

A Protestant Irishman, born in Dublin, at one time *lecteur d'anglais* at the École Normale Supérieure in Paris and later, briefly, assistant to the Professor of Romance Languages at Trinity College, Dublin, Beckett has written the bulk of his most important work in French because, as he once put it: '. . . en Français c'est plus facile d'écrire sans style'; because, that is, when writing in a language in which he has to concentrate on saying what he wants to say, there is less temptation to be carried away by sheer virtuosity of language for its own sake. Nevertheless, Beckett's earlier writings in English and his later work in French (most of which he afterwards translates into English himself) form a single whole and cannot be separated in describing his literary personality.

Because among his earliest published writings there are essays on Proust and Joyce, and because he belonged to Joyce's circle, it has become one of the endlessly repeated clichés of literary reviewers that Beckett is a follower of Joyce, or has been influenced by Proust. In fact, even a fairly casual examination of his work must show that he owes little to either of these writers. As Beckett himself once pointed out in conversation, Proust is an analyser, Joyce a synthesizer. But if Proust dissects reality by examining it minutely, if Joyce builds a new reality by the creative use of language, Beckett does neither of these things: he is searching for the nature of reality itself by eliminating and discarding layer after layer of accidental qualities, by peeling off skin after skin of the onion to reach the innermost core, the nothingness at the centre of being. For Beckett, as he says in his essay on Proust, 'the artistic tendency is not expansive but a contraction. And art is the apotheosis of solitude. There is no communication because there are no vehicles of communication.'[1] To Beckett, therefore, the novel is not an act of communication or storytelling, it is a lonely and dedicated exploration, a shaft driven deep down into the core of the self. It is a self-contradictory, Quixotic, but because of this an infinitely heroic and noble attempt at expressing the inexpressible, saying the unsayable, distilling the essence of being and making visible the still centre of reality. Demokritos the Abderite, in one of Beckett's favourite apophthegms, said: 'Nothing is more real than nothing.'

This exploration has nothing to do with mere description, it rejects 'the grotesque fallacy of realistic art—"that miserable statement of line and surface", and the penny-a-line vulgarity of a literature of notations' (*Proust*, p. 57), the efforts of 'realists and naturalists worshipping the offals of experience, prostrate

---

[1] Samuel Beckett, *Proust* (New York, Grove Press, n.d.), p. 47.

before the epidermis and the swift epilepsy, and content to transcribe the surface, the façade, behind which the Idea is prisoner' (ibid., p. 59).

Yet how is the unsayable to be said, the uncommunicable to be communicated? As Beckett himself put it in describing the difficulties of one of his earlier heroes, Watt:

> ... the only way one can speak of nothing is to speak of it as though it were something, just as the only way one can speak of God is to speak of him as though he were a man, which to be sure he was, in a sense, for a time, and as the only way one can speak of man, even our anthropologists have realized that, is to speak of him as though he were a termite (*Watt*, p. 84).

Having left the surface of reality, Beckett's later novels deal with archetypes, they take place in a '*présent mythologique*' as Molloy puts it. Beckett's later novels have no story, no beginning and no end because they examine archetypal situations that are ever-present attributes of the human condition.

Nor are Beckett's protagonists, from Belacqua, Watt, Murphy, to Molloy, Malone, and the nameless heroes of his later works, fictional characters in the usual sense. They are emanations of his own personality who appear and reappear throughout his books. Belacqua, the main character of his earliest work of fiction, *More Pricks than Kicks* (1934), a sequence of stories about the same tragi-comic hero, reappears in his latest work, *Comment c'est* (1961), or rather is mysteriously referred to, without apparent reason or explanation.

The ten Belacqua stories, picaresque sketches of the life of impecunious Irish intellectuals haunting the pubs of Dublin, already contain a good deal of the essential Beckett. Belacqua himself has the difficulty of locomotion that afflicts so many of Beckett's characters: 'a spavined gait, his feet were in ruins, corns, hammer-toes' (*More Pricks than Kicks*, p. 10). Even more characteristically, he has pre-natal memories: 'I want very much to be back in the caul on my back in the dark forever' (ibid., p. 32). That Beckett himself retains what he believes to be a memory of his pre-natal life in his mother's womb is an established fact. Peggy Guggenheim, who confesses in her memoirs that she was at one time 'terribly in love' with Beckett, a 'very fascinating, lanky Irishman with green eyes and a thin face and a nose like an eagle', also reports that 'ever since his birth he had retained a terrible memory of life in his mother's womb. He was constantly suffering from this and had awful crises, when he felt he was suffocating. . . .'[2] The terrible situation of the embryo in the womb, which Beckett himself describes as one of nameless dread, all the more horrible because it is wholly inexpressible, concerned with a situation utterly beyond the grasp of the sufferer, a fear for which there can be no alleviation because the terrified self knows neither its own identity nor can ever know of even the possibility of help and eventual salvation—this, the most basic of all anxieties, is one of the underlying, ever-recurring *motifs* of Beckett's world.

If Beckett were not an artist of supreme power, however, this ante-natal memory would remain a mere psychological curiosity. It is his achievement that he has transmuted it into an image of universal significance—a summing-up of the entire human condition. For, once born into our world, man ultimately remains as unable to grasp the why and wherefore of his situation, the nature of his own identity, as the foetus in the womb; and like the foetus he is utterly incapable of even trying to form a conception of the unknown dimension on whose threshold he is perpetually balanced: death. The image of death as the unknown into which man is about to be expelled, suddenly and violently, from the warm squalor of his present state, is one of the dominant themes of Beckett's later novels. The helpless, mutilated, moribund old men who populate them are in fact also helpless foetuses in nameless dread of the cataclysm of such a second birth.

The eponymous hero of *Murphy* (1938), Beckett's second work of fiction (and one of the greatest comic novels in the English language), still inhabits a recognizable world: West Brompton, the World's End (on the fringes of Chelsea) and Brewery Road, between Pentonville Prison and the Metropolitan Cattle Market. Murphy is an Irishman trying to lose himself in London (as

---

[2] Peggy Guggenheim, *Confessions of an Art Addict* (London, André Deutsch, 1960), p. 49.

Beckett did when he threw up his post at Trinity College after a few terms of teaching), pursued by a number of others who want to bring him back to respectability. His chief pursuer however is Celia, the charming prostitute who loves Murphy, wants to marry him and is trying to make him take up work, so that she can give up her own profession. But when he finally does find a congenial job as a male nurse at the Magdalen Mental Mercyseat, he is so enthralled by the superior state of mind of the patients that he is doubly and irrevocably lost to Celia and the world. Every hour in the wards of the mental hospital increases,

together with his esteem for the patients [Murphy's] loathing of the text-book attitude towards them, the complacent scientific conceptualism that made contact with outer reality the index of mental well-being.... The definition of outer reality, or of reality short and simple, varied according to the sensibility of the definer. But all seemed agreed that contact with it, even the layman's muzzy contact, was a rare privilege. On this basis the patients were described as 'cut off' from reality.... The function of treatment was to bridge the gulf, translate the sufferer from his own pernicious little private dungheap to the glorious world of discrete particles, where it would be his inestimable prerogative once again to wonder, love, hate, desire, rejoice and howl in a reasonable balanced manner and comfort himself with the society of others in the same predicament. All this was duly revolting to Murphy, whose experience as a physical and rational being obliged him to call sanctuary what the psychiatrists called exile and to think of the patients not as banished from a system of benefits but as escaped from a colossal fiasco (*Murphy*, pp. 176-8).

Playing chess with a hypomanic, Murphy has a mystical experience. He

began to see nothing, that colourlessness which is such a rare postnatal treat, being the absence (to abuse a nice distinction) not of *percipere* but of *percipi*. His other senses also found themselves at peace, an unexpected pleasure. Not the numb peace of their own suspension, but the positive peace that comes when the somethings give way, or perhaps simply add up, to the Nothing, than which in the guffaw of the Abderite naught is more real ... (ibid., p. 246).

Soon after this, in a gas explosion, Murphy dies. His ashes are taken back to Dublin but, before they can be disposed of in the manner willed by Murphy, they are scattered on the floor of a pub in a brawl.

In *Murphy* we can clearly discern an important element of Beckett's literary inheritance: the bitterness, the hatred of the physical side of existence, which can be traced back to that other great Protestant Irishman, Swift.

What Beckett has in common with Swift is the combination of the deepest moral earnestness and artistic integrity with what in its essence is a comic talent. However much he may appear to be exploring the depths of human squalor and degradation, Beckett always remains a master of sardonic humour. Those critics who accuse him of unrelieved gloom and pessimism merely reveal that they lack the sense organs required to see how hilariously funny much of Beckett's vision can be: the audiences who rocked with laughter at *Waiting for Godot* had a very much clearer perception of the true nature of Beckett's genius—which lies precisely in his ability to produce the liberating catharsis of laughter by confronting his public not only with the sordidness of the human condition but also with a vision of its utter pettiness and inanity: that is why Beckett calls Demokritos' saying about the reality of nothingness a guffaw. When we see that all is vanity we can laugh even at the horrors of existence.

From the real Dublin of the Belacqua stories and the real London of *Murphy*, Beckett's own progressive retreat from external reality led him into a world of myth and allegory: the world of *Watt* (written 1943–5). Mr. Knott's farmhouse where Watt, the pathetic, ageless tramp, mysteriously finds work as a servant—only to lose it again as mysteriously when the allotted time is up—lies in a Kafka-country with an admixture of Irish colours and Irish humour. Mr. Knott is mysterious and unpredictable: his world is ruled according to iron laws that are as inexorable as they are absurd; it is a delicate mechanism each part of which is intricately geared to all others; but at its centre there is complete arbitrariness and absurdity. Two dogs are specially kept to eat Mr. Knott's surplus food, for example, but sometimes there is no surplus food from Mr. Knott's table for long periods and the dogs die. Sometimes there is too much: then the dogs die from overeating. So there is a complicated and intricately organized machinery for the replacement and care of these dogs: a whole family devoted to this service. The endless permutations of Mr. Knott's systems are echoed in the permutations of Watt's own thought, always deeply preoccupied with reasoning out the changing possibilities of intricate situations. This preoccupation with permutations, of which Molloy's sucking-stones are perhaps the best-known example, is a recurring feature of Beckett's mind. Molloy had sixteen stones distributed in four pockets:

Taking a stone from the right pocket of my greatcoat, and putting it in my mouth, I replaced it in the right pocket of my greatcoat by a stone from the right pocket of my trousers, which I replaced by a stone from the left pocket of my trousers, which I replaced by a stone from the left pocket of my greatcoat, which I replaced by the stone which was in my mouth, as soon as I had finished sucking it. Thus there were still four stones in each of the four pockets, but not quite the same stones . . . (*Molloy*, in *Three Novels*, p. 69).

Such permutations (and the example quoted is only the beginning of a long and involved calculation of probabilities) are a symbol of reality in flux, at the same time being a form of compulsion neurosis and a sheet anchor of the mind. In *Watt* the universe keeps its stability through a number of such series, 'the series of dogs, the series of men, the series of pictures'. It is the stability of permanence through flux:

Watt had more and more the impression, as time passed, that nothing could be added to Mr. Knott's establishment, and from it nothing taken away, but that as it was now so it had been in the beginning, and so it would remain to the end. . . . Yes, nothing changed in Mr. Knott's establishment, because nothing remained, and nothing came or went, because all was a coming and a going (*Watt*, pp. 144-5).

Watt, written while Beckett himself, hiding as a member of the Resistance, worked as a farm labourer in the neighbourhood of Avignon, marks the transition from conventional narrative to the mythological present of his French novels. Among the *parerga* and *addenda* to *Watt* there is a short poem in which Beckett has summed up the book as follows:

> Watt will not
> abate one jot
> but of what
>
> of the coming to
> of the being at
> of the going from
> Knott's habitat
>
> of the long way
> of the short stay
> of the going back home
> the way he had come
>
> of the empty heart
> of the empty hands
> of the dim mind wayfaring
> through barren lands
>
> of a flame with dark winds
> hedged about
> going out
> gone out . . . (p. 276).

These verses state the themes of Beckett's subsequent work: dim minds 'wayfaring through barren lands', the flame of life hedged about with dark winds—and going out.

At the end of the war, and after a brief visit to Ireland, Beckett returned to his home in Paris. He began to write in French and between 1945 and 1950 produced the fruits of the most creative period of his life: the novels *Molloy*, *Malone meurt*, *L'Innommable*, *Mercier et Camier* (so far unpublished), the three stories and thirteen fragments of an unfinished work collected in the volume *Nouvelles et Textes pour rien*, as well as three plays, *Eleutheria* (unpublished), *En attendant Godot*, and *Fin de partie*.

Of these the trilogy of novels is undoubtedly the most important, the centre-piece of Beckett's *œuvre*.

Molloy (1951) is a curiously constructed book. It consists of two parts of almost exactly equal length. In the first Molloy, a lame and dim-witted tramp on a bicycle, is in search of his home town and his mother. In the second Moran, a suburbanite bourgeois, receives the order of a mysterious organization whose agent he is to set out in search of Molloy. He leaves his home with his son, fails to find Molloy, and suffers a curious change: at the end when he is back home he walks on crutches like Molloy.

Molloy is a book rich in comic incident: the lame, barely conscious tramp lost in the town he believes to be his own home town yet cannot recognize or remember, constantly frustrated in his quest, appears as a latter-day Ulysses trying to reach the haven of his home; like Ulysses he is held captive for a while by a woman—an old lady whose dog he has run over with his bicycle and who now tries to mother the old tramp instead. There is at the same time a mystical, religious element in Molloy's quest: the idea of going to see his mother comes to him when he sees two men meeting at some deserted cross-roads. He later refers to them as the two thieves, so that they may represent the fifty-fifty chance of salvation which so fascinates Beckett and which also plays so important a part in *Waiting for Godot*. The origin of this pattern of thought is the saying of St. Augustine that calls upon mankind not to despair, for one of the thieves on the cross was saved, nor to exult, for one of them was damned.

That Moran is another aspect of Molloy can hardly be doubted. When Moran receives the order, through Gaber the messenger, from Youdi the mysterious boss, to seek out Molloy, he recognizes that he knows him already and yet 'I had no information as to his face. I assumed it was hirsute, craggy and grimacing. Nothing justified my doing so' (*Molloy*, in *Three Novels*, p. 114). And yet Moran has been visited by Molloy: 'This was how he came to me, at long intervals. Then I was nothing but uproar, bulk, rage, suffocation, effort unceasing, frenzied and vain. Just the opposite of myself, in fact. It was a change . . .' (ibid.). Moreover, Moran quite clearly states: '. . . my own natural end, and I was resolved to have no other, would it not at the same time be his?' (ibid.). So Moran conjures up an image of Molloy from the dark recesses of his own mind. But Molloy has multiple aspects:

Between the Molloy I stalked within me thus and the true Molloy, after whom I was so soon to be in full cry, over hill and dale, the resemblance cannot have been great. I was annexing perhaps already, without my knowing it, to my private Molloy, elements of the Molloy described by Gaber. The fact was, there were three, no, four, Molloys.

He that inhabited me, my caricature of same, Gaber's and the man of flesh and blood somewhere awaiting me. To these I would add Youdi's were it not for Gaber's corpse fidelity to the letter of his messages. Bad reasoning. For could it seriously be supposed that Youdi had confided to Gaber all he knew, or thought he knew . . . about his protégé? Assuredly not . . . I will therefore add a fifth Molloy, that of Youdi. . . . There were others too, of course. But let us leave it at that. . . . And let us not meddle either with the question as to how far these five Molloys were constant and how far subject to variation. For there was this about Youdi that he changed his mind with great facility (ibid., pp. 115-16).

Is Molloy then the subconscious part of Moran's own personality—which is the opposite to himself and when released drives him to uproar and frenzy? Is it that part of himself of which he can only get a caricatured image, but which can also be perceived differently by the outside world and by God Himself, who, capricious and arbitrary, can make everything change as everything receives its being by *His* beholding it? Is the book the twofold quest of the subconscious in search of its resting place, the peace of oblivion, and the conscious mind's quest for the subconscious?

It is easy to go too far and to interpret a complex poetic image, such as is presented by *Molloy*, too closely or too literally. Let it be said that these are elements in the picture, but they are themes woven into a symphony; they sometimes rise to the surface, sometimes they are overlaid by others that belong to the pattern which constitutes the whole, but must for ever remain complex, ambiguous, multi-dimensional, and therefore incapable of being reduced to an interpretation in purely conceptual terms. The meaning of a poetic structure of this kind is coterminous with its expression: its ambiguities, hidden parallelism, associations, and assonances *are* its meaning. Thus Molloy is Molloy and Moran Moran; and yet, as Moran says, Molloy is within him.

Molloy's quest for his mother ends in a ditch. His mind goes back to his encounter with the two travellers, the two thieves. He longs to return to the forest; but then he takes that statement back. 'Molloy could stay, where he happened to be.' In fact he has reached his goal. For as the opening sentence of the book informs us, he is writing his story in his mother's room.

As for Moran, his report starts with the words: 'It is midnight. The rain is beating on the windows.' He too is writing a report. But the last words of his section of the book return to the opening passage. They run: 'Then I went back into the house and wrote, It is midnight. The rain is beating on the windows. It was not midnight. It was not raining' (ibid., p. 176).

Thus the last sentence of the book casts doubts on the veracity of Moran's whole report. Or does it? Is this not rather an indication that Molloy and Moran themselves, aspects both of one personality, are also, in the last resort, mere emanations of a third personality—Beckett's own . . .?

In *Malone meurt* (1951) the arbitrary nature of the names and personalities in Beckett's work is even more clearly apparent. Malone, an old man lying somewhere in a hospital or asylum, is dying. He amuses himself by making up stories about people he remembers or invents. Like Molloy and Moran, like Beckett himself, Malone, in his dying moments, is under a compulsion to write down his thoughts, his fantasies, his memories. We hear about Saposcat, the prim and proper boy, and the Lamberts, a squalid family of farmers, and MacMann, another old and infirm man in an asylum, with his keeper and later his lover, Moll—and after Moll's death Lemuel: but then 'the Murphys, Merciers, Molloys, Morans and Malones' also make an appearance. Here then is Malone, making up names and characters. But he himself, in exactly the same manner, is being made up by the author of the book. Moran may have been in search of his deeper, hidden self, Molloy. But so is Beckett whose own search for his self has led to the creation of them all.

For it is this search for the answer to the question: 'Who am I?' or 'What am I saying when I say I?' that provides the impulse for Beckett's explorations. The multiplicity of Molloys that Moran was confronted with when asked by the messenger of a higher power to find him constitutes the basic problem behind this search. What is the self? It is not outward circumstance—for that can change. It is not appearance—that too can change. Is it what I believe to be myself? That may be an illusion. Is it everything that I can think of and imagine, including all the vast crowd of characters I can make up? It is to scoop up all these, in all their infinite possibility, that Beckett is compelled to write. That is why, in one of the very enigmatic and yet highly revealing *Textes pour rien*, he says of his life:

> Words, words, my life was never anything but words, pell-mell, a Babel of silences and words, that life of mine, that I call finished, or still going on, according to the words, according to the hours, provided this still goes on, in this strange way. Apparitions, guardians, what childishness, and ghouls, do I know what that means, surely not, and what is happening in the meantime, as if I did not know it, as if there were two things, anything but that thing, what is it, that unnamable thing, that I name, name, name, without using it up, and that I call words.[3]

Or again, summing it all up in another passage:

> Where should I go, if I could go, what would I be, if I could be, what would I say, if I had a voice, who speaks like this, calling itself me? ... He tells his story, every five minutes, saying it is not his, admit that it's a sly thing to do. ... He makes me speak, saying it is not me, admit, that's an impertinent thing to do, he makes me say that it is not me, me who says nothing. Even, if he still allotted me the third person singular as to his other chimeras, but no, he wants only me, for his ego. ... His life, let's talk about it, he does not like that, he understands, so that it is not to be his, it is not he, think of it, he would not do that to himself, that is good for Molloy, for Malone, there you have mortal beings, happy mortals, but he, you would not think of that, to pass that way, he who has never budged, he who is me, all things considered, and what things, and how considered, he only needed not to go that way ...
> (pp. 153-156).

Textes pour rien was to be a further and even more daring foray into the region to which Beckett had penetrated in the third novel of his great trilogy, *L'Innommable* (1953). Going to the very limits, it provides an illuminating commentary to that most elusive of Beckett's books, but also perhaps his greatest achievement.

Here it is no longer Molloy speaking, or Moran, or Malone: and we have also left the half-world of mythology and allegory. The voice that is now speaking is a voice which, like the one we

---

[3] Samuel Beckett, *Nouvelles et Textes pour rien* (Paris, Éd. de Minuit, 1958), pp. 172-3.

heard in the passages from *Textes pour rien*, is unnamable because it is the voice of a self in search of its own identity. For what is the self? The part that is speaking? Or the part that is listening? There is not *one* voice in our minds, but a multitude of voices, a complex conversation of speakers, listeners, observers, critics, some vocal, some silent. It is thus as a matrix of possibilities that we must see our own consciousness, and the subconscious layers that lie beneath it. In *L'Innommable* it is that unnamable voice speaking, the voice of that deepest, unidentifiable self:

I am neither, I needn't say, Murphy, nor Watt, nor Mercier, nor—no I can't even bring myself to name them, nor any of the others whose very names I forget, who told me I was they, who I must have tried to be, under duress, or through fear, or to avoid acknowledging me . . .' (*The Unnamable*, in *Three Novels*, p. 328).

All these personalities, with their infirmities, their difficulty in moving about, their poverty and simplicity of mind, have only been explorations of the self, attempts to divest it of accidentals, experiments designed to see what would remain of the self if it were lame and dull-witted, without status in the world, a tramp without a home, alone, unsupported, abandoned . . . sick, dying, covered in sores, half-blind. . . . What would remain? The essence and true nature of the self?

In *L'Innommable* that exploration is carried on—but now quite openly, with the cards laid on the table:

All these Murphys, Molloys and Malones do not fool me. They have made me waste my time, suffer for nothing, speak of them, when, in order to stop speaking, I should have spoken of me, and of me alone . . . I thought I was right in enlisting these sufferers of my pains. I was wrong. They never suffered my pains, their pains are nothing, compared to mine, a mere tittle of mine, the tittle I thought I could put from me, in order to witness it. Let them be gone now, them and all the others, those I have used and those I have not used, give me back the pains I lent them and vanish, for my life, my memory, my terrors and shames . . . (ibid., pp. 305-6).

Now, therefore, if in the course of the search another self has to be experimented with, it is quite openly presented as a fantasy. Is this new self to be called Basil? 'Decidedly Basil is becoming important, I'll call him Mahood instead, I prefer that, I'm queer.

It was he told me stories about me, lived in my stead, issued forth from me, came back to me, entered back into me . . .' (ibid., p. 311).

Mahood is a limbless creature, living in a jar, on the corner of some Paris street: so far has the self now been stripped down. But even this does not go far enough. However degraded and deprived Mahood is, he is the ruin of something that had a definite shape. The time has come to go one step further and to explore the self as pure potentiality—as the unborn, not yet determined case of humanity.

Quick give me a mother and let me suck her white, pinching my tits. But it's time I gave this solitary a name, nothing doing without proper names. I therefore baptize him Worm . . . Before Mahood there were others like him, of the same breed and creed, armed with the same prong. But Worm is the first of his kind . . . (ibid., p. 340).

But after Worm's situation has been explored, the narrator can discard him too, as he has discarded Mahood.

. . . Mahood, he was called Mahood, I don't see him any more, I don't know how he lived any more, he isn't there any more, he was never there in his jar, I never saw him, and yet I remember, I remember having talked about him, the same words recur and they are your memories. It is I invented him, him and so many others, and the places where they passed, the places where they stayed, in order to speak, since I had to speak, without speaking of me, I couldn't speak of me, I was never told I had to speak of me, I invented my memories, not knowing what I was doing, not one is of me. It is they asked me to speak of them, they wanted to know what they were, how they lived, that suited me . . . (ibid., p. 399).

The compulsion to speak. Their voices incessantly demanding to be heard. The multitude of selves that ask to speak and to be spoken of. Nothing would be easier than to present this as a clinical picture of neurosis or psychosis. Nothing could be more wrong and more misguided. These tendencies certainly are present, but—and this is the point—they have been magnificently sublimated and turned into a work of art. The wound was there, but so was the genius to heal it, to make it fruitful and a source of healing power for others. The deeper and the more real the wound, the greater the achievement of the mind that could make the aching tissues grow and close the scar. All fiction is in the last resort a matter of voices within the writer that ask to be heard, parts of his own personality that become detached and start a dialogue. But there has been no other writer so deeply possessed and compelled and, at the same time, so triumphantly detached that he could dare to face the problem of the self in all its vertigo, its infinite recession of self-reflecting mirrors.

In Beckett's great trilogy we witness the process of the exploration. We start with fiction and we end in the most ruthless self-revelation, the agony of a soul in search of its own identity. There has been speculation as to why so many of the names in Beckett's novels start with M: Murphy, Molloy, Malone, MacMann, Mahood; there have been those who thought the M may have stood for *Man*. This is to underrate the subtlety and complexity of Beckett's mind—and of his real theme. In fact the M is a Greek Sigma stood on its side. The Sigma stands for Beckett's own first name: Sam. And so of course, the other way about, does the W of Watt and Worm:

> I thought I was free to say any old thing, so long as I didn't go silent. Then I said to myself that after all it wasn't any old thing, the thing I was saying, that it might well be the thing demanded of me, assuming something was being demanded of me . . . I did what I could, a thing beyond my strength, and often for exhaustion I gave up doing it, and yet it went on being done, the voice being heard, the voice which could not be mine, since I had none left, and yet which could only be mine, since I could not go silent, and since I was alone, in a place where no voice could reach me. Yes, in my life, since we must call it so, there were three things, the inability to speak, the inability to be silent, and solitude, that's what I've had to make the best of. Yes, now I can speak of my life . . . (ibid., p. 400).

L'Innommable is thus the culminating point of a progressive exploration of the self: it reveals, in the end, that very centre of nothingness, that state of pure potentiality by which Sartre defines Being-for-Itself. The multitude of characters and personalities which the narrator's voice can assume and conjure up from the void represent so many choices of being, but the core of the self is pure potentiality, *le Néant*, that very nothingness that Murphy delighted in when he had escaped from all his commitments, that pure potentiality represented by Worm, man about to be born. There is no evidence to indicate, and it seems unlikely, that Beckett has ever been consciously influenced by Sartre's philosophy. His genius is far too personal, his method of creation far too compulsive, to allow him to model his writing on some philosophy he may have heard of or read about. It is all the more remarkable that, without doubt, Beckett is the greatest creative writer ever to have put this aspect of existential philosophy into the concrete shape of a work of art. It is as though by some mysterious osmosis the currents of abstract thought and creative vision in our time had interpenetrated each other.

It seemed almost impossible, after *L'Innommable*, to continue on the path of ruthless self-exploration. *Textes pour rien*, as we have already pointed out, was an attempt at going on in the same direction. It produced some of the most beautiful pieces of Beckett's prose poetry (for all of Beckett's writing, it must never be forgotten, is poetry, with sweeping rhythms, complex patterns of sound and imagery), but was doomed to stay unfinished.

After the five years of his creative frenzy that culminated in *L'Innommable* and *Textes pour rien*, there followed a period of silence in French. After the great public acclaim of his play, *En attendant Godot*, Beckett returned to writing in English. He wrote a number of radio plays, the work on which he regarded as a relaxation, as they did not probe the depths or demand the effort that he associates with his work in French.

The novel *Comment c'est* (1961), however, does represent both a continuation of his previous efforts and a new beginning. Written without a single punctuation mark and in strophic paragraphs of varied length, this strange book fuses the mythical elements of *Watt* and *Molloy* with the *motif* of the compelling voice we find in *L'Innommable* and *Textes pour rien* in a vision of truly Swiftian bitterness.

The voice is heard by an again unnamed narrator. He is, or perhaps only tells the story of, an old man who painfully makes his way, crawling on all fours, through a sea of mud (*E fango è il mondo*—the world is mud, was the quotation from Leopardi that Beckett used as the motto for his study of Proust thirty years earlier). The little old man, who does not know how or why he got into his prostrate position, drags with him a little sack filled with tins of fish from which he derives his sustenance—thanks to his possession of a tin-opener which he is in constant dread of losing. Visions from a world of light sometimes penetrate the darkness. And then, so the voice goes on, in intervals of incessant panting which pervade the whole book, the wayfarer in the mud (or is it a vast sea of excrement?) suddenly touches another human figure. Is it alive? Or dead? When poked with the tin-opener it screams—or sings?—so it is alive. Another little old man, face downwards, crawling through the mud. His name is Pim. For a brief span the two prostrate figures lie alongside each other. The narrator learns that he can make Pim talk by hurting him with the tin-opener, and can make him shut up by pushing his face into the mud. Having thus learned how to manipulate his partner, he makes him tell him what he remembers of his life in the world of light, memories of his wife, Pam Prim, and their loves. . . . The narrator loves Pim, who is his victim and whom he torments. He is happy, 'c'était de bons moments'. But then the inexorable laws of nature assert themselves. By a curious, and to himself inexplicable *tropisme*, the narrator is compelled to crawl on, pursuing a preordained course. Pim is left behind. In the third part the narrator, or the voice who speaks through the panting, speculates on the laws that govern their world. Perhaps there are hundreds of thousands crawling through the mud along a preordained route and meeting, at regular intervals, others crawling in the opposite direction. Perhaps each is destined to be executioner and victim in turn in an endless chain of fleeting relationships, between those who stick tin-openers into their victims and those who are thus made to sing. . . . And that perhaps is how it is, *comment c'est*. . . .

*   *   *

Beckett's work is entirely *sui generis*, unclassifiable, disturbing, funny, cruel, and inspiring. It defies all attempts at interpretation —like the world of atomic particles where the introduction of an observer itself changes that which is to be observed. Like Michelangelo, who chipped away the rock to reveal the delicate beauty that had always been imprisoned within it, Beckett works by discarding layer upon layer of conventional narrative material: description, character, psychology, incident, plot, to lay bare the secret workings of the human mind. But here too he can only work as it were, by measuring out the limits of the sayable so that the unsayable may be guessed, hidden behind the last, impenetrable barrier.

Beckett's novels and plays are not easily accessible. They must be approached with due humility, read more than once, wrestled with and fought for. Beckett is a poet working for his own salvation. Public relations and an easy urbanity in the presentation of his work are not included in his basic brief.

And yet, although he has made no effort at achieving fame or creating a following, he has become famous and has won relatively wide support. Perhaps the most difficult writer of his generation, he has reached his public as a dramatist, as a writer of the most poetic radio plays of his time, and as a novelist. This is a fact that goes a long way towards restoring one's faith in the power of the dedicated pursuit of truth and beauty.

Here is a poet who has never made the slightest concession, never sought acclaim, never explained himself, who has never bowed to the demands of fashion or publicity. He merely said what he felt himself compelled to say. What he had to say was difficult, obscure, repellent (for the landscapes of the mind he has revealed were bound at first to appear as horrid and frightening as the dark valleys and ravines of the Alps before their sombre beauty was accepted at large). But, because he had something real and important to say, he has not lacked those who come, eager to hear him.

Works of fiction by Beckett originally published in English:
More Pricks than Kicks, London, Chatto & Windus, 1934.
Murphy, London, Routledge, 1938.
Watt, Paris, Olympia Press, 1958.

Novels originally published in French:
Molloy, Paris, Éd. de Minuit, 1951.

Malone meurt, Paris, Éd. de Minuit, 1951.

L'Innommable, Paris, Éd. de Minuit, 1953.

(The above novels were issued in English translation as *Three Novels*, Calder, 1959: *Molloy* (trs. Patrick Bowles); *Malone Dies* (trs. the author); *The Unnamable* (trs. the author).)

Comment c'est, Paris, Éd. de Minuit, 1961.

Short stories:

Nouvelles et Textes pour rien, Paris, Éd. de Minuit, 1955.

MAURICE BLANCHOT
b. 1907

BY GEOFFREY HARTMAN

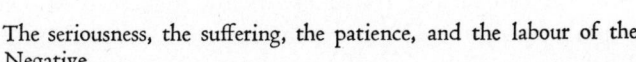

> The seriousness, the suffering, the patience, and the labour of the Negative.
>
> HEGEL

BLANCHOT'S work, says one of his few interpreters, offers no point of approach whatsoever. Today, twenty years after his first novel, he is still the most esoteric writer of contemporary France. There have appeared only three or four essays on his fiction; his novels remain untranslated. This is the more remarkable as Blanchot is also a prolific and well-known critic: besides his three novels, a number of *récits*, and a dyad of short stories, he has published five thick volumes of criticism. But then his criticism has its difficulties too.

One could draw on his criticism to illumine his novels. Such an inquiry, however, though helpful, would also be reductive. I will only use one clue provided by it: Blanchot, as critic, always goes from the work under discussion to the 'problematic' nature of literature. He illumines, therefore, the literary activity in general as well as this or that text. Literature, for him, is problematic in that it cannot be taken for granted: it is an activity hedged with contradictions, plagued by philosophic doubt, and shadowed by prophecies of obsolescence. This establishes a presumption that his novels will also deal with this area of concern, with the problematic status of literature.

They certainly tease us with the question of whether they are novels, or even literature. The difficulty is not in the prose, which is eloquent, or in the characters and world which are physically (if not entirely) ordinary. It is, as in Kafka, the atmosphere and action that puzzle, yet all charmy realism is absent. There is little plot, little characterization, and the ordinariness may be breached by the fantastic. If Blanchot must be attached to a tradition, it involves rather than derives from Kafka, and goes back to the rebirth of romance and the beginnings of surrealism in the Romantic period. Between Flaubert's *réel écrit* and Blanchot's *irréel récit* there is a distance as great as between Mlle de Scudéry and Flaubert. It has recently been argued that the change from the romance to the novel proper had a distinct philosophical cause; and I will eventually suggest that there is also a philosophical analogue to the apparent reversal of direction, the return of the novel to a romantic or surrealistic form. The German Romantics encouraged it by bringing the novel closer to fairy-tale and novella, and the reverse development passes via Novalis, Poe, Nerval, and Baudelaire, to Mallarmé's *Igitur*, and the quasi-confessional literature of Gide, Breton, Leiris, and Bataille.

The ranging of Blanchot within a certain tradition is a comforting but hardly an illuminating state of affairs. For that tradition, and what it intends, are still somewhat obscure. It may be that Blanchot, understood, will focus it more sharply; but one cannot begin with it. A last extrinsic resort lies with the interpreters of Blanchot; and these also do not take us beyond our starting-point: that the novels somehow have themselves, or the activity of art, as their subject. Sartre, for example, calls *Aminadab* (1942) a new type of fantasy and secular ghost-story. He notes in it an evasive mood of finality, and identifies this as the ghost of transcendence floating loose in a world deprived of transcendence.[1] What Sartre means by 'evasive finality' I can best show via a short passage from a later novel, *Thomas l'obscur* ('nouvelle version', 1950):

The book rotted on the table. Yet no one moved about the room. His solitude was complete. And yet, as surely as there was no one in the

[1] '*Aminadab* or the Fantastic Considered as a Language', *Literary Essays* (Wisdom Library, New York, 1957), pp. 56–72. Another interesting critic is Georges Bataille, 'Ce monde où nous mourons', *Critique* XIII (1957), pp. 675–84. On Blanchot and Kafka cf. M. Goth, *Kafka et les lettres françaises* (Paris, Corti, 1956), ch. iii.

room and even in the world, so surely someone was there, who occupied his sleep, dealt intimately with him, was around him and in him. Naïvely, he sat up, and tried to eye the night . . . but nothing would let him catch this presence as a form or as an other. . . . It was a modulation in what did not exist, a different mode of being absent, another void in which he came alive. Now, for certain, someone was coming close, who stood not nowhere and everywhere, but a few feet away, invisible and sure. By a movement which nothing stopped yet which nothing hastened, a power was coming toward him whose contact he could not accept (pp. 36–38).

I leave aside the question of whether an English or American mind can tolerate even Blanchot's maturest prose. The French have a higher level of sympathy for experimental philosophical fiction: and I shudder to think what F. R. Leavis might say. But we can, on the basis of the later novels, move beyond Sartre's rather professional insight. The subject here is clearly art, and its relation to consciousness. The dilemma rendered is the artist's own, that of a mind that seeks to overcome itself from within, to pass into reality rather than into more and more consciousness; and it is through art that it intends to become real rather than more conscious. The evasive, ghostly finality Sartre has noted is projected by the mind while seeking to confront itself as a real body. Something of the agony of its quest to get out of itself without ceasing to be itself is given by this further passage from *Thomas l'obscur*, in which the hero

felt himself bitten or struck, he did not know which, by a thing that seemed to be a word, but resembled rather a gigantic rat, with piercing eyes, pure teeth, an all-powerful animal. In seeing it a few inches from his face, he succumbed to the wish to devour it, to make it the most intimate part of himself. He threw himself on it and, digging his nails into its entrails, tried to make it his own.

The melodious horror of this combat is sustained for another page, at the end of which we realize that Thomas is fighting, like the writer, with the nature of consciousness.

This quest, to make the mind real rather than more conscious, involves, as the above passage shows, an attempted self-estrangement. The old question, of whether the artist is more conscious or less conscious than the thinker, is resolved in an interesting manner. Art, Blanchot suggests, is consciousness in search of an unselfconscious form, consciousness estranging itself as in a dream, which is still a dream of itself. In a beautiful phrase he describes the movement of his characters, and perhaps of his novels as a whole, as that of a strange and burning wheel without a centre, 'l'étrange roue ardente privée de centre'.

I need hardly add that this attempt to transmute consciousness always fails, that success is only its asymptote, and that, according to the image of the wheel, the effort is continually renewed. But there is an inner principle of progression. The writer's failure increases, by a kind of peripety, his burden of consciousness, so that the ghost figure, or the mind thirsting for concreteness, exercises a constantly stronger allure. This ghost figure, just like its avatars, demands flesh and blood; yet being consciousness, being 'ce refus d'être substance', it cannot be incarnated, and therefore actually haunts some characters to their death. To die may become a ruse for giving a body to its void (see *Thomas l'obscur*, p. 130).

The most puzzling as well as the most imaginative features of Blanchot's novels are linked to this dialectic of emanation, of strange intimacies and intimate estrangements. The distance between any two human beings in his novels is infinite and yet nothing. The magic of chance crystallizes and dissolves relationships. The shifts between familiarity and estrangement or, occasionally, life and death, are so quick and pervasive that they affect the very nature of the symbols used, and put the essence (the ontological status) of words in doubt. Blanchot is difficult to interpret because we can never say that *here* he reflects the world we know and *here* an imaginary world. He endows his symbols with a middle and unresolved quality, and he does this in part by a judicious use of the improbable, and an only exceptional use of the sheer fantastic. His latest *récits*, in fact, move purely in the realm of the improbable, and contain no fantastic incursions or overt breaches of the tenuous realism. The improbable, being a special case of *chance*, keeps the mind within the story, teasing it with the hope that all details together might solve the mystery, since no single event is quite absurd. But no resolution occurs, and the reader is obliged to take the mystery as an integral rather than resolved part of the whole; and since the whole is simply the novel, he thinks of the latter as the space in which a mystery is revealed, but *as* a mystery.

Sartre has interpreted the improbabilities to which we refer as depicting a revolt of means against ends, and so constantly inciting, yet denying, the idea of finality. There is a labyrinth of corridors, doors, staircases, and messages that lead to nothing. Locked doors open, a person summoned to appear is asked why *he* requested the interview, and characters or narrator find themselves returning to the point they started from. But if these and similar improbabilities keep us fascinated, it is because they point obliquely and inexhaustively to a specific mystery. They could be explained by positing an all-pervasive forgetfulness. And this seems to be a part of the general pattern of self-estrangement. Blanchot's personae never walk the straight line between two points: they seem imbued, physically and mentally, with a spirit of oblivion, and his novels strike us as being the most un-Aristotelian ever written—they are all *middle*. To be in Blanchot's world is to err: to follow something, to be involved in a maze of words or passageways, to encounter chance openings, to be attracted and distracted continually, to forget to remember, to remember to forget.

With this we come to our first substantive philosophical link. Blanchot's emphasis on forgetfulness harmonizes with what Heidegger calls the mystery of oblivion. Heidegger himself has sources in Hegel and the Romantic period; and it is quite possible that Blanchot assimilates Heidegger through the perspective of a common literary tradition, reaching from the German Romantics to the French Symbolists and Rilke. The mystery of oblivion is described by Heidegger as follows.[2] Historical existence,

---

[2] My summary is drawn primarily from 'On the Essence of Truth' (1943), 'What is Metaphysics' (1929 and 1943), and the various essays on Hölderlin published between 1937 and 1943. I present Heidegger's thought as homogeneous, but this is a simplification: the writings on which I draw post-date *Sein und Zeit*, and there is evidence that both in them and again in recent years Heidegger has modified certain of his views. Some concepts mentioned below, e.g. 'error', have an acknowledged source in Nietzsche and other Romantics and

or man's attempt to live fully in the here and now, would not be possible without an intrinsic oblivion on his part. He learns about the earth by being practical, by attending to each thing as it appears necessary or interesting to him. Yet to do this he must forget the possible wholeness of things, and rest content to substitute continually the part for the whole or being for Being. But how, asks Heidegger, can he forget the whole? There must be, first of all, a dissimulation in Being itself, one that offers him the possibility of mistaking the part for the whole. The part comes to be or appear only in so far as the whole sets it off, but invisibly, without overshadowing. Man's turning towards the part or anything apparently 'open' to him (Heidegger plays on the Greek for 'truth', a word cognate with 'unhidden') means a turning away from the whole; yet he is attracted to the part precisely because it also promises a whole, albeit a different one: the earth in its fullness. Thus the direct search for wholeness (the metaphysical quest) is displaced by an historical appropriation of the earth (the existential quest), and by means of a movement which Heidegger calls *error*, because it is an erring, a wandering from part to part, and because it is erroneous, the mistaking of being for Being.

But besides this dissimulation of the whole there must also be a dissemblance of the dissimulation. A mere veiling of the essence of things would only spur us to pierce the veil, to become mystics rather than existentialists. To accept our human nature we must become freely blind, and dissemble the original dissimulation. And when our eyes are occasionally opened, it is to the existence of dissimulation rather than to Being itself. The mystery of oblivion is an oblivion of mystery, and this alone enables us to live humanly and dynamically and to keep making errors and so gradually to explore and possess the earth.

It will already be clear that Heidegger is giving a very subtle version of Plato's mythically expressed theory of reminiscence, but shifting the emphasis to an involved process of discovery and

post-Romantics. For Blanchot's own summary of Heidegger's thought, and in relation to Hegel's, see esp. *L'Espace littéraire*, pp. 263ff.

forgetfulness. Plato's myth is revived in all its potency in the Romantic period; there is hardly a great writer, from Novalis to De Quincey, who does not explore both the existential and metaphysical implications of—shall we say—sleep. I mention this because, though I think Blanchot is indebted to Heidegger, his understanding of the latter's philosophy is likely to have been mediated by a larger and predominantly literary tradition. If there is any one trait that unifies literary movements since the Romantic period, it is their quest for an adequate theory of unconsciousness or creative self-oblivion.

Blanchot certainly gives Heidegger's concepts a rather exact presence. The oblivion that besets his characters alienates them from various finalities, intensifies their erring motion, and brings them into a freer contact with life, a contact having the surprise, sharpness, and inconsequence of 'chance'. Yet his novels' endless estrangement of every final term raises a double nostalgia which Heidegger also describes: a nostalgia for the concrete, the here and now, and for something greater than every here and now. The first, a tenacious holding on to the part as if it were the whole, Heidegger names insistence (in contrast to existence); and the second is the revived metaphysical desire for the vision of the whole. Heidegger shows, however, that the latter cannot be attained except by first passing through and standing outside everything; or projecting, as he also expresses it, into Nothing. Human life in its freedom is a transcendence towards Being, but always as this Nothing, this eclipsed or veiled form. Certain passages in Blanchot seem to translate Heidegger's dialectic of finitude almost word for word:

I saw immediately [says the narrator in *Celui qui ne m'accompagnait pas*] that I must stay in this place. Perhaps the insight did not teach me anything I had not known. Perhaps in showing me the only point by which I could hold to something real, it screwed the anxiety of the void tighter on me, as if, these words being the only ones I could live in, I had felt them slipping away, as if they were the last abode from which I could control this errant coming and going ['le va-et-vient errant']. I understood well enough, or seemed to understand, why I had to take root here. But, here, where was I? Why near him? Why behind everything I said and he said was there this word: 'Surely everything, where we are, is dissembling?' I heard and did not hear; it was beyond being understood (pp. 98–99).

If the realistic novel puts man wholly into his physical setting, then the 'irrealistic' novel may be said to put him wholly into Nothing. A good part of the action of the *récit* quoted above is the narrator's attempt to describe his physical setting and the inability to do so. The narrator cannot embody himself. In *Thomas l'obscur*, similarly, Thomas seeks various embodiments, and in vain. The sea and earth reject him, and one is reminded of the Old Man in Chaucer's 'Pardoner's Tale' who knocks on the gate of his mother earth, seeking death, imploring her to let him in. Yet Blanchot's value is not in the transcription, however imaginative, of a philosophy such as Heidegger's. This would make his novels a kind of allegory, which they are not. What is perhaps hard to understand is that they participate in the dilemma they describe. They are a passion imitating an action. Blanchot does not merely represent 'Nothing', or the dissimulation of Being as dissimulation. He endures it, and fiction is his durance. In one of the *récits* this is given literal form by the author moving self-divided through his pages, seeking to attain unity of Being, yet questioning the symbols that promise it. But all his novels create a void rather than a world, an *espace littéraire* as ontologically equivocal as mind itself, and which neither reader, author, nor characters can cross to reach Being. What Ortega y Gasset said of Proust can be applied, with a slight though important change, to Blanchot: 'He stands as the inventor of a new distance between symbols and ourselves.'

But how, exactly, do Blanchot's novels participate in what he calls, in *La Part du feu*, 'the realization by literature of its unreality' (p. 306)? Let us consider shortly certain conventional carriers of meanings, such as book, genre, character, and plot. It will be seen that Blanchot uses these to criticize the very realism from which they spring, and which, as part of literature, they must retain.

A 'book' is a portable and condensed experience. For Blanchot it involves the questioning of the idea that portable and condensed experiences are possible: the *œuvre* of an artist is the path he takes to realize his *désœuvrement* (see *Le Livre à venir*, p. 253). It is true that Blanchot's books are separate entities, individualized by title. Yet he has written two versions of *Thomas l'obscur* (1941 and 1950), and in a note prefacing the second version says that a work has an infinity of possible variants. This multiplication (by the modern painter also) of sketches and states, though perhaps linked to Balzac's retake of characters, to the *roman-fleuve* and devices of perspective, may also have an opposite intent. The difference turns on whether the mimetic power of the artist is strengthened or questioned. Balzac's novels add up, they increase the depth and 'realness' of his world, but Blanchot's novels stand in an abstractive relation to one another. What the second *Thomas l'obscur* removes from the first is analogous though not identical to what Cézanne subtracts from Delacroix. Rather than a literary and exotic realism Blanchot purges a literary and exotic 'irrealism', or, to give it the more popular name, 'surrealism'. He is concerned only with the unreality in reality itself.

That is also why Blanchot uses the *récit*, a form strongly associated with Gide. The *récit* is a first-person confessional narrative, a kind of dramatic monologue in prose, and through it Blanchot attacks the Achilles' heel of realism, the notion of the sincere and even of the authorial 'I'. Like the soul, the 'I' is not a simple substance. In the case of the alienated man, who suffers from the 'disease of consciousness' (Dostoievsky), the 'I' is one of many faces, and at most a dialectical component of the whole man. 'The whole history of fiction since Arnim,' writes Breton, pointing once more to the Romantic origins, 'is that of liberties taken with the idea of "I am".' Blanchot, however, is less interested in personality as such than in the personality of words, their deceptive dual character of veil and revelation. His *récits* in their essence are simply (or not so simply) a critique of word-notions that at once motivate and seduce the artist: the *je*, the *ici*, the *maintenant*, the *nous*, the *fin*. To resist them is to restore the space (between the artist and words, between him and the world) which art seems expressly created to deny.

To illustrate this questioning and distancing power of Blanchot's I choose a passage from *Celui qui ne m'accompagnait pas* (1953), similar in some respects to the one quoted previously from this book. The narrator is reflecting, as he does throughout, on the words of an interlocutor, who has no presence except through cryptic replies, echoing silences:

> It is true that from his mysterious word of encouragement I could draw another more persuasive idea, namely, that I need not fear a false approach, the itineraries of error; I did not have one way, I had all, and this should have served to put me on my way with exceptional confidence. 'All! but on condition that I have time enough, all the time I can bear.' He did not demur, for of course the essence of a way is to furnish a short-cut across 'time'; it was this short-cut I sought, with the unreasonable idea that I should find thereby not a continued length of wayfaring but the shortest interval, the soul of brevity, to the point that on taking the first steps, it seemed to me, refusing to go further, that I had the right to tell myself: 'This is where I stand, this is what I'll stick to', and to him this is what I said with increased firmness: 'This is where I stand, this is what I'll stick to', which he happened to answer with a kind of élan and without my being able to resent it: 'But you have all the time you want!' (pp. 16-17).

This is part of a development still hinging on the first line of the book, 'I tried, this time, to approach him directly'; and practically everything in the sentence, the I, the him, the notions of time, way, and directness, are questioned by the *récit*, which moves forward by the force of its questions. The opening (we shall return to it later) expresses an attempt at immediacy, and, as in Kafka, the narrative ironically unfolds in the space that shows immediate contacts to be impossible, though the hope for them cannot die. But while Kafka draws us into his world, giving it circumstantial and symbolic flesh, Blanchot uses fictional counters as literal as words, and as abstract. Though we ask: who is the narrator? who is his companion? when does it happen? we never reach more than this conclusion: the narrator is the one who narrates, his companion someone inseparable from the act of narration, time and space simply that of narration itself. As such everything remains unreal or virtual, and the theme itself points to the perplexity of 'living' in such a condition, again called error. It is, in fact, a comedy of errors, but one that draws us into it insidiously. Though the novel, by its inherently negative progress, leaves us with as little at the end as we started with, it does make the *void* of thought visible as the *space* of art. A space, of course, anything but spacious; rather an effort of distance, as if the writer were constantly in danger of being tricked by the nature of words, or crushed by some endless automatic process of mind-murmur, of mental conjunction.

To suggest the unreality of his characters—who are like the space they inhabit—Blanchot sometimes uses a word with a strong neo-platonic flavour. They are said to lose *resemblance*: 'He saw them lose under his eyes all resemblance, manifesting a small wound on their foreheads whence their faces escaped' (*Thomas l'obscur*, p. 57). It is as if the Idea, whose image they are, suddenly disappears. The characters lose their transcendence, are unable to reach an *au-delà*, whether this is nature, supernature, or symbolic existence. Shades doomed not to rest, they wander through the author's pages as if neither his nor any world would receive them. But they gain therefore a caricature of immortality. They cannot die. Thomas the Obscure digs his own grave and hangs a stone about his neck as if to *drown* himself in the earth. Yet he is forced to 'exist', to stand outside himself till the end of the novel.

It would be untrue, however, to say that Blanchot's characters exist only in art; at least they do not 'live' in art any more than in reality. They have no inn to live in; they are literally outsiders. They are shown not as alive but rather as deathless, or as afraid of being deathless and so seeking death. I hope to find a fuller explanation for this later; here I can only say that art for Blanchot is intrinsically linked to the quest for and impossibility of *realizing* the self via symbols; and what does not have real body and yet is, must be a species of ghost. 'The symbol', he writes in *La Part du feu*, 'has no meaning . . . it is not even the embodied meaning of a truth otherwise inaccessible, it surpasses every truth and meaning, and what it gives us is this very transcendence which it seizes and makes felt in a fictional work, whose theme is the impossibility of fiction to realize itself' (p. 86).

In following through, finally, the plot or action of one of these ghostly novels, we come upon a second philosophical link, this time with Hegel, or primarily with him. If my description of Blanchot's theme is correct, and he shows consciousness seeking to be real rather than more conscious (and failing in this), we already have a Hegelian *donnée*. For that the mind should need to realize itself shows it is estranged from reality, and this estrangement is then seen to be in its very mode of existence: it desires to have itself external or opposite or invested with 'reality'. The starting-point, therefore, seems to be what Hegel calls the unhappy consciousness (which craves complete consciousness of reality and cannot attain it) or the self-estranged consciousness (whose true self seems split or estranged as if of necessity).[3] Yet we have said that the novels are problematic, and have themselves or the activity of art as their subject, rather than consciousness *per se*. The distinction may seem slight but can now be explored further. It is of some importance to determine exactly what the relation of art to consciousness may be. For religion, according to Hegel, shows a higher state of consciousness than art, and philosophy the highest. The great challenge, in fact, to the autonomy of literature, and hence the real enemy to any *rapprochement* between philosophy and art, is Hegel's prediction of the end of art. Only if the two activities are thought co-substantial is the true dignity of either assured. I will now seek to show that Blanchot wants to negate this prediction of obsolescence, that his *récits* are conceived as an answer to it.

Hegel, though he considers it necessary for the mind to suffer a long history of self-estrangement, yet insists that progress can be made which affects not only the quantity but also the quality of consciousness, and that the philosopher, coming towards the end of this history, will conceive the real as the rational, and so overcome the felt difference between the real world and the world of the mind. Art, however, is not a product of the philosophical but rather of the phenomenological imagination: it is an exile form of consciousness and cannot realize its truth. Blanchot, accepting this characterization of art, will argue that art must, if necessary, work against the grain of history. Even should the real approach the ideal, art must remain 'unreal'. It is inherently a project of self-alienation.

With this in mind, let us trace the action of *Celui qui ne*

[3] See *Phenomenology of Mind*, tr. J. B. Baillie (2nd ed., 1949), pp. 241ff. and 507ff.

m'accompagnait pas. Here, by a tour-de-force as amazing as it is profound, Blanchot exhibits the artist 'projecting' art in our presence. We actually see the narrative evolving as a debate, dialectical in form, between the narrator and his estranged self. The narrator tries to overcome the distance between them or to draw from it a third and impersonal person, the unselfconscious unity of both. But we soon learn that neither the self nor its need for an opposing self can be surpassed: that art remains an impossible project, aiming at the 'concrete universal', aiming at true unselfconsciousness, yet always preventing its own success.

How does Blanchot proceed? He enlists, first of all, the support of the greatest apostle against Hegel, Sören Kierkegaard. The unexplicit motive-power behind the narrator, as behind all of Blanchot's characters, is *despair* in Kierkegaard's definition: the uncertainty, increasing with every increase of consciousness, that one has a true self. 'The despairing man', says Kierkegaard (in *The Sickness unto Death*), 'cannot die; no more than "the dagger can slay thoughts" can despair consume the eternal thing, the self, which is the ground of despair, whose worm dieth not, and whose fire is not quenched.' Blanchot's people are unable to die for this reason. And for the same reason they are unable to be born or reborn into life; they suffer an endless purgatorial state, a death-in-life identifiable with the alienated consciousness. Their quest for a true self must go through self-estrangement, and this increases their uncertainty in an inviolable self. Hegel's Philosopher is anathema to Kierkegaard and a stumbling-block to Blanchot because he is inviolably self-assured. If, as Blanchot says, 'the void is never void enough' (*Le dernier homme* (1957) p. 164), who can plumb self-estrangement deeply enough to arrive either at pure reality or pure self? The Philosopher, were he possible, would be the last man.[4]

In *Celui* the desired self becomes, specifically, the self of the

[4] See *Le dernier homme* (1957). The 'last man' is Hegel's Philosopher. Blanchot conceives of him as having no 'existence', i.e. no Being-for-others, which makes him, paradoxically, the central enigma for the other two characters of the novel—the writer or narrator and a young woman. The latter moves from the sphere of the narrator towards the last man, perhaps because her naïve realism, her desire to die intact, at the strongest point, sorts better with the

Writer. The latter does not wish to die, only to *write*. To be a Writer—to be that Self—is the impossibility he seeks to realize by means of the *récit*. Adopting, perhaps, another idea of Kierkegaard's, that to break an enchantment (here of words) one has to retrace one's path exactly, and at every error begin again, Blanchot undoes the spell of language in order to be able to write. With shuddering naïveté, with an eternal *ressassement*, he tries to step backwards from words to the reality of the word. But desiring to write, he is already writing, and falls under the spell he would escape from.

The *récit* begins with the narrator turning towards an unnamed 'other'. He complains; says that he is at the end of his tether, that he wants to write and is afraid to write, that through writing he becomes so interested in the Other that he stands in danger of losing himself. . . . In short, he wants to resolve a situation in which he is neither himself nor not himself. But the Other, whom he wants to appeal to directly and who is very clearly a redeemer-figure, created to make word or thought flesh, obliges the narrator to linger in uncertainty, to stay in the equivocal space of fiction, and be (like his own characters) neither quite living nor quite dead.

Therefore, in one sense, art becomes the enemy of the artist and denies him the realization he desires. The Other, or Persona, is only negatively transcendent ('celui qui *ne* m'accompagnait *pas*'). Though the writer wants to be led into an absolute, this other self shows a curious interest in real things, asking no more of the writer than to stay in his room and to describe it. But he feels this is impossible (he does not want to make the real Words but the Word real?); becomes curiously forgetful; moves nervously about (as in the earlier novels of mistaken rooms and identities, false entries, strange corridors); and also keeps glimpsing 'someone' in the room or just behind the window. This new ghostly Other is probably the fictional double on the point of passing from a state of negative to that of real transcendence, as

Philosopher (who seems to link the realms of death and life) than with the Artist (who tries to remain outside both). Cf. G. Bataille, *L'Expérience intérieure*, pp. 48ff.

the writer is tempted to pass from the first person (*Je*) to the third person (*Il*) form, and thus into full self-estrangement ('l'alibi du Il indifférent', *Le Livre à venir*, p. 199). This, of course, is a necessary movement, if he is to find that original impersonal Word he seeks. Yet, by various means, the double (the second person) prevents him from losing touch with himself and passing totally into a symbol. The tension of relationship, of what Martin Buber calls the I–Thou situation, is maintained. As the narrator is asked to describe the face of this third person, the very effort of visualization makes him aware how much the figure may still depend on him. He cannot, as a writer, attain Being, only being-for-another (himself); and this difficulty of visualizing a face which has no resemblance or a word which has no relation will haunt him even more in *Le dernier homme*: 'Face of Nothingness, perhaps. That is why you [the Other?] must watch over this empty space to preserve it, as I must watch to alter it . . .' (p. 115).

The *récit*, or art itself, is simply keeping this space open. It is using the act of writing to invent forms and situations that maintain the writer in the negative despite the strongest contrary pressure. For the *récit* is, at the same time, the writer's movement towards the reality of the double, his desire to identify. And though the Other repeats, 'I can't do anything for you', he does admit being linked to the writer through writing ('par les *écrits*'). The essential, the inherent temptation is to desert the labour of the negative by going over into one's symbols. The artist posits a transcendence (metamorphosis) of this kind, but his art exists in order to resist him.

Art, therefore, cannot succeed in making the mind real rather than more conscious. A tension in its very nature prevents this. But it discloses the strength of the desire for a reality beyond consciousness. And in Blanchot's other novels the possibility of really transcending consciousness is expressed as follows. There is generally one character (a woman) who manages to die, while all others are deprived of death. The woman, by an act of will, by a metaphysical *Liebestod*, aims at a live transcendence: she seeks to pass whole from life to death, and there is, Blanchot suggests, one chance, only one, of doing so. Perhaps the artist in the space of his art also approaches that one chance of transcendence. Perhaps he can truly realize his other self and draw his mind from Consciousness into Being. It is this hope, however slender, however mystical, which moves him to write. If he fails, like Orpheus, it is because he does not dwell patiently enough in the space of alienation, and so cannot 'convert the negative into Being'.[5]

But most of Blanchot's characters, like Kierkegaard's despairing men, are sick unto death yet deprived of the ability to die. Their sickness is consciousness. They suffer an alienation from life within life, and the milieu in which they look for death or else suffer their death-in-life is related to various ancient and modern hells, to Purgatory, the Waste Land, the T.B. Mountain and the House of the Dead. (The milieu of *Le dernier homme* is indubitably a Sanatorium.) It is not surprising, therefore, that Blanchot's plots retain features of the prototype of the Quest, but how it begins and what it seeks are peculiar. The mind-errant, having sought life and found death-in-life, now desires an authentic death. The Faustian mind also begins with a perception of death-in-life (in Hegelian terms, with self-consciousness or thought) and proceeds ironically by a wager *against* life, although this wager dialectically affirms the thing it denies. Among similar ancestors of Blanchot's characters are the many wandering Jews and Mariners of the nineteenth century, figures deathless (immortally mortal) like the Sybil of Cumae. Blanchot's earliest complete story, 'L'Idylle', has as its central figure that *étranger* who is the modern equivalent of Mariner, Wanderer, or Faust—in short, a type of the alienated mind.[6]

Our study of Blanchot has led us to a concept of man and a concept of art. His novels evoke a curious middle-world, or rather middle-void. The noble assumption of the Renaissance,

---

[5] *Phenomenology*, p. 93. For the inversion of the Orpheus myth, see esp. *L'Arrêt de mort*, pp. 40–60, and *Thomas l'obscur*, pp. 112ff.: 'Anne thought of crossing over to death alive. . . .'.

[6] 'L'Idylle' bears direct traces, in the names of some of its characters, of Dostoievsky's *Memoirs from the House of the Dead*. On death and deathlessness, see also 'L'Œuvre et l'espace de la mort' in *L'Espace littéraire*, esp. pp. 161ff. Blanchot is fully acquainted with Rilke, Broch, Beckett, and others.

that man is a late creation, standing between heaven and earth and sharing the attributes of both orders, is held to but modified. Man is not a mixed mode, though having the seeds of all life in himself, but one who keeps the realms apart, who avoids the contamination of both earth and heaven. Art helps him to find a 'between' and to preserve it as the sphere of his liberty. This is a new and hard concept of mediation, which defines man purely by the quality of the void in him, and the artist by a resistance to symbols, human or divine, that would fill this void. Standing in the midst of things, and specifically in the midst of the treachery of words, the artist bears the curse of mediacy.[7]

Blanchot, moreover, relates art to the mind's need or capacity for self-estrangement. Art is not consciousness *per se*, but rather its antidote, evolved from within consciousness itself. And though this view has been gained by bringing to bear on Blanchot a particular philosophic tradition, the latter is only one of many having a common base in Romanticism. The nineteenth century yields a profusion of 'anti-self-consciousness' theories. But none, I think, has been quite so influential or provided a better foundation for understanding art generically. In England the nearest approach to a similarly adequate theory is Yeats's concept of the mask, the persona theory of Pound, and the impersonality theory of Eliot. American criticism has added the idea of the poem as an ironic structure. These have some truth and belong to a distinctive branch of inquiry, call it problematics, which should be as important as thematics or the history of literary ideas and forms. To study the problematics of art would be to consider each work as standing in a dialectical relation to consciousness and a critical relation to the whole activity of art.[8]

---

[7] For a complete exposition of the idea, see the commentary on Hölderlin (in *L'Espace littéraire*, pp. 283–92) which is deeply indebted to Heidegger. The latter has coined the term '*Zwischenbereich*' (mesocosm rather than microcosm!) to indicate the 'between' status of man. I borrow the phrase 'the curse of mediacy' from Ernst Cassirer, who says that language 'harbors the curse of mediacy and is bound to obscure what it seeks to reveal' (*Language and Myth*, 1925; tr. 1946).

[8] The only study of English poetry from a dialectical viewpoint that I know is by Harold Bloom, who approaches Shelley with Buber's dialectic in mind: see

Hegel's prophecy of the end of art, like Plato's older grouse, in no way originates these special relations. But it has made critic and artist more attentive to them, and above all in France where Marxism gives Hegel a redoubled voice. French critics tend to be over-philosophical: they have to fight Marxism on its own ground, to preserve art by a philosophy of art. In the meantime, of course, the cure being worse than the disease, literature may itself succumb to the philosophical habit. But perhaps it will suffer no more in this case than it did, for example, from neoplatonism. Blanchot's own curious strength is that his *récits* are neither philosophy nor straight fiction but an autonomous middle-form. In a very tentative way his work is like the organon Schiller called for, one that would mediate between philosophy and art. He who knows fiction will be led by it to consider philosophy, and vice versa: and this suggests that there is a new genre, or even type of literature, in the making. Yet Blanchot, it must be admitted, is not uniformly successful as an artist; sometimes, in fact, I have a sinking feeling that a few verses from Rilke or from Valéry express all he has to say. But this feeling, in turn, may show that Blanchot has taught me to read more strongly and relevantly such lines as Rilke's description of poetry: 'Ein Hauch um nichts. Ein Wehn im Gott. Ein Wind', or Valéry's many beautiful renderings of the sense of self-estrangement: 'Qui pleure là, sinon le vent simple, à cette heure/Seule avec diamants extrêmes? . . . Mais qui pleure,/Si proche de moi-même au moment de pleurer?' Blanchot's *récits*, and especially the latest ones, are sombre and bewitching works, not without tedium, but teasing us vigorously out of thought.

Shelley's Mythmaking (New Haven, 1959). Charles Feidelson, *Symbolism and American Literature* (Chicago, 1953), was, I believe, the first to point out the distinctively *problematic* ('not merely in the sense in which every literary symbol is indeterminate, but more specifically in the sense that its characteristic subject is its own equivocal method') nature of a nineteenth-century American tradition, comparable in this to the French Symbolists. Other relevant studies are Erich Heller's treatment of the 'ontological mystery' in *The Disinherited Mind* (American ed., New York, 1957), and Paul de Man's questioning of the 'incarnationist' assumption in modern English and American criticism: 'Impasse de la critique formaliste', *Critique*, XII (1956), pp. 483–500.

Novels and *récits* by Blanchot:

Thomas l'obscur, Paris, Gallimard, 1941. (A 'nouvelle version' of this novel was issued by the same publisher in 1950.)
Aminadab, Paris, Gallimard, 1942.
Le Très-Haut, Paris, Gallimard, 1948.
L'Arrêt de mort, Paris, Gallimard, 1948.
Au Moment voulu, Paris, Gallimard, 1951.
Celui qui ne m'accompagnait pas, Paris, Gallimard, 1953.
Le dernier homme, Paris, Gallimard, 1957.

Short stories:
Le Ressassement éternel, Paris, Éd. de Minuit, 1951.

SIMONE DE BEAUVOIR
b. 1908

BY MAURICE CRANSTON

———————★———————

LIKE George Eliot, Simone de Beauvoir is both a philosopher and a novelist. Unlike George Eliot, who spoke with a bold positivistic voice in her philosophy and a prim Victorian voice in her fiction, preaching chastity and practising adultery, Simone de Beauvoir has only one voice; her work—and her life—is all of a piece. As an artist, she has less sheer genius than George Eliot, but she is a better philosopher and her novels are more consciously and elaborately intellectual. She has also been the more fortunate woman. George Eliot's companion in life was that egregious polymath George Henry Lewes. Simone de Beauvoir has Sartre. All her work is permeated by Sartre's influence. At the same time it must be said that all Sartre's work has been affected by her presence. Neither of them published a book until well over the age of thirty, and after they had, so to speak, developed intellectually together.

Simone de Beauvoir was born in 1908 into a prosperous and civilized, if not exceptionally distinguished, family living in Paris. Her father was a lawyer who dabbled in the theatre, as both actor and director, but who was too mindful of his status as a gentleman to do so for profit. He was a devout and earnest Catholic, who upheld the traditional ethos of the *haute bourgeoisie* with something of that same fervour and rigidity—not to say fanaticism—with which his daughter afterwards attacked it. In the first volume of her autobiography, *Mémoires d'une jeune fille rangée* (1958), Simone de Beauvoir dwells on the comfort and decorum of her early life; and one may readily imagine her playing with her friends and their nurses in the Jardin du Luxembourg like a happy, sweet, angelic child in a painting by Renoir. Two circumstances break into the tranquillity of that image. When Simone de Beauvoir was six, World War I began. A few years later she lost her faith in God. The war hardly touched her life at the time, but the other experience was immediately shattering. In her *Mémoires* she recalls the seriousness and moral intensity of her nature, even as a child. She was one of those for whom religious feelings are not only the most acute, but also the most 'real'. Hence when she came to use her powers of reflection, and to doubt the existence of God, the emotional effect was extremely disturbing. The Nietzschean expression 'God is dead'—as meaningless to the ordinary rationalist as it is blasphemous to the ordinary Christian—enshrined for her the bitter truth of that dramatic personal experience; for she had had a revelation of Nothingness, which was quite as sensational, in its way, as the proverbial unbeliever's sudden vision of God.

In this experience, too, we may see the beginning of Simone de Beauvoir as a philosopher. A universe in which 'God is dead' seemed to her incomprehensible, and she felt an urgent need to understand it. Perhaps she also hoped to find in metaphysics some alternative emotional satisfaction to that of religion. Her parents and teachers did little to encourage an interest in what, in their opinion, was 'not a woman's subject', but she made philosophy her speciality at both school and university, and became in time herself (somewhat to the dismay of her father) a *professeur de lycée*, teaching, however unconventionally, the conventional 'philo' syllabus to the young in Marseilles and Rouen and eventually for a time in Paris.

As a student she made the acquaintance of Simone Weil, but friendship did not ripen between them, and the reason may perhaps be seen in a remark of Simone de Beauvoir that while Simone Weil was wholly concerned with the problem of social justice, she herself was entirely taken up with the problem of the meaning of existence. Simone de Beauvoir was destined in time to become intensely interested in questions of social justice, but she never regarded them as distinct or isolated questions: political problems, as she saw them, derived from moral problems, and morals in turn derived from metaphysics. Even in her most 'political' phase, it was still philosophy which most concerned her. In the second volume of her autobiography, *La Force de l'âge* (1960), Simone de Beauvoir describes how, during the worst months of the Occupation, when Sartre was in a prison camp in Germany and she was alone in Paris, she went to read the works of Hegel at the Bibliothèque Nationale; in a curiously memorable sentence she tells us: 'Hegel me calmait.'

This is not to say that she had ever been, except in a most indirect and partial sense, Hegelian. Hegel is himself too calm, too confidently rationalistic to have furnished the needs of a young mind tormented by the thought that 'God is dead'. The philosophers who were asking the questions which worried Simone de Beauvoir from her childhood onwards were the existentialists; and it is hardly surprising that she was swiftly and instinctively drawn, while still a student, to the theories and person of Sartre, who was by some three years her senior. When he was placed top of the list in the competitive *agrégation*, she appeared second. And already as students they formed that bond which, though carefully distinguished from 'bourgeois marriage', has remained a settled partnership in life.

Simone de Beauvoir has never claimed to be an originator in philosophy, in the sense that Sartre is; she has written nothing as weighty or as formidable as *L'Être et le néant* or his *Critique de la raison dialectique*, but she has been no less successful in the expression of philosophical ideas through the medium of the novel. In her essay 'Littérature et métaphysique'[1] she gives us some clues as to what her intentions have been. She admits that the expression 'metaphysical novel' is alarming, and that it would be foolish to imagine an Aristotelian, a Spinozistic, or even a Leibnizian novel, because every one of those metaphysical systems 'excludes subjectivity and temporality'. On the other hand, she suggests that a philosopher who fully admits subjectivity and temporality is almost bound to become, like Plato and Hegel and Kierkegaard, a literary artist. The form of the novel has a particular attraction for the existentialist, because only the novel

[1] In *L'Existentialisme et la sagesse des nations* (Paris, Nagel, 1948), pp. 103-24.

allows a writer 'to evoke the original *jaillissement* of existence'. She pleads for the metaphysical novel to be given its due place beside the psychological novel, on the grounds that it has as good a claim to acceptance and that it may be judged in much the same way: 'If a psychological novel set out to illustrate Ribot, Bergson, or Freud, it would be worthless.' But if psychological principles are assimilated into an artistic whole, the novel will succeed: 'Proust as a disciple of Ribot bores us; he tells us nothing; but Proust, the true novelist, reveals truths of psychology unperceived by the theorists of his time.' As for her own novels, Simone de Beauvoir says she does not attempt to expound in literature principles already established in philosophy, but to present those aspects of 'metaphysical experience' which could not otherwise be communicated. Her aim is to put across a vision which is not broken down by the analytic processes of the philosophical method, but is present in all its fullness, *dans son intégrité*.

It is not difficult, I think, to see why existentialists like Simone de Beauvoir and Sartre should attach such importance to the novel (and equally the play), if one compares their philosophy with that of a British empiricist, such as Hume. In many respects their theories are identical. Hume is as much an unbeliever as they, and indeed more so. He can see no rational proof of the existence of God, or of any given purpose in human life, or of a Moral Law, or, for that matter, of the existence of the external world. But the great difference between Hume and the existentialists is that Hume does not mind. He loses no sleep because Reason fails to prove the existence of God and the Moral Law. The philosopher who doubts goes on living and behaving just as other men do, who believe. This is not to say that Hume 'reposes his head on the pillow of doubt'; on the contrary, he reposes his head on the pillow of habit and custom and tradition. And this is where Hume and the British generally have the advantage over French philosophers. In a country where there is security, where the law is effectively enforced, and where convention upholds a decent moral order, it does not matter if the abstract truths of classical philosophy are found to be empty. But in a country where there is no political stability, where the Germans repeatedly invade one, and the franc does not hold, there is no refuge to be found in habit, custom, and tradition. If in such a situation the universe itself is found to have no rational order, the discovery will understandably be felt as a disaster. Thus, the same ideas which an empiricist like Hume expresses drily, and without any kind of emotional involvement, are expressed by an existentialist in highly dramatic terms. Indeed a large part of the existentialist's task is to seek out the emotional implications of what Simone de Beauvoir calls 'metaphysical experience'; for what we are confronted with here is not just knowledge or opinion, something believed or doubted, but something deeply *felt*.

English critics of existentialism such as Professor Ayer find it easy to mock the notion of *le Néant*. This specimen of 'bogus metaphysics', they claim, has been neatly disposed of by Lewis Carroll in that celebrated dialogue between the White King and Alice, when they are waiting for the messenger:

'I see nobody on the road,' said Alice.
'I only wish I had such eyes,' the King remarked in a fretful tone. 'To be able to see Nobody! And at such a distance, too!'

French existentialists are accused by their English critics of making the mistake the White King made; of thinking that the words 'Nothing' or 'Nobody', stand for a thing or a person, whereas in fact they are only linguistic devices for denying the presence of a thing or a person. But to argue in this way is to miss the point the existentialist is making. The situation of the existentialist when he becomes aware of *le Néant* is not like that of Alice seeing nobody on the road; rather it is like that of a widow returning from her husband's funeral, and becoming aware that there is nobody in the house. The sensation of emptiness, of absence, of a void, fills her with acute distress. Her concept of 'nothingness' owes its nature to a positive being that she had once known, but it is not for that reason any less real. Similarly, for the French mind, nurtured in the confident rationalism of Descartes and the Enlightenment, the discovery that there is no rational order in the universe can be understood to be an important and also an extremely unnerving experience.

Simone de Beauvoir maintains that one must live through that experience to the full; and then pass on to the next stage, which is that of building our own foundations for our own beliefs; each of us must devise his own philosophy afresh. It is usual for existentialists to speak of the world, and of our existence in the world, as 'absurd'. What they are saying, with this somewhat extravagant language, is simply that life as such has no meaning. As against this notion of absurdity, Simone de Beauvoir holds that our existence is 'ambiguous', by which she means that it has no *one* meaning, but many possible meanings. The significance of life is whatever each one of us can discover, or create for himself: 'the meaning must be ceaselessly revindicated'. There is a strong emphasis here on the need for *effort*. In her short treatise on ethics, *Pour une morale de l'ambiguïté* (1947), she makes a similar point. Moral values, she says, exist only in so far as men create them: there is no God to give commandments, no Moral Law revealed to the eye of reason; and therefore every time we act we must create anew 'a meaning and a truth which carries within itself its own rigorous demands' (p. 24).

Simone de Beauvoir has confessed in her autobiography how much the idea of immortality once meant to her, and how difficult it was for her to reconcile herself to the finality of death. This problem is the theme of one of her most successful novels, *Tous les hommes sont mortels* (1946). Its heroine, Régine, yearns for immortality; she pursues and seduces a pathetic lunatic because he believes he is immortal, and because he makes her believe it too. Régine has every worldly satisfaction—love, fame, money, beauty, health—but she dreads death and longs for that ineffable something which faith alone can give. In the course of the novel Régine learns that death is not a fate to dread, but is, on the contrary, a mercy. And she is left with the sense that she must find in life itself what she had hoped for in immortality; and the end, in this novel as in Mr. Eliot's poem, 'n'est que le commencement'.

Once again we may notice the contrast between Simone de Beauvoir and David Hume. The thought that there was no immorality did not disturb Hume; James Boswell, who visited him on his deathbed, was struck by the sang-froid with which the old atheist contemplated his own extinction. Hume, we may fancy, would never have understood the uneasiness of the existentialist on the subject of immortality. But Hume, one must in fairness remember, died in bed at the comfortable age of sixty-five. When Simone de Beauvoir wrote *Tous les hommes sont mortels* she was living in occupied Paris; the Gestapo was in the city and the gas-chambers and the firing squads were not far away; blackmail and treason and betrayal were commonplace. As Sartre himself wrote in his article, 'La République du silence': 'Every second we experienced, in the richest sense, the meaning of that banal little phrase "All men are mortal". And the choice which each one of us made in himself was a genuine choice since it was made in the presence of death, and since it could always have been expressed in the form "Rather death than...".'[2]

Existentialism considers itself (not unreasonably) to be a philosophy of crisis, and it is not surprising that both Simone de Beauvoir and Sartre should have made their names as writers during the most critical years of modern French history. Their fame will always be linked in people's minds with the Resistance. And yet one might well ask: what is the connexion between being an existentialist and supporting the Resistance? Undoubtedly in the case of Simone de Beauvoir, as much as of Sartre, there did seem to be a connexion. For the answer we may look to *Le Sang des autres*, published in 1944. The central characters of this novel are Blomart, a man of bourgeois birth who joins the Communist Party in the 1930s, and Hélène, an eager girl of humble origins who hankers after metaphysical certainty. She tells Blomart: 'When I was young, I believed in God. It was wonderful; something was demanded of me every instant. Then it seemed to me that I simply *had* to exist. It was a necessity.' Blomart replies: 'I think your trouble is that you imagine the reasons for living must come down from heaven to you ready made. The truth of the matter is that the reasons for living are for us to create ourselves' (p. 67). Unfortunately Hélène is not much good at creating reasons for living. She begins by falling

[2] In *Situations III*, p. 12.

in love with Blomart himself, who rejects her. Next she goes off with an ageing voluptuary; and then has to come to Blomart's flat for an abortion. Compassion stirs love in Blomart's heart, but he is soon separated from Hélène. War breaks out and he is posted to the Maginot Line. Hélène follows him, only to be sent back. She arranges a soft job for him in Paris and is bitterly disappointed when he will not take it. She thinks their love ought to matter more than patriotism. The defeat of France isolates her in Paris and she accepts a German protector. Then one evening over dinner she experiences a sudden 'moment of truth'. She realizes the evil of Nazism and joins the Resistance. She is reunited with Blomart but soon afterwards she is killed on a Resistance mission. The book ends with Blomart contemplating her dead body, and thinking of his love. He tells himself:

If only I dedicate myself to the defence of that supreme good . . . freedom, then my passion will not have been useless. You have not given me peace; but why should I want peace? You have given me the courage to accept for ever the hazards and the *Angst*, to bear my crimes and the guilt which will torment me for ever. There is no other way (p. 224).

The main philosophical argument of the book, then, is first, that freedom is the supreme value in life; and second, that it demands great courage to be a free man. Let us see how this position is arrived at. God (on this view) does not exist; there is no law governing the universe. From this it follows, among other things, that determinism is false. The life of man is subject neither to the will of God nor to the principles of 'scientific necessity'. The future is open and man's will is free. And precisely because the will is free, it is possible for man to be a moral being.

One condition of man's being free is that he should *believe* that his will is free. Belief in determinism saps the resolution to make one's own fate, it breeds a kind of oriental fatalism. Simone de Beauvoir voices more than one objection to determinism. She not only considers it false; she considers it mischievous in so far as it encourages this attitude of passive resignation towards evil. A thoroughgoing determinist like Zola can neither praise nor blame; he sees men as the creatures of circumstance who cannot be judged. Simone de Beauvoir does not admire Zola. She prefers Sade, and in her essay 'Faut-il brûler Sade?'[3] she claims for that scabrous writer a place among the ranks of the moralists precisely because he thought it essential to find a *justification* for all he did and said. In trying to prove that his crimes were not wrong, Sade was appealing all the time to morality. He was thus very different from Zola, who simply eliminated morality. This is why Simone de Beauvoir sees Sade as being, if not on the side of the angels, at least on the side of philosophy and, in a perverse way, of humanity as well.

She admits that the determinism of Zola and his kind is a much more comfortable doctrine. For if the determinist cannot blame others, neither need he blame himself. To believe in the freedom of the will is to acknowledge one's own responsibility and one's own guilt. That is why courage is called for. For it is the consciousness of oneself as a responsible being that breeds anxiety and despair. It is always a difficult task, and sometimes it is a heroic task to bear this responsibility. But there is no escaping from it. 'Chacun est responsable de tout devant tous', she quotes at the beginning of *Le Sang des autres*, and these words of Dostoievsky's might serve as an epigraph to all her work.

And yet, much as she dwells on the effort and the courage that freedom exacts, Simone de Beauvoir rejoices in freedom. If the will is free and the future open, it is possible for men to break away from their bondage to the past. The shackles may be strong, but they are not unbreakable. 'People like to believe that virtue is easy', she writes in *L'Existentialisme et la sagesse des nations*. 'They also resign themselves quite readily to the thought that virtue is impossible. What they hate to recognize is that it is possible, but difficult, to be good' (p. 44).

There is no doubt about it: Simone de Beauvoir is a thoroughly didactic writer; she is preaching. She is not the kind of philosopher who has a detached interest in knowledge. She wishes to influence conduct. Her existentialism, as she puts it, 'réclame de l'homme une tension constante'. On the other hand, she is not telling her readers what they ought or ought not to do,

---

[3] In *Privilèges* (Paris, Gallimard, 1955), pp. 11–89.

beyond the demand that they should *be* moral beings. Apart from the case of supporting the Resistance, she defines very few specific moral duties. Indeed in her first novel *L'Invitée* (1943), she seems to be saying that sincerity alone is what matters. Like Sartre's *Huis Clos*, *L'Invitée* has for its plot the conventional triangle made into a circle by the intrusion of homosexuality. A theatrical couple, Françoise and Pierre, are happily in love. They have passed their first youth and they are not married, but apart from 'insignificant' unfaithfulness, they are sufficient to each other. Xavière, a young girl from the provinces, visits them in Paris. To the reader's surprise—for Xavière is depicted as a charmless bitch—Françoise and Pierre invite her to live with them. As her behaviour worsens, their love for Xavière grows. Françoise, who wonders wretchedly whether Xavière loves her in return, becomes ill, and in the nursing home she elicits from the girl the signs of tenderness she yearns for. She gets better and for a time the three of them live together happily, the love of Françoise and of Pierre for Xavière platonic but avowed. The question inevitably arises: will Xavière sleep with Pierre? She does not. She sleeps instead with a boy named Gerbert. The existence of the trio is threatened. So, to enable Pierre to regain his hold over Xavière, Françoise carries Gerbert off to the Alps. It is no good. Pierre is called up for the army, and Françoise realizes that Xavière has destroyed the one thing that gave meaning to her life—her relationship with Pierre; and she kills the girl. The last words of the book concern the murder she has done: 'No one could condemn her or absolve her. Her act belonged to no one but herself. "It is I who desire it." It was her own will which was being accomplished; there was nothing now that divided her from herself. At last she had chosen. She had chosen herself' (p. 418).

The argument here is extremely paradoxical. Françoise realizes herself as a moral being by doing an evil deed. She becomes conscious of herself as a free—undetermined—being in the execution of one wholly autonomous act. It is no part of the author's intention to exculpate her. Indeed, it is a continuing theme of all Simone de Beauvoir's books that there is no exculpation; precisely because we can choose, we are culpable. Nevertheless there is something unsatisfactory about a novel which leaves its central problem unsolved and merely brings the curtain down, so to speak, with an act of theatrical violence. Simone de Beauvoir herself came to feel this. In the second volume of her autobiography she writes: 'The ending of *L'Invitée* did not satisfy me: it is not through murder that one can overcome the difficulties engendered by our co-existence with others' (*La Force de l'âge*, p. 622). She thinks better of her second novel, *Le Sang des autres*, where instead of evading the problems of living together, she tried to face them squarely: 'I tried to define our proper relations with other people' (ibid., p. 622). In the same paragraph, Simone de Beauvoir says, apropos of her third novel, *Tous les hommes sont mortels*: 'I tried then to rectify the moral optimism of my two earlier works, in describing death, not only as a relation between each man and all, but also as the evil of solitude and separation.'

A similar point is made at the end of Simone de Beauvoir's fourth novel *Les Mandarins* (1954). After an unsuccessful love affair, the narrator, Anne Dubreuil, decides to commit suicide. But at the last moment she changes her mind. She thinks of her husband and her friends: 'I cannot impose my corpse, and all that would come after my death, on their hearts. . . . Death is present; but the living are even more present' (p. 578). And later Anne says to herself: 'Since my heart continues to beat, it will have to beat for something, for someone. Since I am not deaf, I shall one day hear people calling to me. Who knows? Perhaps one day I shall be happy again. Who knows?' (p. 579).

The moral sentiment of this ending is acceptable enough, but it is hard to see in what sense it is specifically existentialist. The talk of happiness and concern for others savours rather of utilitarianism. Sartre's ethical theory, never fully elaborated, can be seen to have undergone a sudden—or 'dialectical'—transformation, from a form of nihilism, which recognized sincerity or authenticity as the only standard of moral judgement, to a strange mixture of Kantianism and Marxism, which identifies moral virtue with commitment to the freedom of others, or of all.

Simone de Beauvoir has moved in the same 'social' direction without giving her metaphysics the revision needed to support these new imperatives.

Les Mandarins, however, has little of the philosophical interest of the author's other work. It is a novel about life among the French intellectuals in the 1940s. It has proved the most popular of Simone de Beauvoir's books and has undoubtedly appealed to many readers as a *roman à clef*, a novel which gives the inside story of the conflicts and passions of the literary and political intelligentsia, the *mandarins*, of France in the heroic—and anti-heroic—years of the Liberation and after. It is a very long book, and in method more synoptic than analytic. The influence of American 'realist' novelists, of John Dos Passos in particular, is marked. Like those writers the author has sought to depict the life of a society rather than of individuals. The scene is crowded with characters and there is an abundance of incident. A number of the characters are obviously drawn from living people, and many of the incidents are at least as close to actual history as are those of Defoe's *Journal of the Plague Year*. The world that Simone de Beauvoir portrays is smaller than Defoe's London or the New York of Dos Passos's *Manhattan Transfer*; but it is her intention to present that world as a kind of organic whole; each individual and each incident is significant only in relation to the others.

A few of the characters nevertheless stand out from the rest. One, Henri, a young idealistic intellectual who has a certain resemblance to Albert Camus, is the *jeune premier* if not the hero of the piece. The Anne Dubreuil who appears in some chapters as narrator, is a woman psychoanalyst and also the protagonist of the central sexual drama: in this character the author has plainly invested more than a little of herself. Anne's husband, Robert, is a professional philosopher (rather like Sartre) who intervenes at decisive moments in the narrative but who is never more than sketched as a personality, never—and this is one of the faults of the book—never given the dimensions that a key figure in any novel ought to have.

Henri is the editor of an independent left-wing newspaper, *L'Espoir*. His constant problem is to keep his paper independent and to keep it going. As the first enthusiasm of the Liberation wears off, it becomes increasingly difficult for a serious paper to compete with commercial rivals. Henri is offered 'discreet' help: first American money; then Communist money. But he will neither sell out to America nor surrender to the Communists, though his sympathies are, in general, with Russia. He allies himself to Dubreuil's independent Marxist movement, but loses even that support when, after a *crise de conscience*, he decides to publish—as Dubreuil thinks, inopportunely—the facts about the Russian forced labour camps.

Rigid in his morality, Henri loses his paper; only to find in his private life that he is driven to compromise with his principles after all. He has an affair with an actress, Josette, who was once a collaborator, and to save her from disgrace he gives false evidence at the trial of a pro-Nazi informer. He secures the man's release in return for the suppression of the evidence against Josette. Henri is henceforth regarded with suspicion by some of his best friends from the Resistance days. His conscience is uneasy and one day he confesses to Dubreuil what he has done. Rather to Henri's surprise, Dubreuil does not reproach him but invites him to learn from his experience that moral principles are not fixed for ever but have to be adapted to actual situations. The book ends with a *rapprochement* between Henri and the Communists on a common platform for liberty in Madagascar; and the marriage of Henri to Dubreuil's (and Anne's) neurotic daughter, Nadine.

The most promising, but finally most disappointing, character in the book is that of Anne herself. She is clearly a woman of great intelligence and emotional maturity, and for this very reason the story she tells of her love affair with an American writer named Lewis—an affair initiated and prolonged by her will more than his—is a curiously unreal story. As Anne cannot make Lewis want her on her own terms—which include her living in France and with her husband—she becomes progressively more hurt and disillusioned, and so moves to the brink of suicide. But there is no sign that she understands Lewis's side of the case, or that there is, on his side, a case to be understood. Much also might be expected in the way of explanations from Anne; but the author's special tenderness towards this character seems to have hindered her from doing what she might otherwise have felt it necessary to do.

In all, I do not myself feel that *Les Mandarins* is the best of Simone de Beauvoir's novels, although it has been the most widely acclaimed. As a 'metaphysical' novel it is far less concentrated than any of the three earlier works; and the influence of Dos Passos seems to have led the author away from the pursuit of her own objectives. Breadth has been achieved at the cost of the depth. In *Tous les hommes sont mortels* there is nothing much in the way of a story, and the heroine Régine is a puzzling, difficult character. But Régine is a full character. Her metaphysical experience—or, one might say, her metaphysical obsession—is indeed revealed 'dans son intégrité'. Of no one in *Les Mandarins* can the same be said. Where this last novel does succeed is in its treatment of politics. No work of fiction published since the war gives such an insight into the political dilemmas of the French intellectual. At this level it might even be said to carry on where Sartre's unfinished *Les Chemins de la liberté* breaks off. But the fact remains that politics is *not* Simone de Beauvoir's chief concern. Her chosen subject is philosophy at a higher level of abstraction: and it is when it is judged in terms of her own critical principles that *Les Mandarins* is found most wanting.

It is even arguable that Simone de Beauvoir comes closer to realizing the novel she wished to write in the second volume of her autobiography, *La Force de l'âge*. For this is a book with a heroine—the narrator—and a hero—Sartre; and its central narrative is the story of their life together. Although it does not dwell, as a novel might, on the sexual *rapports* between its chief protagonists, it has much to say about human relationships and the connexion between the world of ideas and the world of personal experience. It is, in a way, a romantic story. During their early years together Sartre and Simone de Beauvoir were much separated, with Simone de Beauvoir in Marseilles and Sartre in Laon or Berlin. But later, when she was working in Rouen and he at Le Havre, they could meet regularly and when Sartre found work in Paris they were able to take rooms in the same hotel. They never set up house together and a great deal of their time was spent in cafés (something hardly conceivable in any country but France). Simone de Beauvoir did all her writing at café tables, and it was in cafés—notably the *Flore*—that they held court after they became successful and before an even greater fame drove them into a more retired way of life. Simone de Beauvoir explains that she and Sartre would have married if there had been a question of having children; as a childless couple, they could find no valid reason for compromising with their anti-bourgeois principles. She declares that she herself never felt any desire for children, but from the life she describes in her memoirs and the situations which recur in her novels, it is obvious that parental relationships in some transmuted form have had an important place in her experience. Sartre and she have together moulded more than one young person's life; and these young protégés and protégées were, in a sense, their children, just as their favourite cafés were their home.

However, when one turns to Simone de Beauvoir's book on Woman, *Le deuxième sexe*, one cannot help feeling that it has been, in a way, impoverished by the author's repudiation of motherhood and family life. This is another long book, fortified by a great wealth of psychological, sociological, and other empirical material, but its actual argument is a simple one. Again freedom is seen as the supreme ideal; and the author claims that in past and present societies women as a sex have been and are still being denied freedom. Simone de Beauvoir joins issue with Freud on his theory of the castration complex. She disagrees that woman feels inferior to man because she has no penis. Women feel inferior because they *are* inferior; and men, she says, have made them inferior. Woman is designed, not by nature but by society, for the passive role in life. A young girl is trained to please and serve men; marriage is woman's most usual profession; and marriage, with its endless round of child-bearing and domestic chores, has nearly always been a form of servitude. The unmarried woman is hardly more free: making herself presentable absorbs much of her time, and if she wants a husband she is not allowed to take the initiative in finding one. In sexual relations, the woman 'gives herself'; the man takes.

Simone de Beauvoir expresses vigorous dissent from the views on women expressed by those male novelists generally supposed to 'understand women'. She discerns the homosexuality behind D. H. Lawrence's doctrine of the woman's subordination to the phallic principle. She sees in Montherlant's contempt for women only false heroics and hysterical narcissism. Claudel's poetry and soulfulness, she claims, merely serve to conceal the old Catholic desire to sustain the prerogatives of the male. In general, she holds, the past belongs to men; but she wants the future to be shared equally between the sexes. Equality would not worsen the position of men; on the contrary it would 'free men from those shameless acts of cruelty to which women have hitherto had to resort to defend themselves in a man's world'. Women are at present educated for submission; the spirit of revolt is crushed in them. Simone de Beauvoir believes that they should be educated just as boys are and, as she puts it, 'educated for liberty'.

Le deuxième sexe is a brilliant and belligerent book; but precisely because it goes on and on about women being like men, and thus fails to explore the *uniqueness* of woman, it is something of a disappointment as a study of its subject. Unmarried, and uninterested in motherhood, living, in fact, to all intents and purposes just like a man, Simone de Beauvoir is not ideally qualified by experience to write the kind of book she hoped to write; but read as a corrective to the old-fashioned patriarchal ethos which still prevails in Latin societies, *Le deuxième sexe* must at least be acknowledged as a forceful and opportune polemic.

In all existentialism there is a strong element of stoicism; and Simone de Beauvoir is no exception. In *La Force de l'âge*, describing an occasion when she saw Sartre sitting happily in some ugly, squalid place near Marseilles, she says: 'Sartre aimait l'inconfort.' The reader of her autobiography may be tempted to suspect the same of Simone de Beauvoir herself. The rooms she describes having chosen to live in; her spartan recreations, walking and climbing for sixteen hours a day; her indifference to sickness and pain; her capacity for travelling the roughest way and for sitting up night and day talking metaphysics—in all this there is precious little of the sybarite, and much of the dedicated, self-denying, self-punishing dissenter that we recognize in England as a Puritan.

Novels by Simone de Beauvoir:
L'Invitée, Paris, Gallimard, 1943.
    She came to stay (trs. Roger Senhouse and Yvonne Moyse), London, Secker & Warburg, 1949; New York, World Publishing Co., 1954.
Le Sang des autres, Lausanne, Marguerat, 1944, and Paris, Gallimard, 1945.
    The Blood of Others (trs. Roger Senhouse and Yvonne Moyse), London, Secker & Warburg, 1948; New York, Knopf, 1948.
Tous les hommes sont mortels, Paris, Gallimard, 1946.
    All Men are Mortal (trs. Leonard M. Friedman), New York, World Publishing Co., 1955.
Les Mandarins, Paris, Gallimard, 1954.
    The Mandarins (trs. Leonard M. Friedman), London, Collins, 1957, and Collins (Fontana Books), 1960; New York, World Publishing Co., 1956.

JEAN CAYROL
b. 1911

BY CARLOS LYNES

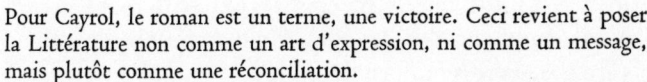

> Pour Cayrol, le roman est un terme, une victoire. Ceci revient à poser la Littérature non comme un art d'expression, ni comme un message, mais plutôt comme une réconciliation.
>
> ROLAND BARTHES

CRITICS of modern literature frequently divide sharply on the question of the 'poetic' novel. Some of these critics, especially in England and America, still cling to notions inherited from traditional nineteenth-century views, insisting that a 'proper' novel must show human beings in their social environment and be plausible in a direct social and psychological sense. Such observers look with suspicion or outright disapproval on novels which exist within the domain—paradoxically both freer and more rigorous—of poetry. Moreover, they seem unable or unwilling to distinguish between novels in which poetic embellishments are 'added on' and works of fiction conceived and accomplished within the modes of poetic creation.

Whatever one may think of this question, it is a fact that the novel from Proust to the present has developed, at least in its most creative figures, as a new form of poetry, nearly always with metaphysical overtones. Even Stendhal and Balzac—to the consternation of many whose literary views were formed under the influence of the older critics—are today admired for the poetic quality of their novels and for their unique personal vision of man and his destiny.

Maurice Blanchot emphasized the gulf between generations of critics when, fifteen years ago, he reproached René Lalou for taking psychological *vraisemblance* as a criterion of value in the novel. Blanchot himself 'defined' the novel, at that time, in these terms: 'The novel . . . can exist without most of the elements which tradition ascribes to it—plot, characters, orderly narration—but every important novel offers us an image of our condition in its *ensemble* and is an attempt to show its meaning or its absence of meaning.'[1] This remark could doubtless be applied, in a broad sense, to all the great works of prose fiction, from *Don Quixote* to *A la recherche du temps perdu*; its most precise and specific application, however—especially in its negative aspect—is to the most original and representative French novels of the past few decades. It characterizes the novels of this period still more accurately, perhaps, if supplemented by Jules Monnerot's observation: 'Our novels are the expression, privileged for a time, of an interrogation which knows no end other than itself—they are *vehicles*.'[2]

This interrogation, which is more often metaphysical or spiritual than social or psychological, frequently assumes a kind of mythic form and function. Our myths differ from those of the past, however, in being unique personal creations, fashioned by individuals out of their intimate need to impose a structure of meaning on the chaotic mass of experience in a world where no body of truth seems any longer to be 'given'. It has become a commonplace to point out that these individual myths fail to give social integration to our experience or to give us the sense of 'belonging' in a solid, coherent universe which we all 'understand' in the same way. This is true enough; yet, as R.-M. Albérès shows in *L'Aventure intellectuelle du XXe siècle*, the writers of our time reveal a remarkable similarity in their apprehension of the human predicament, despite differences in ideology and in language or style which often mask this accord.

A number of the outstanding French writers of the last few decades have felt the need not only to incarnate their personal myths in the concrete imaginative worlds of poems, novels, and plays, but also to deal more abstractly with these myths in essay form. The most poignant and moving of these writers, to my mind, is Jean Cayrol, who in several collections of poems, in a novel trilogy, and in six other novels, as well as in essays, has

---

[1] Maurice Blanchot, 'Autour du roman', *L'Arche*, no. 9 (Sept. 1945), p. 109.
[2] Jules Monnerot, 'Malraux et l'art', *Critique*, no. 22 (March 1948), p. 206.

expressed, with his myth of 'Lazarus in our Midst', a profound vision of man's condition in our contemporary 'univers concentrationnaire'—a poetic vision more disturbing even than the documentary reports on concentration camp horrors but at the same time pregnant with the hope of resurrection, or reconciliation, implicit in the name Lazarus.

Born in 1911, Jean Cayrol belongs to the generation of French writers who have reached a vigorous maturity during the fifteen years since the Liberation. A librarian in his native Bordeaux before the war, Cayrol had already founded a short-lived literary review and published two slim volumes of poetry strongly influenced by Surrealism. During the Occupation he was active in the famous 'Réseau de Rémy', was seized by the Gestapo, imprisoned for a year at Fresnes, then deported to the concentration camp of Gusen, near Mauthausen, where he was held for nearly three years. Out of those experiences came some of the most moving poetry of the decade: *Et nunc* (poems from Fresnes, published in the same volume with *Miroir de la Rédemption*, (1944)), *Poèmes de la nuit et du brouillard* (1946), the searing record of the poet's inner experience in the concentration camp, and *Passe-temps de l'homme et des oiseaux* (1947), the first poems written after Cayrol's return to the world of the living.

In 1947 Cayrol, whose stature as a poet was already impressive, published the first two parts of a novel trilogy under the collective title *Je vivrai l'amour des autres*. Even without the third volume (which did not come out until three years later), this work revealed a new voice of remarkable resonance, though too disturbing, perhaps, to be heeded immediately by a public which had been quick to acclaim what Gaëtan Picon once called the 'metaphysical naturalism' of Sartre or Camus. Critical recognition did come promptly, however, in the form of the Prix Renaudot, which has often been more truly a sign of creative originality than the Prix Goncourt. Another novel, *La Noire*, appeared in 1949. In 1950 two essays, 'Les Rêves lazaréens' and 'Pour un romanesque lazaréen', after prior publication in periodicals, were brought out in a little volume under the collective title *Lazare parmi nous*; later in the same year came the concluding volume of *Je vivrai l'amour des autres*. Since 1950 Cayrol has published five additional novels, which have given him an important place as a slightly older contemporary of the 'new' French novelists: *Le Vent de la mémoire* (1952), *L'Espace d'une nuit* (1954), *Le Déménagement* (1956), *La Gaffe* (1957), and *Les Corps étrangers* (1959). Cayrol has also published essays, new collections of poems, and the extraordinary recent book—neither novel nor prose poem nor essay but an unclassifiable new form—*Les Pleins et les déliés* (1960). After providing the title and the unforgettable spoken text of Alain Resnais's film on the concentration camps, *Nuit et Brouillard* (1955), Cayrol has more recently been exploring the possibilities of new forms of creative expression in the film medium, with several remarkable works already completed and more to come.

With each new novel, Cayrol's unmistakably personal tone, a strangely incantatory atmosphere, a unique fictional world in which a certain spontaneity is fused with the fluid inevitability of the dream, have imposed themselves more and more on the imagination of readers disposed to *enter* the world of a novel as they would a poem or a surrealist *récit*, instead of making the vain effort to *understand* it in terms of the traditional social or psychological novel. Though Cayrol's fictions are not tales of magic or fantasy or the supernatural—at least not in the usual sense—they do suggest, by contrast with works that follow the modes of realism or naturalism, the older tradition of the marvellous tale, of certain medieval romances, of fairy tales, and stories preserved by oral transmission. Thus the reader whose sensibility is alive to poetic resonances quickly finds himself coming under a strange, dreamlike spell; he recovers something of the feeling of a child listening, with rapt attention, to a favourite fairy story that is ever new, though he already knows its every detail.

In Cayrol's absorbing fictional world we find, by implication or suggestion at least, a symbolic *prise de conscience* of man's condition and the hint—sometimes the ardent promise—of reconciliation and redemption. The Biblical image or myth of Lazarus enables Cayrol to evoke the fundamental themes of his apprehension of the *misère* and the *grandeur* of man's nature. At first this myth is linked closely to the deportee, returned from the concentration camps to the pale, opaque world of the living. But even in those novels where this connexion is unmistakable, it is discreet, being rendered not by the detailed narration or description of concentration camp horrors, but by suggestive images of a world of absence. After the first few novels, the myth ceases to be linked directly to the remembered horrors of the actual camps. The banal but at the same time hauntingly strange 'space' of Cayrol's fictional world becomes the whole 'univers concentrationnaire' of absence—corresponding to, but not deriving from, the world of *ennui* evoked by Bernanos. In this Cayrolian universe ineffectual figures move pathetically, vaguely aware of the loss of something precious which they have never known, wandering aimlessly, encountering objects and other bewildered figures, and sometimes grasping clues, signs which put them on the road towards maturity—a maturity which is not loss of innocence, but the assumption of love. These clues, these signs project the faint but warming light of hope, suggesting the possibility of reconciliation, of redemption through a miracle of grace that seems more akin, at least poetically, to what André Breton and his group call the *surréel* than to the supernatural grace of Catholic theology.

Cayrol, who is not pietistic, not in any sense a novelist or poet of 'edification', is, however, a fervent Catholic believer, of the stamp of Bernanos or the late Albert Béguin. For him there is no such thing, in creative literature, as the 'Catholic writer' ('l'écrivain catholique'); there is only the Catholic who is a writer ('le catholique écrivain') in the same way, basically, that anyone else is a writer. By this Cayrol means that the role of the Catholic who is an artist is not to prove or preach the religion which remains the 'motor' of his action, the foundation of his thought; the writer—and in particular the novelist—is neither a theologian nor an exegetist, but a 'witness' ('un témoin').[3] Our contemporary world being what it is, the novelist—Christian or not—can only be a witness to Evil ('le témoin du Mal'). He *must* speak out ('dire le Mal'), because Evil is omnipresent, in the concentration camps and prisons of yesterday, or today, in war, brutality, and cruelty, in

---

[3] Cayrol has made this point in several lectures, including one given in Marseille in 1950 and reported on briefly in the *Cahiers du sud*, no. 304.

disease, in poverty and other social ills, in all forms of human anguish and vice. Though he does not speak of 'engagement' in the Sartrian sense, Jean Cayrol declares that the novelist must bear witness to evil because, in our time above all, he cannot be complacent and secure, he cannot ensconce himself in a static faith, cannot hope for salvation by closing his eyes and his heart to the ills of human beings in this world. Like Bernanos or Graham Greene, Cayrol denounces every mask of *pharisaïsme* or hypocrisy, everything which dries up the sensibility, the spirit of those who seek a false, unearned security, who take refuge in moral or intellectual 'comfort'.

But Jean Cayrol, in his own novels, does not merely bear witness to evil, he does not concern himself primarily with the naturalistic portrayal of the surface of our unlovely society. He evokes the disorder of our world, but this is not his goal, his limit. Through the poetic qualities of his fictions, through the style, in the deepest sense of that expression, he reveals occasional glimmers of hope, of possible reconciliation and redemption. His major concern in this perspective is, perhaps, as he wrote to me in a letter of 28 January 1957, 'to recover, on the far side of abuses, an order' ('retrouver, à travers les abus, l'ordre').

This phrase, which must not lead to the supposition that Cayrol's books are *romans à thèse*, or even novels of ideas, recalls the writer's preoccupations in *Lazare parmi nous* (1950) and, in particular, the jacket comment characterizing these two essays as 'a diagnosis of present-day humanity, and a diagnosis which, beyond all the shadows and disorders, permits hope'. The essay on 'Les Rêves lazaréens' goes beyond surrealist interpretations to affirm that at the point of intersection of the subconscious and the conscious mind in dreams, one is in possession of the total self or, as the jacket comment puts it, of one's 'soul desirous of salvation'. In the concentration camps, where men's dream life was as rich as their waking life was impoverished, Cayrol believes 'dreams came . . . to let us know that we were never abandoned' (*Lazare parmi nous*, p. 61). In the essay 'Pour un romanesque lazaréen'—which is less a manifesto for a new art of the novel than an evocation of a new novelistic universe—Cayrol suggests the themes of his novel trilogy and, beyond this, the poetic ambience of the novels which were to follow and, above all, the strange coupling of 'le merveilleux' and 'le réel', the dreamlike yet real freedom of 'allure' which will characterize all his novels and make them hard to describe in conceptual language:

Habit no longer engenders anything. Every creation becomes unforeseeable, unhuman, for it comes into being or is dissipated without apparent reason. No longer will anything be *surprising*; every situation may appear or disappear, be re-formed or de-formed, outside the being who sees them, in a kind of incantation which is the special property of this diffused Lazarian magic (*Lazare parmi nous*, p. 62).

The first volume of *Je vivrai l'amour des autres* bears the title *On vous parle*. In this long monologue, the impersonal *on* of the title is peculiarly appropriate for the depersonalized, dehumanized voice speaking directly to each of us (for the reader is the *vous* of the title) in a torrent of words which seem to be trying to fill the terrible void in which the speaker has neither name nor visage. The voice is that of a sort of *clochard* without status in the world of others. Still a young man, he is ageless as the night; enveloped in the shroud of his solitude like Lazarus risen from the grave, he drifts about the city, encountering other waifs and wanderers as alien as himself, never able to remain long with another in this nightmare world of impenetrable beings clinging to their poor 'secret lives' in pathetic desperation.

This nameless speaker has been a deportee, but only by chance, having been picked up by the Gestapo as he waited in line at a cinema. It is significant that he recounts nothing of his existence in the concentration camp except the relentless chase for cigarettes which represented his only 'resistance' in that inhuman place (serving, on a lower level, somewhat the same function as the dreams—*les rêves concentrationnaires*—which Cayrol describes in his essay). In a deeper sense, this speaker has been a 'deportee' from the beginning of time. As child and man he has existed outside a world in which he has no place, clinging to his solitude as his most precious, his only possession. He remains a 'stranger', an alien wanderer in a more desolate 'waste land' than the one evoked by Eliot long before our mid-century 'univers concentrationnaire' brought the reality of total destruction of body and spirit close to us all.

For this disturbing, sometimes repellent 'héros lazaréen', only words and objects exist with solidity, with plenitude. His words are never really *heard* by others in this world; yet they continue to pour forth, sometimes muted by weariness, sometimes in spurts of anger or exaltation, almost hysterically, or with the monotonous rhythms of an obsession. The absence of any real contact with living beings that characterizes the spiritual malady of the speaker has as its counterpart the intense, almost hallucinatory, presence of *things*. This presence imposes itself on the reader—the *listener*—in frequent passages of poetic intensity, which plunge far beneath the threshold of sensory experience and yet evoke the most humble and banal objects. These objects are not monstrous and frightening as in Sartre's *La Nausée*; if they seem to possess 'magic' properties, this magic is benign. They bring the speaker, in his solitude, intimations of a link between his inner world and the outer world of sense perceptions, and sometimes they seem to point towards a faint glimmer of dawn, a narrow slit opening into the world of others.

The haunting voice in these pages speaks mostly of the past, for the past—even a frightful or desolate past—has something of the form and solidity of objects, a kind of stability and substance which the speaker and the shadowy human forms around him lack. Occasionally there is a reference to the present, but only as a void or a nebulous, inchoate mass of perceptions and impressions. Not until the final page is there any mention of the future: after having been 'saved'—if only provisionally—by a humble and compassionate café proprietor, the nameless narrator-protagonist murmurs these first words of hope: 'There is a tomorrow . . . you hear, there is a tomorrow . . .' (p. 179).

This tomorrow belongs to the second part of Cayrol's trilogy, a more ample volume with the fitting title *Les premiers jours*. Here the form shifts from the anonymous monologue of *On vous parle* to a somewhat more objective third-person narrative, though the point of view remains close to that of the hero. The speaker without name or visage has now recovered his name, Armand; at the end of the volume he also recovers, for himself and for others, his human visage. Here too the ambivalent meaning of the general title, *Je vivrai l'amour des autres*, begins to emerge. Armand, like the mythical 'héros lazaréen' evoked in the essay 'Pour un romanesque lazaréen', 'can discover only in others the profound meaning of love, its harmony, its joy, its plenitude' (*Lazare parmi nous*, p. 90). Incapable at first of creating his *own* love for another person, he tries to attach himself to a love that already exists, to love Lucette *through* Albert. This 'amour parasitaire', Cayrol says in his essay, is a malady peculiar to our world without God, in which 'substitutes [*les ersatz*] are intermingled with the purest products of our hearts and our spirituality' (ibid., p. 90). This malady comes not from fear of love, but from 'nostalgia for Love in a love without an object, a love in which the carnal is no longer linked with the supernatural' (ibid., p. 91). In such a dissociation, no authentic act of creation is possible.

Before the end of *Les premiers jours*, however, the 'héros lazaréen' experiences at least a partial awakening of his human faculties—a transformation magnificently realized by the novelist in a long, dream-like sequence—and becomes capable of tears and of love *for* (instead of *through*) others. Armand's resurrection is still precarious, for he is just beginning to live his 'first days' in a world in ruins where love alone appears as the saving grace—and love for a young woman like Lucette is a fragile thing on which to found a man's life. There are intimations, perhaps, that Armand's nascent love for Lucette is but a stage on the way to a higher love (to Love, as Cayrol would put it, the capital letter being made to bear this weight of meaning). The notion of divine love, however, is evoked only by an *absence*: Cayrol, as novelist, accompanies or follows his protagonist, but does not precede him or force his hand. Armand, on awakening from the dream sequence, asks softly, 'Who has just left me?' and then murmurs, still deeply moved by his dream experience (like the men in the concentration camp dreams described in *Lazare parmi nous*): 'I have lost someone... I have lost someone' (*Les premiers jours*, p. 250).

Just as *On vous parle* had ended on the word 'tomorrow', so *Les premiers jours* concludes with this same word of hope. Armand can now envisage not merely the possibility of a tomorrow, but the reality of *living* this tomorrow in the world of others. The rigours and above all the uncertainties of this world of others are not overcome, however, by the fact that the 'héros lazaréen' is now beginning to feel less alien, less solitary:

With Albert gone, Armand no longer knew what might happen; after him there was the unknown.
—Tomorrow, I know nothing of tomorrow, thinks Armand (p. 309).

Three years elapsed between the publication of the first two parts of *Je vivrai l'amour des autres* and the appearance of the final volume, *Le Feu qui prend*. This interval was not surprising, since composing a conclusion to the trilogy must have been far more difficult than writing the earlier volumes. No facile conversion of the hero could have been envisaged, for this is not a novel of 'edification', but a serious, deeply-felt metaphysical 'interrogation' that demands a resolution on the same profound level of complexity and authenticity. Of course no novelist could be expected to furnish a final answer to such an interrogation. All that could be asked of Cayrol, no doubt, is that the faint spark of hope kindled in the first two volumes should show promise of eventually producing a clear flame within the hero's spirit, without, however, giving us the feeling that this development is contrived or didactic. This is accomplished in *Le Feu qui prend*, though perhaps the subtly symbolic texture of *On vous parle* and *Les premiers jours* sometimes approaches more abstract allegory here.

As the story begins, Armand is knocking at midnight on the door of his mother's dilapidated house in an unnamed—or nameless—French city: 'He had reached, one evening, the final refuge. Suddenly he thought of his mother's arms' (p. 32). But this family living in sombre squalor can offer little comfort, little courage, little security to the sorely beset 'héros lazaréen'. The mother is weighted down by the burdens of a past even more sordid than the present; Monsieur Flouche, who has replaced the 'father' of Armand's childhood, is a hypocritical weakling and a drunkard; Tom, Flouche's son, a boy with the 'astonishingly fragile' visage of 'the youth of today', is already involved with an underworld band.

But in this microcosm of the 'monde en ruine' there is one saving grace. At the first family dinner Armand meets Francine, Flouche's daughter, and immediately comes under the spell of this girl with the pure profile, the strangely luminous brow beneath masses of dark hair: 'It was truly a countenance which gave forth a secret radiance' (p. 47). Armand and Francine are drawn to one another from the start, but both must grow in strength and confidence, both must live through shattering experiences in their squalid world, before they can face the future together in the rekindled brightness and warmth symbolized by the *fire* of Cayrol's title.

The climax of these experiences comes in the long chapter on the mother's death. Here, too, the symbolism of the title becomes clear. Armand comes home late one afternoon to find the house silent, cold, deserted. He tries to light a fire in the dining-room, but there is only smoke: the fireplace is a dummy, without a chimney. At last, however, a tiny flame appears, and even a bit of warmth: 'These embers could not last long, but this humble blaze gave forth hope' (p. 174). Drawn by a slight noise to his mother's room, Armand finds the old woman in agony, alone and unable to call for help. She wants a priest, but Armand first gets a doctor, who can do little for the dying woman. Armand wanders into the street again, trembling at the thought of going into the unfamiliar darkness of a church. Back at the house, he finds the front door ajar: 'When he entered the room, a big fire was blazing with the sound of crackling bark. The miracle had taken place. Death had been disarmed. Francine had come home' (p. 189). This fire clearly symbolizes the hope implicit in the title: *Le Feu qui prend*. It presages, of course, no facile victory; when the priest arrives, Madame Flouche is already dead. Then begins the dramatic scene between Armand and the priest, a 'wrestling with the angel' reminiscent of a more poetic Bernanos. This encounter ends not in conversion, however, but in a kind of frightened retreat on the part of Armand.

Two more ordeals remain to be met. Francine, whose light is

intense but fragile, strays off into an obscure theosophical sect for a time; Armand finally discovers her one morning in a café, weak and exhausted, but ready now to face life courageously with him at her side. Then Lucette, who had left Armand before he returned to his family, arrives late one night, bleeding from a wound inflicted by a member of the underworld band to which Armand had once belonged. Her symbolic role is revealed through her words to Armand: 'Today you know how to walk beside someone. It is I who taught you' (p. 239). Francine emphasizes Lucette's role, for herself and for the now fully resurrected Armand: 'Thank you for having come with us. Now we are together as one' (p. 247). The dying Lucette is taken to a hospital, while Armand and Francine wait together for daybreak. With a new sympathy for the lives of others, they watch the early morning activity beneath their window. The doorbell rings and Armand goes down to get the bread from the baker's boy, but 'not without again taking in his arms the one who saw him at last in full daylight, in the heart of man's misery' (p. 253). As Armand starts downstairs, Francine looks in the mirror, smiling, in full confidence, not just for herself, but also for 'the window open at her back, for the daily sunlight, in short for the things of this earth which needed her peaceful gaze in order to believe in a better lot' (p. 254). And the book concludes: 'Everything was being played in a pair of laughing eyes, once again' (p. 254).

With Francine's pure and human light to give him confidence, Armand is now ready to assume his human condition in full maturity, on the far side of apathy and despair, even though the 'monde en ruine' which succeeds the 'univers concentrationnaire' still remains to be rebuilt. Undoubtedly Cayrol's sincerity and integrity both as a believing Catholic and as an artist kept him from forcing the conclusion by taking Armand further along the route on which he had halted, out of timidity and fear, in the scene with the priest. There is a spiritual affirmation in the last pages of *Le Feu qui prend*, however, which reveals a deep and grave optimism about the irreducible value of the human person. Lazarus risen from the dead is, after all, a pregnant symbol of reconciliation and hope.

In all three volumes of *Je vivrai l'amour des autres* there is a kind of surrealist climate which makes this work representative, I think, of an important current in the contemporary French novel. Armand, like the hero of Breton's *Nadja* or Aragon's *Le Paysan de Paris*, wanders about the streets of the city in an atmosphere of strangeness and mystery which comes from a certain free, spontaneous, direct perception of the real (that is what the *surréel* is). He meets other figures as 'lost' as himself, the objects about him take on forms as marvellous as the ones they assume in dreams, chance plays unaccountable tricks after the manner of the surrealists' 'hasard objectif'; rational explanations and mere logic seem to offer only degraded caricatures of the rich complexity of immediate experience. One thinks of Restif de la Bretonne's *Les Nuits de Paris*, of certain pages in Balzac and in Baudelaire, of Dostoievsky, of Duhamel's Salavin, as well as of the surrealists, Sartre's Roquentin, Camus's Meursault, even Queneau's *Pierrot mon ami* or *Loin de Rueil*—not as 'sources', but simply as parallels for certain aspects of Cayrol's hero and his unique fictional world. Cayrol's poetic transfiguration of his vision of 'Lazarus in our midst' bears the stamp of a profoundly human and perceptive creative spirit; his trilogy, more than a decade after its original publication, must be recognized as one of the earliest and still one of the most admirable accomplishments of the 'new novel' in France.

Like the concentration camps that one senses behind *Je vivrai l'amour des autres*, the war of 1939–45 furnishes, in *La Noire*, the background for the symbolic portrayal of man's desolation in the modern world of estrangement and dissociation. Here again we are in a world of *absence*, all the more poignant because Cayrol's characters seem so remote from the actual war and, indeed, from any participation in the world of others. Evoked with luminous intensity, these figures belong to a kind of dream world; they are figures from a poet's vision, having little in common with the world of appearances or the social comedy of the realistic novel.

On the surface, the story of *La Noire* appears simple. In August 1939 Armande is living with her mother and two sisters in a bizarre, dilapidated villa overhanging the waters of a mysterious lake somewhere in the south-west of France. Her lover—she has given him the name 'Tristan'—comes to say good-bye. His mobilization orders have given this uncomplicated man the courage to break away from Armande's demanding love—a love which, as she herself later admits, was a vain attempt to satisfy her need for an absolute.

Armande's mother and sisters soon return to the city, seeking the refuge of habit and convention against the nameless horrors of war. Armande remains behind, lacking the force to abandon the solitude and desolation which correspond to the ruins of war, to her impossible love, to the 'univers lazaréen' in which she exists. Slowly the months go by, marked only by the changing face of the lake—closely linked to Armande's inner life—and by rare incidents. She encounters a mysterious little girl who tries to drown her in the black, deep waters—'la noire'—of the lake. One day a soldier with a ghastly wound appears. A banal letter from Tristan and a perfidious one from her sister arrive. Armande leaves in a trance-like state to search for Tristan in the city, returns soon to the lake, then flees towards the sea as an 'issue immaculée'. Finally, through her dreams, she enters an impregnable realm of the spirit in which she feels that she is reunited with Tristan through an interpenetration of their dreams (here again one notes Cayrol's use, in his novels, of the belief affirmed in his essay, 'Les Rêves lazaréens').

On the day the armistice is signed, Armande was to leave the lake to join her family in town: 'She was leaving the lake, the forest, her dwelling, like a hiding place exposed to everyone; her love was now going further away, wandering endlessly, already a victim of that malady of ruins which was to attack the most secret hearts' (p. 215).

But this is not the end of the novel. There is another dimension to the story, which gives the whole work a more complex, a more profound meaning. Suddenly a 'speaker' interrupts the 'objective' narrative to reveal that he is the one who is drawing on his knowledge of the 'real' events to create a story and to search out the deeper truth about Armande. Soon this speaker is seen as the principal figure in the 'reality' behind the story; his own story is developed in italicized chapters, slowly at first but with increasing rapidity in the latter part of the book, where chapters of the two stories alternate in an atmosphere of growing tension. The full meaning of *La Noire* emerges only from the juxtaposition of these two stories, from their confrontation in the reader's mind and sensibility, from the complex synthesis which results.

The nameless speaker whose monologue forms the 'other' story belongs—like the heroine—to the same race of 'héros lazaréens' as Armand in *Je vivrai l'amour des autres*, but this speaker's spiritual malady is even more hopeless. His too is a case of 'amour parasitaire': he dares not assume his love, like other men, but tries to live in its shadow by telling the story of Armande and the half-mythical Tristan. The twofold story undergoes an intricate development; more and more the speaker's inner life, which can be imagined from the increasing tension of his inserted monologues, becomes the principal theme. Armande dies, and the speaker goes back to the villa by the lake, a few years after the war. The house itself has been destroyed by bombs, but certain objects associated with Armande remain more or less intact, as a kind of 'frightful tomb' revealing the shameful secrets that had been hidden during Armande's lifetime. Now at last the speaker realizes why he and Armande had placed Tristan between them like a protective screen against their love: 'We were seeking an alibi; it was I who had wounded Armande more than Tristan; it was Armande who had forgotten me to the point of dying from it' (p. 221). Almost hysterically, the speaker refuses to believe in the finality of his loss, to accept 'winter for myself, prayers on a tomb, pilgrimages' (p. 221).

His 'solution' is to marry Anne, Armande's malicious sister: 'Now Armande can also be *Anne* and nothing will prevent me from seeking her in this distorting mirror' (p. 222). Anne will make him suffer, she will try to destroy the memory of Armande, he knows; yet is it not possible that some day she will become 'une Armande retrouvée'? And, more in desperation than with any hope, he ends with this cry: 'No one on earth can make me believe that even in a world in ruins one can live only the caricature of one's love' (p. 222).

In its atmosphere, *La Noire* has even more of a mysterious, surrealist quality than *Je vivrai l'amour des autres*, and the total meaning of this novel depends even more upon the intermingling of the nocturnal world of dreams with the world of waking reality. But here the tonality is darker: instead of the 'open' conclusion of some of the texts of the 'heroic' period of Surrealism or that of *Je vivrai l'amour des autres*, one finds in *La Noire* something like a dialectic of damnation. It is as if the author—whose earlier 'héros lazaréens' had at least begun to realize the promise of resurrection contained in the Biblical myth—were here obsessed with the evil in our 'univers concentrationnaire', our 'monde en ruine', against which even faith cannot always prevail.

In Cayrol's five novels published since *La Noire*, the war and the concentration camps have disappeared into the remote background and even the myth of Lazarus, though still implicit perhaps, need no longer be invoked to account for the heroes. These more recent books, like the earlier ones, are nevertheless novels of *absence*, of confused, *vulnerable* men and women living in estrangement from other human beings and from the world— the world 'in ruins' which is the legacy of our times. These insubstantial figures are also separated from any transcendent or 'higher' love, for while, as already noted, Cayrol never uses the novel to propagate his Catholic faith, one sometimes senses that the bewilderment, the vulnerability, the pathetic fragility of love in the lives of those who move restlessly and obscurely in his fictional universe are the corollary of the absence of God in the modern world. Cayrol is not, however, merely recapitulating the banal theme of modern man's condition as a creature divided within himself and hopelessly alienated from a cosmos which he apprehends only as chaos. His works are not novels of despair, but creative aspirations towards reconciliation, towards the rediscovery by man of himself and of the world. Even in the obscure lives evoked in this 'monde distrait'[4] there are occasionally faint gleams of light, and now and then one feels that it may still be possible for these vulnerable creatures adrift in an

---

[4] This term occurs in Cayrol's two-paragraph comment on his novels in *La Pensée française* (December 1956). My quotation is from the author's typescript.

opaque world to attain some precarious fulfilment in life. The *resistance* of Cayrol's fictional beings is humble, unspectacular, more instinctive than deliberate; yet somehow, like the old Negro woman Dilsey in Faulkner's *The Sound and the Fury*, they *endure*, in both senses of the word. Even in a 'monde en ruine', in the desolate world of absence, this endurance contains the germ of hope. The alternative to a certain 'revolt' which has been the preoccupation of many European writers of the twentieth century is here apprehended not as resignation to 'abuses', but as the *reconciliation* of man with himself, with the world from which he has alienated himself, and finally, perhaps, with the 'higher' love which, for Cayrol, is God. This ultimate reconciliation, however, is only implicit in 'le romanesque lazaréen'; the domain of the novel, for Cayrol as for his contemporaries, remains the existential world of men and things.

In *Le Vent de la mémoire* (1952) the protagonist is a writer, approaching middle age, living falsely on the reputation acquired from his one published novel but inwardly tormented by shameful memories he has tried to suppress. The things he has thrust out of his consciousness have nevertheless found expression in an autobiographical manuscript which he has apparently written without being consciously aware of it. The 'wind of memory' blows up a storm, and Gérard can no longer evade his past life of cruelty, selfishness, and the inability to love others or even himself. The humble, patient love of a young woman—who refuses to abandon this man who treats her as badly as he had treated all the other human beings whose lives had touched his —offers, at the end, a hope of reconciliation or redemption. If Gérard 'assumes his half-consumed destiny', Cayrol's jacket comment on the book suggests, perhaps he will find, through this love freely offered, 'respect for himself and the tender and vulnerable possession of life'.

L'Espace d'une nuit (1954), which Cayrol once characterized as a 'little novel of presentiment',[5] is a story of recognition and of liberation. François, whose childhood has been dominated by a

---

[5] Cayrol used this expression in the *dédicace* on the fly-leaf of a copy of the book which he sent me in the spring of 1954.

hypocritical, sadistic, blindly possessive father, returns home, on his thirtieth birthday, in answer to an ill-understood summons. He gets off the train from Paris shortly before it reaches his father's village, wanders through the *space* of an ordinary yet mysterious *night*, and meets, at the end, the dénouement of his obsession along with the morning light which presages, beyond the death of the father, the continuation, the renewal of life. François achieves his tardy coming-of-age, in a world which he finally accepts and assumes; freed from his buried childhood fears, his 'complexes', he can now face life, in the world of others, as an adult.

This book is one of the most absorbing and one of the most perfectly realized of Cayrol's efforts to discover, through creative fiction, the reality, the *presence* of a world transcending desolation and despair. The title suggests the author's link with the 'phenomenological' mode of the most original present-day French fiction. For the dream-like progression of François through the strange yet familiar countryside, during which he loses his way and encounters other beings as 'lost' as himself, is not merely symbolic or metaphysical. It is movement through 'real' space and time (or space-time), through a world of *things* which are *present*, in their irreducible immediacy, before becoming, as Cayrol says, *leitmotives* which serve as roots to hold 'a floating, sometimes vague, always unpredictable plot'.[6]

Le Déménagement (1956) reveals, like *Le Vent de la mémoire*, a protagonist—this time a young woman—who has tried to impose a false rigidity on life, thereby drying up love in herself and in those around her, refusing charity, negating hope. The experience of moving from the deceptive refuge of the apartment where she had lived since childhood, first with her parents and a brother and sister, then with her husband alone, becomes a harrowing, nightmarish adventure which stirs up all the mean and sordid memories, reveals the emptiness of a marriage to which Cate had never brought the warmth of love, leads her finally to the realization of her inhumanity, to despair, and to the brink of death in an attempted suicide. But with the dawn,

---

[6] From Cayrol's statement in *La Pensée française*—see footnote 4.

after Cate's final night of anguish, there comes a faint glimmer of light as she regains consciousness and hears her husband's voice calling her, as if from a distance, though he is now once again at her side. In this book, as in the others, there are undoubtedly symbolic meanings, metaphysical resonances. But we first become aware of space, objects, moving forms, the irreducible space-time world which comes into *existence*, which is apprehended as a *presence*, before we 'structure' it in terms of rational, moral, or philosophical meanings. There is nothing *a priori* in this novelistic world: silence becomes language, absence becomes presence only as we advance with the characters into a future which does not exist at all until each instant comes into focus as a present.

The young medical student who is the protagonist of *La Gaffe* (1957) has left Paris for a little summer resort in Brittany on impulse, on a pretext, without any precise goal, but really impelled by his subconscious desire to throw off the life of habit, of ambiguity, of falseness—and of immaturity—which he has always led. Like François in *L'Espace d'une nuit*, he wanders about in a world of space and time which is at once commonplace and strange; he becomes involved in adventures, in other lives. He commits a 'blunder' (this gives the book its title), discovers love and, with this discovery, seems at last to be on the way to assuming life in the world of others as an adult. As always, in Cayrol's novels, we leave the protagonist at the precise moment when he perceives a faint, hopeful gleam of light. Through this light, through his meeting with the young girl Christiane, Jean grasps the possibility of attaining recognition, assent, reconciliation. This reconciliation will be precarious, we know, for human beings will always remain fragile, vulnerable; they cannot attain, in this world, what the critic Bernard Dort once called 'une impossible divinité'. But in Cayrol's universe, at least, they remain free to change, free to seek the light, capable, perhaps, of finding it, not so much by deliberate, conscious effort as by a kind of grace for which the most favourable conditions seem to come from the breaking of habit, of routine, and from a certain receptive disposition which must precede, no doubt, an active search. Here, at the end of the novel, the hero can affirm: 'I was born yesterday morning, at about eleven o'clock, of a blunder' (p. 190).

In all his novels, Cayrol—like most other contemporary novelists—uses the technique of 'restriction of the field', choosing a 'post of observation' close to or even identical with that of the principal character. He uses this technique flexibly, however, sometimes permitting us to hear the inner monologue of the protagonist and thus range freely with him through time and space, sometimes withdrawing slightly so that the angle of vision is somewhat broader, occasionally even shifting the point of view, for a few pages, to another character. With his most recent novel, *Les Corps étrangers* (1959), Cayrol returns for the first time since *On vous parle* to the *récit* entirely in the first person. The man who is speaking here is of the same unhappy race as Gérard in *Le Vent de la mémoire*, Cate in *Le Déménagement*, or the nameless speaker in *La Noire*. He is endlessly telling and re-telling the story of his life, casting out the 'foreign bodies' which fill his memory with things that never happened, replacing them with other distortions or inventions which resist our efforts to disentangle the true from the false, to separate actual events from imaginary ones created by Gaspard—subconsciously, perhaps—to deny his sordid past. Finally we realize that Gaspard's memory, which refuses the passive role of mere recapitulation in order to *create* a past which corresponds to his nostalgia, has become the agent and the expression of hope. We leave Gaspard finally as, catching his breath, he begins once again the long, confused story which has neither beginning nor end. Or if there is an end, it is 'open', as a comment on the book's jacket suggests: 'It is for the reader to continue Gaspard's story, granting him the grace to choose the best of lives in the worst of worlds.'

Jean Cayrol's novels confirm the profound truth of Proust's insight that what we call style, in literature and in art, is ultimately *vision*; they likewise illustrate Mark Schorer's corollary notion of 'technique as discovery'. If it were possible to sketch out here, for Cayrol, the kind of 'existential psychoanalysis' of a man through his literary style which Manuel de Diéguez is attempting to develop,[7] I would suggest that Cayrol's 'réponse originelle au monde', the 'organisation propre de sa plus profonde liberté', his 'comportement originel devant la profondeur tragique'—which we apprehend at their deepest, most authentic level in his style—are defined by a certain *allure*, a certain spontaneity of movement forward in time and space, a certain luminosity even in the darkest moments, the feeling that, advancing along the line of intersection of dreams and waking reality, outside logic and despite material ruins, through banal but mysterious encounters in this 'monde distrait', we may at any moment find ourselves—with the 'héros lazaréen'—on the threshold of reconciliation in a world open to the infinite.

These dream-like stories, which emerge from Cayrol's total being with the immediacy of the surrealist texts which were a significant influence on his early poetry, are defined more by fresh ways of apprehending experience and by a style which incarnates, in a sense, Cayrol's 'choix originel', his unique response to the 'tragic sense of life', than by any formal conventions within the historical or social framework of a literary genre. Gone are the 'preparations' of Balzac, the Flaubertian descriptions with details deliberately chosen to fit into a rigid pattern with a predetermined meaning, the psychological analysis tending to define a kind of essence even in characters marked by instability; gone even is the Proustian architecture which—like Keats's Grecian urn—does not so much 'recapture' as *abolish* time. With Cayrol and the figures moving in his fictions we enter a 'space' which becomes a 'world' only as we become aware of its *presence*, as we begin to 'structure' our perceptions with no regard for *a priori* notions of reality. 'I write as one walks,' Cayrol says. 'I invent my psychology in proportion as I advance in an *inattentive* world ('un monde distrait'.) I know nothing beyond what the inhabitants of my books know, I do not go ahead of them' (also from Cayrol's statement for *La Pensée française*).

The 'inhabitants' of Cayrol's fictional universe, from Armand in *Je vivrai l'amour des autres* to Gaspard in *Les Corps étrangers,* are in constant motion, walking endlessly, seemingly at random, in

[7] See Diéguez, *L'Écrivain et son langage* (Paris, Gallimard, 1960).

the real space of the world of phenomena, a world both familiar and strange, disturbing and reassuring. If this motion seems to *spatialize* man's loneliness, it also incarnates his vague aspirations toward reconciliation and renewal and keeps him free to follow paths where chance encounters—chance for Cayrol being very much like 'le hasard objectif' of the surrealists—may lead to recognition and to love. Love, one should note, is not for Cayrol the exalted passion of the Romantics, but a humble, patient, human emotion which may, nevertheless, bring the modern Lazarus back to life.

The movement toward assent and reconciliation in Cayrol's novels seems to me to be in the line of a certain current in modern poetry from Nerval to René Char; it is akin, above all, to the 'open' view of man and the world, to the optimistic face, of surrealism. Critics of these poets often emphasize their 'Promethean' revolt and their tragic despair over the failure to attain lasting possession of the 'absolute', of which they have, at best, only occasional fleeting visions. But moments of accord, of reconciliation, of confidence in the midst of flux and disorder do exist in the writings of a Nerval, an Éluard, a Breton, or a Char. This accord exists, of course, only in the human dimensions of time and space; it is an existential reality which remains incommunicable unless the one who apprehends it is a creative artist, able to 'translate' it into a style.

Such an assent, such a hope of reconciliation will appear naïve to some. With Jean Cayrol, however, it is not the idle fancy of a man unaware of suffering, ignorant of cruelty and evil; it is not systematic or abstract. It springs from the man's unique sensibility, from his direct and deep experience of the world, as well as from confidence in the poet's imagination and his dreams as instruments for the discovery—or the recovery—of truth; from faith, ultimately, in a certain human power to transcend history. Poetry and the novel, the poetry *of* the novel—these become, for Jean Cayrol, like the whole domain of artistic creation for Malraux, an 'anti-destiny', that is, one of man's highest ways of asserting, of manifesting his freedom and his significance in opposition to any notion of a blind or hostile fatality.

Novels by Cayrol:

Je vivrai l'amour des autres, Paris, Seuil, 1947-50:
    i. *On vous parle*, 1947.
    ii. *Les premiers jours*, 1947.
    iii. *Le Feu qui prend*, 1950.

La Noire, Paris, Seuil, 1949.

Le Vent de la mémoire, Paris, Seuil, 1952.

L'Espace d'une nuit, Paris, Seuil, 1954.
    All in a Night (trs. Gerard Hopkins), London, Faber, 1957.

Le Déménagement, Paris, Seuil, 1956.

La Gaffe, Paris, Seuil, 1957.

Les Corps étrangers, Paris, Seuil, 1959.
    Foreign Bodies (trs. Richard Howard), New York, Putnam, 1960.

ALBERT CAMUS
1913-1960
BY JOHN CRUICKSHANK

———————★———————

CAMUS declared on more than one occasion that he was a moralist only, not a philosopher. It is true, of course, that he was trained in philosophy at the University of Algiers and that he wrote a *diplôme d'études supérieures* on the philosophical links between Plotinus and Saint Augustine. But in many ways his own modest disclaimers are justified. He lacked the genuine philosophical gifts of Sartre and Simone de Beauvoir. His thought is more prone to illogicality and vagueness than theirs; it often fails to measure up to the stringent demands of modern, professional philosophy. And yet, if his mind is not always as keen, in a strictly intellectual sense, as the mind of Sartre, neither is it as rigid. The very fact that Camus combined emotional and moral considerations with intellectual inquiry enabled him to make an outstanding contribution to the life and ideas of his age. Furthermore, despite what Camus says, it is hardly possible to make a sharp distinction, in practice, between metaphysics and ethics. A moralist cannot satisfactorily elaborate theories without having philosophical presuppositions or even, indeed, explicit philosophical beliefs. And when Camus described himself as a moralist rather than a philosopher he was perhaps only saying that he approached metaphysical problems in a particular way and with a particular emphasis. He arrived at general conclusions about human existence through an instinctive distrust of abstractions and a direct concern with human beings in their individuality. Other thinkers and writers have adopted this same kind of approach to the abstract through the concrete for clearly defined philosophical reasons. Camus thought in this way spontaneously and unselfconsciously.

It is a deep-seated, natural attitude which found its equivalent social expression in his pleasure in the company of ordinary people, his distrust of professional intellectuals, and that outstanding gift for friendship which has been emphasized by most of those who knew him well.

Where his speculative essays are concerned—particularly *Le Mythe de Sisyphe* and *L'Homme révolté*—we may agree with Camus that he was more obviously a moralist than a logician or metaphysician. He embodied in these writings, and in much of his journalism, what is best in the moral conscience of the contemporary world. He did so, too, without bombast or humbug. Emmanuel Roblès spoke for many when he described Camus as a moralist whose work presents not a narrow didacticism but a complete style of living.[1] In fact, Camus was a presence and an exemplary figure for his times, as well as a symptom of them. With characteristic modesty he refused the role of guide and keeper of other men's consciences, yet this is the role he fulfilled for many readers. His closeness to his age and to the outlook of ordinary people made it inevitable that his essays and journalism should reflect most of the best, and sometimes unconscious, aspirations of those who read his work—and of many who did not. His outlook on his times was characterized by common sense, by a sceptical attitude towards all ideologies and a deep concern for the well-being of individual men.

Curiously enough, Camus's imaginative writing conveys a different impression from that to which the essays give rise, and this despite their close similarities of theme and style. His novels, in particular, often seem cold and remote from practical human affairs. In them Camus maintains a certain distance, an ironic detachment, from his subject. As a result, his fiction often appears to be more abstract, less humane, than his journalism and speculative essays. Indeed, it sometimes seems more 'philosophical' than the 'philosophical' writings. This is a strange and

---

[1] See his preface to Henry Bonnier, *Albert Camus, ou la force d'être* (Paris, Vitte, 1959). Bonnier himself emphasizes Camus's understanding of the mentality of his contemporaries, calling him 'the perfect topographer, the eternal surveyor' (p. 32).

intriguing paradox which has produced some unfavourable reactions to Camus. More than once he has been praised as a moral voice and adversely criticized as an artist. Such a judgement seems to me to be quite mistaken. It arises, I think, from a failure to understand fully the nature of Camus's whole enterprise as a man and a writer. In order to see more clearly the somewhat complex relationship between his essentially subjective essays and his more abstract, philosophical novels, it is necessary to consider in turn his attitudes to life and to art. The two attitudes are inevitably related, but the nature of the link between them is seen most clearly if they are first separated and their differences exhibited.

*   *   *

In a recording made some time before his death Camus spoke of a dualism running through his life and reflected in his work.[2] This dualism might be described, in very general terms, as a contrast between the instinct for beauty, for physical plenitude, and the experience of tyranny and war. Camus found such a dualism symbolized by the contrast between the village of Tipasa which he knew as a young man, and its appearance when he revisited it twenty years later. The Tipasa of his youth was a community of fishermen and farmers. It overlooked the Mediterranean from the Algerian coast. As one climbed the slopes behind it the air was filled with the scent of roses, tamarisks, and eucalyptus trees. At the summit there were ancient ruins and stone sarcophagi. Here, Camus says, he often lay in the sun during the day, or watched the stars at night. But when he returned to Tipasa from Europe twenty years later the beauty of the ruins was deformed by barbed-wire fencing; and a guard was on duty. Entry during the day-time was only possible by special permission. It was totally forbidden at night. He adds wryly that it was also raining when he returned there. It is clear that this changed aspect of the ruins of Tipasa symbolized for Camus the change that had been progressively wrought in the

[2] 'Albert Camus vous parle': *Festival* (Coll. 'Leur œuvre et leur voix'), FLD 19 M (25 cm., 33⅓ t.). Cf. *L'Été*, pp. 143–63.

world during the last twenty-five years. The dualism also made itself felt in a more dramatic and even more personal way. The day on which World War II broke out—2 September 1939—was the very day he had unwittingly chosen, months before, to begin a keenly anticipated voyage to Greece.

The writings of Camus show that he had a love of simple things, a deep sense of the whole Mediterranean tradition and a certain nostalgia for the past. Such attitudes contributed much to his thought throughout his whole life. At the same time, he was too imbued by the values of this very past to turn his back on the present. He was unwilling to live 'by procuration', as he put it. That is to say, he was not prepared to accept whatever beauty and happiness a life sealed off from contemporary disquiet and the suffering of his fellow-men might have enabled him to enjoy. On the contrary, he determined to maintain the dualism if need be, to reject all evasions, by seeking a path to happiness and beauty through the very heart of his age with its tyrannies, its crimes, its moral nihilism. This is the undertaking —the search for moral affirmations in the face of suffering and despair—which gave shape and purpose to his thought and which greatly influenced his work as an artist.

Camus's own general account of this dualism in his thought and work is misleading to some extent. It implies that the conflict first arose after two contrasting experiences, largely prompted by the fact of war, had succeeded one another directly in time. First of all, he seems to say, there was the perfect happiness, a kind of pagan insouciance, which he associates with Tipasa and his youth and early manhood in Algeria. Later, this happiness was destroyed by violent and tragic public events. Thus the dualism and the conflict first arose from the attempt to regain a happiness which would be as intense as that which war had destroyed yet which would also take account of the realities of the world after Warsaw, Auschwitz, and Hiroshima. It is clear however, when one reads Camus, that conflict characterized his thought and was reflected in his work from an early date. What war does is simply to alter the emphasis placed on the two terms of a dualism already deeply rooted in his experience of life. It is not, I think, an over-schematization to say that in his 'Algerian period' (until 1942) he was continually disturbed by the presence of poverty, suffering, and death immediately below the surface of his happiness, whereas in his 'European period' (from 1942 onwards) the dualism arose from his belief in the possibility of human aspirations being satisfied despite the immediacy, indeed the apparent supremacy, of so many things that encouraged cynicism and despair. In the first period, a predominant happiness was weakened by awareness of strong reasons for anxiety and disquiet; in the second, anxiety and disquiet never wholly dispelled belief in the possibility of happiness. The key-concept of the first period is the idea of *the absurd*; that of the second period is the notion of *rebellion*. To examine these two concepts is to follow the shifting emphases of the dualism that constantly marks Camus's ideas.

The paradox from which a sense of the absurd ultimately derives is to be found in the earliest collection of essays, *L'Envers et l'endroit* (1937). The title itself suggests the idea of contrast, of related opposites, and the five essays are both a paean of praise to physical existence and a sombre meditation on its transitoriness. The terms of the dualism are variously expressed in terms of youthful vigour and the decrepitude of old age, health and sickness, natural riches and material poverty, life and death, man and nature, joy and despair. In one essay Camus tentatively defines happiness as 'perhaps . . . a compassionate sense of our misfortune' (p. 61). The paradox behind this formula is made more explicit towards the end of the book: 'There is no love of life without despair about life' (p. 113).

These first essays tend to assert private experience in objective and universal formulas. Camus's second publication, *Noces* (1939), contains four essays which are more directly personal, in expression as well as feeling. The rich, colourful beauty of life in Algeria, with its appeal to all the senses, is again a major theme. Camus writes with lyrical intensity of 'the beautiful face of the world' (p. 35) and his own sun-drenched youth amid 'the vast libertinage of nature' (p. 16). And yet, this very intensity of the material presence of the world becomes, in time, a kind of absence. It ends by focusing attention on the absence of anything beyond this material presence. By the same token it therefore precludes meaning, an explanation of itself. It may be a weakness in Camus that he should want or expect explanation, but he does so, and the very 'libertinage of nature' eventually becomes an imprisonment—imprisonment in the immediately temporal. At this point, as Camus later pointed out in *Le Mythe de Sisyphe* (p. 88), a succession of present moments lived with intensity gives rise to a sense of the absurd. This is particularly so when, during such an experience, attention is turned from the material world to the world of men confronted by it. By staking all on the flesh and the senses a man also underlines the fact that he is the prisoner of his own brief existence. He throws into striking relief his own inevitable mortality. Thus we find in *Noces* that the reverse side of things is emphasized again— above all the 'mathematical certainty' of death and man's desperate and often unconscious efforts to find deliverance from the idea that death is final and complete. Camus insists on the paucity of our imagination where death is concerned:

> Since we are so ready to display our subtlety in discussing other topics, I am always astonished by the poverty of our ideas on the subject of death. Either it is good or it is evil. I fear it or I welcome it (so they say). But this also proves that everything simple exceeds our understanding. What is the colour 'blue', and what are we to think about it? The same difficulty arises in the case of death. We do not know how to discuss death and colour. And yet what is important is the man I see before me, a dead weight like the earth itself, a prefigurement of my future. But can I genuinely think about this? I say to myself: I must die, but this means nothing because I do not succeed in believing it and can only have direct experience of the death of other people. I have seen people die. In particular, I have seen dogs die. Touching them was what really upset me . . . and I realize that my horror of dying is bound up with my jealous love of living. . . . But for my own part, facing the world, I do not want to lie or to be told lies. I want to maintain my lucidity to the last and contemplate my end with all the richness of my jealous love and my horror (*Noces*, pp. 36–38).

This acute awareness of death, experienced against a background of physical plenitude which offers no spiritual consolations, seems to be the main form in which Camus first met what he later called the absurd. He also wrote: 'My fear of death is related to the extent to which I detach myself from the world and identify myself with the fate of living men instead of contemplating the eternal sky' (ibid., p. 38). This shift of emphasis to 'the fate of living men' is typical of Camus. It is the standpoint he adopted a few years later in *Le Mythe de Sisyphe* when he set out to examine the absurd in more detail and began with the arresting statement: 'There is only one really serious philosophical problem—suicide. To decide whether life is or is not worth living is to answer the fundamental philosophical question' (p. 15).[3]

In so far as Camus described the absurd in terms of a nihilistic attitude tempting his own generation, he wrote with considerable insight and conviction. Individual experience of the absurd doubtless takes its most dramatic form in the 'horror of dying'/'jealous love of living' contrast. But the absurd can make itself felt in other ways: recognition of the remorseless passage of time; a highly private sense of self-alienation; awareness of the gulf, which neither love nor friendship can satisfactorily bridge, between the self and other selves; a feeling that the physical world is alien, that the strength and endurance of nature mock our frail mortality. But any one of these forms of experience of the absurd is only likely to arise when the routine which characterizes most people's lives has been abruptly destroyed. The senseless repetitiveness of social existence, which ought itself to prompt awareness of the absurd, normally seals us off from it. We follow easily enough the continual rhythm of 'getting up, taking the tram, four hours in an office or factory, a meal, the tram, four hours' work, a meal, sleep' (*Le Mythe de Sisyphe*, p. 27), and this pattern is repeated week after week, month after

---

[3] There is a close similarity between Camus's ideas up to the 1940s and those of his friend and teacher Jean Grenier. Grenier wrote: 'Everything contributes to the glory of man. To his glory and to his destruction. If he is of so much value it is because death, rather than the landscape, is the décor of his actions. The one cannot be understood without the other. The only thing that gives shape to desire is a sharp and ever-present sense of man's end. From these two forces (desire and death) a philosophy of tragedy is born.' Jean Grenier, *Les Îles, suivi de Inspirations méditerranéennes* (Paris, Gallimard, 1947), pp. 109–10.

month, year after year. But if something occurs which causes us suddenly to query this existence, to utter the simple word 'why', a link in the chain of daily gesture is broken, meaninglessness breaks in upon us, the absurd becomes a reality.

In the course of his survey of nihilism Camus goes on to speak of the absurd as a more purely intellectual concept. It is here, in its movement away from the concrete towards the abstract, that *Le Mythe de Sisyphe* is least satisfactory. No doubt Camus is right to insist that much of our experience of the world lies outside the reach of rational categories. It is true, too, that the history of thought is a story of conflicting viewpoints, of private convictions masquerading as universal truths, of the failure of speculation to achieve any certainty other than the conviction of its own ignorance and uncertainty. Yet it also follows that Camus's own experience of the absurd is equally irreducible to neat rationalizing. When he moves on to a conceptual account of the absurd it is not difficult to convict him of circular argument, failure to distinguish between more than one sense of the same word, mistaken interpretation of philosophers from the past, identification of words themselves with the things they signify, &c. But one remains convinced of the genuineness of the general position which Camus expresses as follows:

I can feel this heart inside me, and I conclude that it exists. I can touch this world, and I also conclude that it exists. All my knowledge ends at this point. The rest is hypothesis (ibid., p. 34).

This is the attitude to experience which gives rise to a 'philosophy of tragedy'. It also leads to an ethic of quantity since, in the absence of moral absolutes, the intensity and frequency of enjoyable experiences is the only available qualitative standard. *Le Mythe de Sisyphe* is essentially an attempt to justify both a philosophy of tragedy and an ethic of quantity, and to show that they are inseparably linked.

Theoretically, an ethic emphasizing intensity of experience might itself have been sufficient reason for Camus's association with the French Resistance in Lyon at St. Étienne in 1942. In fact, however, he had already turned his back on the morally indifferent ethic of quantity which at first seemed a logical deduction from his philosophical account of nihilism. This is a good example of the way in which the moralist in Camus so often overcame the philosopher. In the concrete circumstances of enemy occupation and the resistance which it provoked, philosophical theorizing gave way to positive and purposeful action in defence of humane values. During his practical experience in the Resistance, Camus began to fashion the notion of 'rebellion' which, after 'the absurd', is the second key-concept of his thought. Rebellion becomes, in fact, the main theme of *L'Homme révolté* (1951). This means that *L'Homme révolté* is, to some extent, an investigation of how the argument of *Le Mythe de Sisyphe* went wrong. Camus naturally does not abandon the fundamental nihilist position of the earlier book. He insists that he had never regarded the absurd as an end in itself but considered it to be a realistic basis on which to build more positive moral ideas. Also, there is evidence in the *Lettres à un ami allemand* (1945) of his realization that nihilism is not only the negative, indifferent attitude described in *Le Mythe de Sisyphe* but that it may grow into something as positively menacing as Nazi ideology showed itself to be. Nazism, he claims, derived much of its momentum from one logically possible interpretation of the metaphysical *cul-de-sac* outlined in *Le Mythe de Sisyphe*. He therefore re-examined his earlier position and concluded that to say the world is meaningless and to deny moral values must imply some measure of value and meaning enabling one to make this very statement. He writes:

I continue to believe that this world has no supernatural meaning. But I know that something in the world has meaning—man—because he is the only being that demands meaning for itself. The world at least contains the truth of man (*Lettres à un ami allemand*, pp. 72–73);

and again:

Although apparently negative because it creates nothing, rebellion is positive in a profound way since it reveals those elements in man which must always be defended (*L'Homme révolté*, p. 32).

As in the case of *Le Mythe de Sisyphe*, the negative half of the argument in *L'Homme révolté* is impressive. Camus's account of the inherent weaknesses of revolutionary political theory—especially his analysis of the tendency of all true revolutionaries to sacrifice humane behaviour to such false absolutes as History and Revolution itself—is striking and convincing. But just as the positive deductions from the absurd led, in *Le Mythe de Sisyphe*, to a position Camus was ultimately obliged to forsake, so in *L'Homme révolté* his doctrine of rebellion, which he carefully distinguishes from revolution in the political sense, must strike one as very unsatisfactory. One can admire, and possibly accept, the idea of rebellion as it is presented, in terms of practical morality, in imaginative works such as *La Peste* and in much of Camus's journalism. But its philosophical formulation in *L'Homme révolté* is again open to various logical objections and, indeed, is too often expressed in disturbingly vague or hermetic language. The nostalgia for Tipasa is evident in Camus's advocacy of 'the Mediterranean tradition', 'solar thought', the lyricism of sunshine and light in the closing pages of the book. This lyricism was a moving and persuasive means of conveying the instinctive epicureanism of the early essays in *L'Envers et l'endroit* and *Noces*. In *L'Homme révolté*, following as it does a series of political analyses, and attempting to embody concrete proposals derived from these analyses, it has all the appearance of an intensely private vision struggling unsuccessfully with the problem of its own practical application.

Philosophically, then, both *Le Mythe de Sisyphe* and *L'Homme révolté* are distinctly unsatisfactory. This is why I said earlier that Camus's speculative essays show him to be a more convincing moralist than logician or metaphysician. Their chief value lies perhaps in the fact that they offer the spectacle of an intensely humane and fundamentally simple man attempting to face honestly some of the most pressing problems confronting the contemporary conscience. They help to illuminate a certain sensibility which is associated particularly with the movement of ideas and course of events during the last quarter-century. But the light they shed is ethical, not philosophical. It is this feature of Camus's essays—his ability to convey the subjective experiences which run parallel to certain philosophical dilemmas—that points to what were to be his particular gifts as a philosophical novelist.

In imaginative writing, as distinct from essays on ideas, the balance between abstract thought and concrete human experience is very different. The natural alignment of this balance in Camus's own case, while it made him an unsatisfactory philosophical essayist, enabled him to achieve an outstanding measure of success as a philosophically-minded creative artist.

*　　*　　*

It is probably not possible to derive a wholly self-consistent aesthetic theory from Camus's writings on the nature of literature and the novel. Nevertheless, one can say that there is a fundamentally close relationship between the ideas described above and his conception of literature. In the latter, as in the former, the notions of the absurd and rebellion play a considerable part. For Camus, the subject-matter of literature today must be the absurd. That is to say, literature must describe those features of the human condition which give rise to a philosophy of tragedy. At the same time, literature (and art generally) is not only a means of portraying the absurd. It is also an expression of rebellion and protest. This rebellion is made possible by the fact that the literary work, in becoming a work of art, gives aesthetic form and coherence to experience which is otherwise incoherent and formless. In this way the work of art is closely bound up with man's sense of scandal and his instinctive rebelliousness in the face of the absurd. Camus's line of argument here is, of course, open to some objections. Apart from the fact that literature does not affect reality in this way (i.e. the work of art does not give order to experience but to our *picture* of experience, which is what religion also does), it is also the case that much of the most impressive and influential art of this century has attempted to reflect incoherence in its form as well as its subject. However, what does clearly emerge from these statements by Camus is the fact that he is an advocate of classicism in art. He is so, above all, in so far as he requires literature to dominate life, having espoused it, 'to enter becoming in order to confer on it the style which it lacks' (*L'Homme révolté*, p. 319). This is one of the reasons for the marked stylistic austerity of much of Camus's imaginative writing. The artist in him seeks to discipline the romanticism of the moral philosopher. Such a reaction is also in keeping with his own definition of classicism (in *L'Homme révolté*) as romanticism brought under control.

Other general features of Camus's imaginative writings spring from this classical view of art. He regards literature as a means of asserting freedom and dignity through this controlled rebellion against the human lot. Thus the more serene and apparently self-sufficient the work of art is, the more it will emphasize both the fact of man's dilemma (which is its subject) and the extent of his protest against that dilemma (conveyed by its form). In fact, detachment is one of Camus's chief ideals as an artist. Its importance is considerable because it enables him to write novels which have a predominantly moral and philosophical content, yet which are neither didactic essays nor *romans à thèse*. In his fiction he does not cease to be a witness to his times, but his approach here is markedly different from that adopted in his essays. In the latter, he investigated causes and proposed solutions. As a result, both the diagnoses and the remedies were inevitably coloured by contemporary pressures and private bias. In the novels and short stories, however, he uses a variety of formal, artistic devices in order to maintain much greater distance from his subject. Personal views about cause and cure are either eliminated or specifically subordinated to the artistic requirements of the work. The timeless problem remains, but temporary explanations and proposals are removed. Generally speaking, too, Camus does not pass clear-cut moral judgements in his fiction. Detachment is accompanied and reinforced by an element of ambiguity. It is perhaps in *La Chute* that ambiguity most obviously works against positive moral judgement. We shall see later, however, that it has a similar effect in *L'Étranger* and *La Peste*. In fact, Camus conceives of art as a means of understanding and justification rather than as a vehicle for passing judgement:

The aim of art ... is not to legislate or to wield authority but, first and foremost, to understand. It sometimes gains authority by dint of understanding, but no work of genius has ever been founded on hate and contempt. This is why the artist, when he achieves his goal, absolves instead of condemning. He is not one who judges but one who justifies.

He is the perpetual advocate of living beings . . . (*Discours de Suède*, p. 58).

The freedom, autonomy, and dignity of art (freedom, autonomy, and dignity are also the aims of rebellion) are ultimately derived from its renunciation of partisan judgements. In the end, literature must steer an even course between the Scylla of superficiality and the Charybdis of propaganda. Only such a course will reveal its proper nature and true freedom. And Camus again justifies his own classicism when he adds at this point that this 'difficult freedom . . . resembles most a form of ascetic discipline' (ibid., p. 61).

At an early stage in his career Camus described the most significant kind of novel as being, in his view, 'philosophy expressed in images'.[4] Later, in *Le Mythe de Sisyphe*, he claimed that 'the great novelists are philosopher-novelists' who 'write in images instead of using arguments' because of their conviction of 'the uselessness of all systematized explanation' (p. 138). In general, 'what distinguishes the modern sensibility from that of earlier times is that the latter took its material from moral problems while the former draws its nourishment from metaphysical ones' (ibid., p. 142). Such comments as these explain why Camus's fiction is about the absurd, but the absurd described in non-conceptual terms. Metaphysical questioning is constantly implied in his novels, but it is conveyed in terms of human testimony and experience. All Camus's imaginative writing comes within the terms of his own definition of the work of art which, he claims, 'is born when the intellect gives up the attempt to account rationally for the human lot' (ibid., p. 134). Description replaces analysis and such description of the absurd is, for Camus, true realism of subject-matter.

At the same time, however, Camus wishes to present this subject-matter in a manner that will satisfy his need to protest and rebel. The artistic form given to the content is his main means of doing so. This form, or style, mainly consists of an

---

[4] Quoted by R. Quilliot in *La Mer et les prisons: essai sur Albert Camus* (Paris, Gallimard, 1956), p. 101.

aesthetic 'correction' of the world by the redistribution into an artistic whole of elements taken from human experience. In this sense, the kind of novel he envisages 'is born at the same time as the spirit of rebellion and exemplifies, on an aesthetic plane, the same aim' (*L'Homme révolté*, p. 320). The novel, and indeed literature generally, is thus neither complete refusal nor complete acceptance of reality. It is both refusal and acceptance within certain bounds, and great art arises from the resulting tension. This is a view which puts considerable emphasis on stylization. The word often occurs in Camus's theoretical writings and he defines it in *L'Homme révolté*:

Stylization presupposes both reality and the mind which gives shape to reality. Through stylization the creative effort remakes the world and it always does so by means of a slight warping which is the hallmark of art and of protest (pp. 334–5).

It is this effort of stylization which has prompted a few critics to speak slightingly of Camus's novels as synthetic sermons, lifeless images or rhetorical creations remote from daily experience. Such objections rely on what is admittedly a long-accepted, but also surely a quite partial, view of what a novel should be. In a loose and undefinable form such as fiction, I see no reason why the novelist should inevitably make character and plot (in the nineteenth-century sense) the major elements in his work. Indeed, by no means all great novelists of the past have done so. A novel in which character and plot remain subordinate to statements about human experience at large may be more 'realistic', in the proper sense, than 'slice of life' fiction. The philosophical novel at its best is as close to life as the best kind of psychological novel. In the case of Camus, stylization is not allowed to degenerate into what he himself called 'pure nostalgia' with no basis in day-to-day reality. Stylization, as he says above, presupposes reality. But it also presents reality in a certain way by using such methods as controlled and ordered language, formal arrangement and shaping, symbolism, ambiguity and irony. It is precisely in this way that Camus, unlike a number of his contemporaries, has written novels that can be regarded both as specially significant for our time and as enduring works of literature in their own right.

*   *   *

Something of Camus's outstanding artistic skill can be seen in the way in which, for each novel, he chooses a form that will serve and promote a particular perspective of the absurd. In *L'Étranger* the vocabulary of objectivity and an abrupt, discontinuous syntax help to convey the incoherence of existence and its resistance to explanation. Vocabulary and syntax are among the various elements that contribute, in a formal way, to that sense of alienation which is the theme of the novel. Camus himself commented: '*L'Étranger* . . . under the guise of first person narrative, is an exercise in objectivity and detachment as its title indeed indicates' (*Actuelles II*, p. 93). Meursault's alienation makes detachment a natural attitude. With the different material of *La Peste* detachment is achieved by almost opposite means. In this case the narrator, Rieux, consciously rebels against the absurd and this positive attitude, unlike the passivity and incomprehension of Meursault, could easily lead the author to write a *roman à thèse*. Camus indicates how he seeks to avoid this: 'Behind its appearance of an objective chronicle, written in the third person, *La Peste* is a confession. Everything is arranged in the novel so that the element of confession will be complete in proportion as the narrative is indirect' (ibid., p. 93). In addition, by exploiting the symbolic possibilities of an epidemic of bubonic plague in Oran (the fight against the plague is both resistance to the German occupation of Europe and rebellion against the absurd) Camus enclosed the particular and the general in a single artistic unity. The use of symbolism both made possible further detachment and allowed the novel, in accordance with his own view of modern tendencies in literature, 'to extend beyond psychology to the condition of man' (*L'Homme révolté*, pp. 338-9). In *La Chute* the ambiguity of the subject, the whole concept of a 'judge-penitent', is another form of detachment. It is reinforced by the use of monologue masquerading as dialogue since this suggests that an important element in the full story of Clamence is being suppressed (i.e. the judgements or comments of a second person). It is here that Camus comes closest to using art as judgement, despite his own theories. Admittedly, an unfavourable judgement of Clamence may not be explicit in the morally ambiguous content of the novel; but it is present in the unusual *form* which the content takes. This is implied in Camus's statement: 'I used there a theatre technique (the dramatic monologue and the implied dialogue) in order to describe a tragic comedian. I simply adapted the form to the subject.'[5] As regards the short stories of *L'Exil et le royaume*, these again vary greatly in form and style according to the demands of the subject-matter in each case.

L'Étranger (written 1939–41; publ. 1942) is first and foremost a statement about the absurdity of experience. In non-conceptual terms it conveys the feelings that can arise from the fact that reason is unable to reduce the world to rational categories, that man is alienated in a world which he does not truly 'know', that genuine self-knowledge and knowledge of other people are both unattainable. It is a vague, subjective awareness of this which Meursault experiences for much of the novel. The following short passage is typical:

A little later, in order to do something, I picked up an old newspaper and read it. I cut out an advertisement for Kruschen Salts and stuck it in an old scrapbook in which I put newspaper-cuttings that strike me as funny. I washed my hands and eventually sat out on my balcony (p. 34).

Meursault's boredom, as it is briefly described here, might be due to any one of a number of different causes. As such passages accumulate, however, consciousness of the absurd is built up. This is the simplest and most obvious way in which, by putting his philosophy of the absurd into images, Camus remains a novelist while conveying his own vision of man's condition. These accumulated images of Meursault performing certain acts, or of the objects that surround him, remain unrelated. They do not contribute either to a pattern of behaviour or to a patterned

[5] Interview with Robert D. Spector published in *Venture*, III, 4 (Spring/Summer 1960), p. 38. Camus wrote his answers to Spector's questionnaire in December 1959, about a fortnight before his death.

background. As a result, they add to the already strong sense of incoherence. Further, since first person narrative is used, they contribute to a feeling of the author's detachment by showing us events eluding Meursault's understanding without Meursault himself telling us so.

It is largely true, in fact, that Meursault is not conscious of alienation prior to the trial. On the contrary, he is well adjusted to the physical world and derives great enjoyment from it. At most, he has a vague sense of being ill-adjusted to society. There is the fact, for example, that he finds much of the social ritual accompanying his mother's funeral to be meaningless. He is also aware that both his boss and his girl friend find him odd in some ways. But a crucial feature of the first half of *L'Étranger* is the fact that it is to the reader, not to himself, that Meursault appears as an outsider. One result is that Camus can thus prepare the reader for the judgements later passed by society on Meursault. He even encourages the reader, up to a point, to side with the prosecution. By the same token, he attempts to forestall any sentimental reader-identification with Meursault. In this way Camus invites a detachment of the reader's sympathies from Meursault and then sets himself the task of justifying his hero while deliberately encouraging the reader's censure. This gives rise to a distinct feeling of moral ambiguity in the novel.[6] It is true that Meursault killed a man—it is possible that he did so in what he thought to be self-defence—but it is also true that he was unfairly tried and condemned to death. Camus is not using this situation solely to attack capital punishment (though this is undoubtedly an element in the novel; it is surely significant that Camus's manuscript contains a drawing by him of a guillotine in one of the margins). More specifically, in the context of the novel, the situation means a confrontation between the simple, direct language of Meursault, who often admits uncertainty and says no more than he means, and the

[6] In a remarkable analysis of *L'Étranger—Sur un héros païen* (Paris, Gallimard, 1959)—Professor Robert Champigny discusses the whole question in detail. He describes Meursault's killing of the Arab as an event rather than an act (pp. 96–97) and shows how Meursault both knows himself to be a criminal and genuinely experiences no guilt (p. 108).

false, assertive public language of the court which often has no meaning that can be confirmed in the individual's life. The court of law, and the society which it represents, cling to concepts and absolutes which have no foundation in reality and which honest adherence to human experience, let alone conscious awareness of the absurd, shows to be void of meaning. This, then, is another indirect but natural means by which Camus conveys his own conception of what the absurd implies.

A complicated instance of the objectivity and detachment which Camus himself attributed to the novel is to be found in his confusing treatment of time. Having begun by recording his mother's death on the same day as he received the news, Meursault goes on to shift the temporal viewpoint with almost bewildering inconsequence. Sometimes he writes of events as they occur and then proceeds to give a retrospective account of other events which undoubtedly happened later. In the second half of the novel, unlike the first, he writes mainly, though not always, from a point in time shortly before his own death. This confused time-scheme is unlikely to be the result of mere negligence on Camus's part. It should be seen, I think, as part of his ironic intention.[7] One might possibly interpret it as further evidence of the absurd through the incoherence of experience, but it is more likely that the continually changing relationship between 'I' the narrator and 'I' as seen by the narrator serves another purpose. It makes difficult any clear separation between the two Meursaults—the Meursault who can understand with his mind the claims of a court of law (and make them comprehensible to the reader), and the Meursault who can make no sense of these claims as applied to his own experience. In the same way, the distinction is blurred between the relatively articulate Meursault of the final pages and the natural pagan of the first part. The result is another form of ambiguity and it supports objectivity and detachment. Two irreconcilable viewpoints are allowed to stand. No doubt Meursault is finally 'absolved' in the sense in which Camus used the term earlier, but this absolution is far removed from any direct and simple moral justification of the

[7] Quilliot, op. cit., p. 38, quotes Camus as saying: 'All my work is ironical.'

main character. His justification is indicated more obliquely by a series of reminiscences of Christ, ending with the reference to 'consummatum est' in the final sentence of the novel.

In *La Peste* (written 1944–7; publ. 1947) detachment is maintained by less complicated means. This is mainly so because the novel is built round the central symbol of the plague. As a result, the two figurative meanings of the plague—the German occupation and the absurd—are not described in a direct and naturalistic way. Both are presented obliquely, symbolically, through a realistic account of the epidemic, and detachment and a measure of stylization easily follow. Other consequences result from the use of a symbol. In the first place, by avoiding a directly realistic account of the Occupation, Camus was able to remain free from the contemporary pressures and personal bias that have disfigured many treatments of this subject. Symbolic representation in *La Peste* discounts partisanship yet retains a genuine sense of moral protest. Indeed, through the generalizing agency of the symbol, the Nazi occupation is put into the wide historical context of all social and political tyrannies and the justification of resistance to them. Secondly, by giving a symbolic account of rebellion against the absurd, Camus is obliged to convey his ideas through images and to avoid conceptual language. Some of the leading themes of *La Peste*—separation, fraternity, goodwill, protest—are thus presented by means of concrete human situations and escape the sentimental overtones which such ideas tended to acquire in the later pages of *L'Homme révolté*.

The use of an all-pervasive symbol in the novel, although it favours detachment, offsets the abstraction to which detachment is prone because of its integrating effect. The Occupation and the absurd, the concrete experience and the speculative idea, are both enclosed and related within the single image of the plague. Thus abstract questions arising from human speculation are closely linked with an actual political experience lived through by human beings. The absurd is not confined to awareness of an alien universe to which men can give no satisfactory meaning. It is also present in one reaction to this situation which prompts some men to enslave other men. By doing so, however, they actively connive at the absurd. They increase the power of the very thing that scandalized them in the first place. Thus the fact emerges that rebellion against the absurd must include rebellion against human systems that give it further social and political extension. There is human hostility, as well as natural hostility, to the fundamental dignity of human beings.

The general air of detachment to which symbolism gives rise is strengthened by Camus's narrative method. Whereas he used direct, first-person presentation in *L'Étranger*, here in *La Peste* he employs a form of detached, anonymous narration. Even when the leading character, Rieux, identifies himself as the actual narrator, he refuses to write in his own name. His argument is that the catastrophe was communal, not personal, and he must therefore write for all, not simply for himself. He says: '. . . the narrator has aimed at objectivity' (p. 200). This effort of objectivity is seen in the highly qualificatory language used by Rieux: 'it seems', 'it is possible', 'in all probability', &c. This attitude obviously holds the reader at some distance from the events described so that once again, as in *L'Étranger*, sentimental reader-identification is discouraged. In addition, an objective account of events and characters serves the symbolic purpose of the novel by encouraging in the reader a detached state of mind which helps to make him more receptive to its figurative implications.

Symbolism and detachment seem to be associated with irony and ambiguity in *La Peste*, though on which specific occasions and to what extent is not easily decided. Ambiguity for ironic purposes becomes possible at various points where Camus's system of symbolic equivalences obviously breaks down. On the plague/Occupation level there are many small inconsistencies. For example, the fact that the cinemas and theatres of Oran are full applies to the circumstances of the Occupation but hardly to those of an epidemic. Again, those who are actively resisting the plague use the isolation-camp incinerators for the cremation of its victims whereas, in occupied Europe, it was clearly the Nazis, not the *résistants*, who burned their own victims in the concentration camps. Other instances of such inconsistency are easily found. In a more general sense, however, the plague seems an unsatisfactory symbol of the Occupation because it over-simplifies the moral dilemmas of the latter and places the inhumanity of man to man, to which it continually points, outside the scope of human responsibility altogether. Similar problems occur at the plague/absurd level, including the obvious objection that plagues are sporadic phenomena whereas the absurd is a permanent feature of the human condition.

I am inclined to think that some of these difficulties are due to the inadequacy of Camus's symbol or to his inadequate handling of it. Yet it is not possible to believe that all such inconsistencies are unconscious. Camus's general theory and practice of fiction make it more likely that just as ironical distance was achieved in *L'Étranger* by choosing as a martyr of the absurd a man who had killed one of his fellows, so, in *La Peste*, irony and ambiguity are intentionally maintained against too direct an equivalence between narrative event and symbolic meaning. Camus blurs the edges of his symbol to ward off excessive simplification. At the same time he keeps intact its general validity.

A familiar form of moral ambiguity—the frequent difficulty of distinguishing satisfactorily between innocence and guilt—dominates the subject-matter of *La Chute* (1956). In this case ambiguity and irony are directly suggested throughout by Clamence's own monologue. There is not the same use of such subtle formal devices as in the two previous novels. At one point Clamence himself says: 'Life is ambiguously ordered' (p. 131) and in this respect his own life resembles his estimate of life in general. He began his career as a successful insider, repeating the confident assertions and accepting the clear distinctions made by public thought and morality. But one event in particular, a failure of courage on his part, changed his whole outlook, reversed his estimate of himself, ushered him into a world of uncomfortable truths and disturbing uncertainties. As a result he now realizes that his former modesty allowed him to shine among his fellows, his championing of underdogs helped him to succeed, his goodness permitted him to dominate. The compromising underside of each of his virtues is thus revealed to him without any decisive principle of evaluation being offered.

A secondary form of ironic ambiguity shows itself in Clamence's reaction to this discovery. He adopts the ambivalent role of what he calls a 'judge-penitent'. That is to say, he confesses his own guilt with an appearance of penitence, but he does so in order that he may convict his listener of comparable guilt and, to that extent, judge him. Camus even adds a further layer of irony to the novel since he himself is clearly judging Clamence for using this stratagem to judge others.

Judgement is also meted out to Clamence in so far as he appears to be an ironic self-portrait by Camus. This aspect is seen in a number of details, not least of all in the relationship between the moral deflation of Clamence and Camus's own discomfort at the moral eminence to which he was raised against his will by enthusiastic readers and commentators. At the same time, of course, Clamence's 'fall' involves reactions on his part which Camus did not approve. What starts as ironical detachment eventually develops into radical separation.

Camus's narrative method in *La Chute* again heightens the ambiguity and equivocation which surround the novel in so many ways. By using the monologue form he does not merely point to Clamence as a 'tragic comedian'. He also sees to it that the reader cannot be certain when, or how far, Clamence is telling the truth. We cannot be sure that Clamence, or Camus, means what he says at any given point. We cannot be sure which of his many roles Clamence, in particular, is playing. This is also true of the ambiguous attitude to Christianity that emerges from the novel. Finally, in a comment like the following, Camus even adopts explicitly ironic detachment towards his ambiguous material: 'I cannot put off the story any longer despite my digressions and inventive efforts which, I hope, you appreciate at their true value' (pp. 80–81). It is clear, then, that *La Chute* contains a most complicated network of ambiguous attitudes and ironic comments. This dominant feature of the novel makes a final appearance in the wry statement with which *La Chute* ends: 'It is too late now. It will always be too late—fortunately!'

The features I have emphasized in the three novels are also to be found, though usually in a more simple form, in the six short stories of *L'Exil et le royaume* (1957). The meaning of the collective title is not wholly clear though I take the 'exile' in question to refer to the fact that all the stories could be said to convey the experience of alienation either from the natural world, or from other men, or both. The precise meaning of 'the kingdom' is more difficult to establish. A momentary experience of deep kinship with the material universe seems to suggest one direction in which it may lie (cf. 'La Femme adultère'). The final story ('La Pierre qui pousse') suggests human fraternity as an ideal kingdom and friendship as a possible means of glimpsing it. But in the end, exile and kingdom merge into one another. In *Le Mythe de Sisyphe* Camus wrote that for a man who is conscious of the absurd 'the hell of the immediate is finally his kingdom' (p. 75). In this sense the dilemma of the human condition arises from the very mingling, the near-identification, of exile and kingdom. The world of nature and men is, for Camus, man's only kingdom, yet awareness of the absurd is awareness of the exile man is bound to experience even within the very boundaries of that kingdom.

There is the usual detachment in these stories in so far as Camus deliberately understates their wider meaning in his anxiety to avoid their becoming philosophic pamphlets. The detailed circumstances of each story often seem far removed from the themes implied in their collective title. Also, there is little attempt to analyse the problems involved. For instance, the idea of inevitable misunderstanding and cross-purpose in human relationships (an idea not necessarily at variance with Camus's emphasis on friendship) is given simple narrative treatment both in 'Les Muets' and 'L'Hôte'. Ambiguity and irony are again present in various particular forms, and more generally in the fact that the main characters in the stories are not allowed to become exemplary heroes. In the last analysis, however, one chiefly admires other aspects of this collection: the remarkably wide range of styles that Camus mastered; the outstanding rendering of the spirit of place; a new firmness and richness in his portrayal of character. In private conversation he referred to these short stories as 'exercices de style'. There is little doubt that apart from their own intrinsic merits they represent a series of experiments carried out with the aim of creating an even more satisfactory artistic form for his philosophical ideas.

In these comments on Camus's fiction I have given a very limited account of it. I have merely pointed out a few formal devices in each novel. It seemed reasonable to do this because so much has already been written about the philosophical content of Camus's fiction yet relatively little attention has been paid to two problems: (*a*) how he saw the connexion between his ideas and his imaginative writing; (*b*) what devices he used to maintain a satisfactory balance between his thought and his art. It is, I think, in a study of such devices as detachment, ambiguity, irony—and the general stylization resulting from them—that the nature of his thought and achievements of his art can best be seen. They provide the fascinating spectacle of a novelist attempting to be a philosopher by means of a subtle and original deployment of the resources of prose fiction.

Novels by Camus:

L'Étranger, Paris, Gallimard, 1942.
> *The Outsider* (trs. Stuart Gilbert), London, Hamish Hamilton, 1946, and Penguin Books, 1961.
> (This same translation issued as *The Stranger*, New York, Knopf, 1946.)

La Peste, Paris, Gallimard, 1947.
> *The Plague* (trs. Stuart Gilbert), London, Hamish Hamilton, 1948, and Penguin Books, 1960; New York, Knopf, 1948.

La Chute, Paris, Gallimard, 1956.
> *The Fall* (trs. Justin O'Brien), London, Hamish Hamilton, 1957; New York, Knopf, 1957.

Collected short stories;

L'Exil et le royaume, Paris, Gallimard, 1957.
> *Exile and the Kingdom* (trs. Justin O'Brien), London, Hamish Hamilton, 1958; New York, Knopf, 1958.

(All the above items, in the translations listed, are published in a single volume, *The Collected Fiction of Albert Camus*, London, Hamish Hamilton, 1961.)

ALAIN ROBBE-GRILLET
b. 1922

BY JOHN WEIGHTMAN

————————★————————

OF the group of writers who have made their names recently as exponents of that elusive entity, *le nouveau roman*, Robbe-Grillet is the most remarkable. In the space of seven years he has produced four novels, *Les Gommes* (1953), *Le Voyeur* (1955), *La Jalousie* (1957), *Dans le labyrinthe* (1959), and two striking manifestoes. In public lectures and newspaper interviews he has proclaimed again and again that the time has come to bring about in the novel the aesthetic revolution that has already been accomplished in music and the fine arts. At first, both his books and his theoretical statements aroused considerable opposition, and he had the honour of being publicly chided by François Mauriac for dehumanizing literature. By now he has won a considerable measure of acceptance; he is established as an authoritative figure on the Parisian literary scene, and the English translation of his third book, *Jealousy*, recently awakened admiring interest in this country. Yet the philosophical implications and the artistic value of his work are not easy to determine. One can waste a lot of time trying to find analogies between him and the other main figures of the experimental trend, particularly since he has gathered them around him at the Éditions de Minuit, of which he is principal reader. Nathalie Sarraute, Michel Butor, Claude Simon, and others are sometimes classed as a school of which Robbe-Grillet is supposed to be the centre. Actually, the chief resemblance between these various writers is their opposition to the so-called 'traditional', 'bourgeois', or 'Balzacian' novel and the view of life it is said to convey; and even this opposition is complicated, because Butor declares himself to be a passionate

Balzacian. As regards their positive activity, each of these experimental novelists has to be taken separately. It is not certain that they admire each other or even read each other's works. Therefore the study of the others—apart from Butor, who is to some extent an imitator of Robbe-Grillet—has little bearing on the understanding of Robbe-Grillet himself. A further difficulty is that his theoretical statements are much clearer than his actual practice and, in fact, do not refer to the most puzzling aspects of his work. In spite of his readiness to defend his version of *le nouveau roman* in public debate, he seems to me to be reticent about his basic impulses. These I cannot deduce with any confidence from his novels, and I may as well admit the limitations of my approach at the outset. I find his ideas interesting and his French beautifully precise, but I cannot fully respond to any of his novels, at least if I try to read them as novels. Each is enigmatic, and I am uncertain about the quality of the enigma; all the more so, indeed, since Robbe-Grillet himself has declared, rather perversely perhaps, that he dislikes mysteries.

* * *

Theoretically he has two main attitudes which concern, respectively, our view of the external world and our grasp of the internal reality of the mind. The first of these he has expounded excellently in his two manifestoes, published in *La Nouvelle Nouvelle Revue Française*—'Une voie pour le roman futur' (July 1956) and 'Nature, humanisme et tragédie' (October 1958). The second he mentions incidentally, without defending it in such a convincing way.

He has never admitted any special indebtedness to Sartre, but he can be placed in the post-Sartrian line of development because of his sense of the alien character of the world and his anti-bourgeois reflexes. When asked about his literary ancestry, he replies: 'The first fifty pages of Camus's *L'Étranger* and the works of Raymond Roussel'. (Roussel is a comparatively unknown writer who died in the early 'thirties and was eccentric to the point of madness.) A scientist by training and more especially an expert in tropical agriculture, Robbe-Grillet shows no signs of wide literary reading, but it seems probable that he was also influenced by Kafka, Simenon, and Graham Greene, to mention only three names that come to mind as one reads his books. Yet he is nearest to Sartre in his obsession with inanimate objects, while going one step farther than Sartre in asserting that our normal apprehension of the external world is corrupted by a long tradition of bourgeois humanism. In fact he criticizes both Sartre and Camus (after the first fifty pages of *L'Étranger*) very vigorously for yielding to the sentimentality of the traditional view, when they are in the very act of proclaiming the irreducible nature of the material universe. They are guilty of using metaphors, and in Robbe-Grillet's opinion a metaphor is either a falsehood or a capitulation. To speak, for instance, of the 'majesty' of a mountain or of a village 'nestling' in a valley is to postulate, between man and the material world, an emotional relationship which does not exist, or only exists through an illusion. The mountain has a certain height and a certain form; majesty is a conception foisted on to it by us. The village nestles only if, for a moment, we transfer our human personality to it. Of course, such a metaphorical use of language goes a long way back before the beginnings of bourgeois humanism and, if pressed, Robbe-Grillet will even admit that all language was originally metaphorical. He probably singles out the bourgeois humanist for attack because the confident humanist, more than anyone else, has assumed that the world is man's domain. In Robbe-Grillet's view, this is not so. The material creation just is, independently of man. Language can be used to define it from the human angle of vision provided we are careful to show that there is no complicity between things as they are and our human emotions. Hence his now famous descriptive passages, which consist of minute definitions of shapes, colours, and distances.

What Robbe-Grillet is condemning is obviously the anthropomorphic use of nature as a sounding-board or a reflector. We have referred to this in English, since Ruskin's day, as the pathetic fallacy, a term for which there is no convenient equivalent in French. His objection to it really takes two different forms: he sees in it (*a*) the germ of tragedy and (*b*) the first step towards the illicit creation of God. He cannot reproach Sartre, the atheist, with any weakness for God, but he can, and does, suspect him of describing the absurdity of the world in such a way that the description itself has the cathartic effect of producing a form of reconciliation. The hero of *La Nausée* lives in a highly dramatic relationship of discordance with his surroundings, and this causes him to make a plentiful use of metaphor. Roquentin deluges the chestnut tree in the municipal park at Bouville with comparisons, all unfavourable but all indicative—according to Robbe-Grillet—of a sort of appropriation through hatred. For him, the general tone of *La Nausée* is one of intense uneasiness metaphorically defined, and therefore accepted with suspicious tragic resignation:

... Roquentin's melancholy bachelorhood, his lost love, his 'ruined life', the sombre, ludicrous fate of the Autodidact, the general curse of earthly living, may thus seem to be raised to the level of a higher necessity. But in this case, what becomes of liberty? Those who refuse to accept the curse lay themselves open to the supreme moral condemnation: they will be termed 'stinkers'. It is as if Sartre—who cannot be accused of essentialism—had, in this book at least, carried the ideas of *nature* and *tragedy* to their furthest extreme. Once again the struggle against these ideas has only served to give them new strength (*N.N.R.F.*, October 1958, pp. 598–9).

How far Robbe-Grillet evolved this criticism on his own and how far it may have been suggested by the neo-Marxist critic, Roland Barthes, is uncertain. Before Robbe-Grillet produced any theoretical writing, Barthes had published in *Critique* (July 1954) an enthusiastic analysis of Robbe-Grillet's first novel, *Les Gommes*, which he saw as an original attempt to treat the world without making any concessions to the suspicious softness of tragedy. When Robbe-Grillet came to write 'Nature, humanisme et tragédie' in 1958, he used an extract from another of Barthes's articles as an epigraph, as if he fully agreed with Barthes's analysis of his work and accepted the programme that Barthes outlines:

Tragedy is merely a way of retrieving [*recueillir*] human unhappiness, of subsuming it, and thus of justifying it in the form of necessity, wisdom or purification: the rejection of this process and the search for the technical means of avoiding the trap it lays (nothing is more insidious than tragedy) is a necessary undertaking today (*N.N.R.F.*, October 1958, p. 580).

Other neo-Marxist critics have taken the opposite view that genuine tragedy, which is only possible in the absence of religious belief, is a bracing manifestation of man's Promethean struggle against the unknown. Without entering into the vexed question of the true nature of genuine tragedy, we can assume at least that Robbe-Grillet's objection to the tragic mode is a matter of temperament, quite unconnected with any desire for political action. He has never shown any interest in politics. His anti-tragic conviction is linked with the belief that the tragic softening introduced by metaphor indicates a mistaken contemplative attitude towards the universe. To put it bluntly, if you begin by using metaphors, you may end by believing in God, because God is no more than the most generalized form of the pathetic fallacy. (Sartre has not borne this out, but Camus seemed to be almost on the point of doing so in his last book.) In a striking paragraph, Robbe-Grillet reformulates the Marxist and Freudian view that God is a projection of the human sense of mystery, a hypostatization of the human thirst for an answer to the riddle of the universe. The passage, incidentally, would make a good philosophical commentary on Walter de la Mare's poem, *The Listeners*:

I call out. No one answers. Instead of concluding that there is no one there—which might be purely and simply an ascertainable fact, dated and localized in space and time—I decide to behave as if there were someone there, someone who, for reasons unknown, refrained from answering. From then on, the silence which follows my calling out is no longer a *true* silence; it is endowed with a content, a depth, a soul—and this soul refers me back to mine. The distance between my cry, still ringing in my own ears, and my silent (perhaps deaf) vis-à-vis to whom it is addressed, becomes an anguish, a hope and a despair; it gives a meaning to my life. Henceforth, the only thing I shall attach importance to will be this false emptiness and the problems it sets me. Ought I to go on calling out? Should I shout more loudly? Should I use a different set of words? Again I try . . . I very soon realize that no one will answer; but the invisible presence that I continue to create by calling out forces me to go on forever breaking the silence with my unhappy cry. Soon the reverberating sound begins to confuse me. Spellbound, as it were, I call out again . . . and again. In the end, my distraught consciousness translates my exasperated solitude into a higher necessity and a promise of redemption (*N.N.R.F.*, October 1958, p. 590).

Ultimately, then, Robbe-Grillet objects to metaphors because they are tragic, and to tragedy because it is a veiled form of religion. One may wonder, of course, whether the systematic avoidance of metaphor does not denote a tension, which might be called a religious fear of religion. More happy-go-lucky unbelievers may risk an occasional metaphor as a means of wry communication with their fellows, without feeling that they are capitulating to the unknown. However, we can recognize Robbe-Grillet's initial endeavour as another attempt to 'purify the language of the tribe'. He is really trying to abolish the last vestiges of the primitive magic of the Name.

It is perhaps worth mentioning that, as Robbe-Grillet himself explains, this obstinately concrete view of the external world is not entirely the result of a direct vision of things as they are but rather an effect of the cinema, and would probably have been inconceivable at an earlier period before the cinema or television screen became part of everyday living. He points out that even the most banal film, which merely aims at telling a story, has an unintentional and surprising feature, quite independent of the plot. Conventional scenes, when they are photographed, may take on an unconventional air:

In the original novel, the objects and gestures which formed the substance of the plot disappeared entirely to be replaced by their pure significance; an empty chair was no more than an absence or an expectation, a hand placed on a shoulder was simply a mark of sympathy, iron bars at a window merely signified the impossibility of escape. . . . But now we *see* the chair, the movement of the hand and the shape of the bars. Their significance remains flagrant, but instead of monopolizing our attention, seems to be an addition or even a superfluity, because what strikes us, persists in the memory and proves essential, irreducible to vague mental notions, is the gestures themselves, the objects, movements and outlines to which *reality* has suddenly and involuntarily been restored by the fact of their being photographed.

It may seem strange that these fragments of brute reality unwittingly offered us by the filmed story should strike us so forcibly, when identical scenes in our everyday existence would be incapable of curing our blindness. It seems that the conventions of photography (its two-dimensional character, black and white colouring, the limitations of the frame, the differences in scale according to the type of shot) help to free us from our own conventions[1] (*N.N.R.F.*, July 1956, pp. 81–82).

This explains why, in reading Robbe-Grillet, we so often have the impression that we are not following an action taking place in real life but watching a film, the sound-track of which has gone dead or is working only intermittently. Here again, his assumption is debatable. Some of us may be made uneasy by the documentary content of filmed stories precisely because the cinema can so easily give enormous significance to a branch tossing in the breeze or a shadow moving over a wall. Artistic documentaries exploit this facility quite shamelessly. Robbe-Grillet is clearly not in favour of such a tendency, but does he realize that the pathetic fallacy may be all the more powerful through being inarticulate, or through being expressed indirectly? You may destroy the illusory 'romantic heart of things', jeeringly referred to by Barthes, and yet replace it by an equally dubious form of *lacrimae rerum*, which clings to the surface like a film of dew. For me, Robbe-Grillet's descriptions often have the charm of mathematical spells; that is, his attempt to abolish one form of magic leads to the creation of another.

* * *

Some of the critics who have accused Robbe-Grillet of dehumanizing the novel may have been exasperated by his elaborate visual descriptions, but what they are really disturbed about is the rather different matter of the absence in his work of any recognizable, traditional, psychological content. Both Barthes and Robbe-Grillet pass very quickly over this point, as if its connexion with the objective inventory of the external world were obvious. In his review-article on *Les Gommes*, entitled 'Une Littérature objective', Barthes merely says towards the end that

---

[1] Sartre has admitted to a comparable revelation through the cinema. He says that the satisfaction of watching photographed scenes helped him to grasp the notion of the urge towards coincidence with being.

he is not going to discuss the book as a story except to point out that:

> . . . interiority is put between brackets; objects and spaces and the movement of man from one to the other are promoted to the rank of subjects. The novel becomes a direct experience of man's environment without his being able to claim to have any form of psychology, metaphysics or psychoanalysis with which to approach the objective setting he discovers around him (*Critique*, July 1954, p. 591).

Robbe-Grillet, in his first manifesto, devotes only one paragraph to the question of psychological content. I quote it together with the preceding paragraph to show how the transition, or rather the jump, is made:

Thus objects will gradually lose their uncertainty and their secrets, will abandon their false mysteriousness, the dubious interiority that Roland Barthes has called 'the romantic heart of things'. Things will no longer be the vague reflection of the hero's vague soul, the image of his sufferings or supports for his desires. Or rather, should it happen that things still accept such tyranny, the acceptance will only be apparent, the better to show how remote from it they remain.[2]

As for the characters of the novel, they themselves can admit of a great variety of interpretations; according to the reader's interests, they can give rise to any sort of psychological, psychiatric, religious or political commentary. It will soon be noticed how indifferent they are to such so-called wealth. Whereas the traditional hero is constantly warped, overwhelmed or destroyed by the 'interpretations' the author suggests for him, and constantly relegated to an intangible and unstable *elsewhere*, ever more remote and indistinct, the hero of the future, on the contrary, will stay put. The commentaries will all be 'elsewhere'; compared with his irrefutable presence, they will appear useless, superfluous and even dishonest (*N.N.R.F.*, July 1946, pp. 82–83).

This appears to be all Robbe-Grillet has written on the subject, apart from ridiculing the traditional notion that it is the novelist's business to 'delve deep' into human nature. What he calls 'the old myths of profundity' are to be discredited. As for 'human nature', he treats it in debate as a comic, outmoded expression; he will counter an objection with the remark: 'Ah, vous croyez encore à la nature humaine, vous!' Perhaps he is again going one

---

[2] I notice, on translating this sentence, that it adopts the linguistic form of attributing volition to things. A lapse from doctrinal purity?

step farther than the existentialists by amplifying their concept of freedom to the point of saying that a man cannot be defined except as a behaviour pattern at a given moment. To analyse soul-states confidently in terms of love, hate, ambition, or any other such fluctuating abstractions is no doubt to be as sloppy in one's approach to inner reality as one is in dealing with the external world in terms of metaphor. In these internal applications the traditional vocabulary is even more charged with dubious significance; therefore—Robbe-Grillet might say—get rid of it altogether, show your character in a given situation without committing yourself to any supposition about his inner reality.

He once declared in a newspaper interview that it is not the artist's business to provide an explanation but to create an object, and clearly he wants his books to have the solidity and independent existence of a statue or a picture, which resists any anecdotal or intellectual summary. This is perhaps not as new an ambition as he implies. Camus, in *L'Étranger*, had concentrated on behaviour and had left it ultimately unexplained, and he, one imagines, had been prompted to do this by the example of such writers as Hemingway who emphasized action and treated cogitation as effeminate and therefore to be missed out. As a matter of fact all the great novelists, when one comes to look at them closely, are far more descriptive than explanatory; this, it could be maintained, is true even of Proust, who carried the 'psychological novel' to the farthest point it has so far achieved. When Robbe-Grillet denounces the 'traditional' novel he appears to be thinking of the mechanical repetition of worn-out devices by inferior novelists; as far as I know he has not discussed Proust or Tolstoy or Stendhal. But he is purely 'creative' in that he is not interested in the appreciation of other people's work but only in expressing his own vision. And the only aspect of this vision he has explained fairly clearly is the treatment of objects; his characters are mysteriously non-traditional, not only because we are given fragmentary information about their internal reality but also because the whole texture in which they are set is mysterious. We are uncertain about their objective actions, about the objective relationships between them, about the time in which the events are taking place. Each book, of course, far from being an example of 'objective literature', is a highly subjective pattern, signed Robbe-Grillet.

*   *   *

In his first novel, *Les Gommes*, Robbe-Grillet has not yet got quite into his stride and he even allows himself, perhaps inadvertently, a few metaphors. Barthes says he can see only one: the hero goes into a stationer's shop and asks for a very soft indiarubber—'une gomme très douce' ('douce' = soft, gentle, sweet). There are more obvious ones than that: an alarm-clock stops ringing—'avec étonnement sur quelques sons avortés' (with astonishment, after a few abortive sounds) and a café-proprietor, reflected in the mirrors of his establishment, is likened to a fish in an aquarium. More important still, the characters are fairly traditional. The café-proprietor might have come out of Simenon and there are a score of other characters who are analysed to a certain extent and even hold intelligible conversations with each other. The originality lies in the construction and in some of the descriptions.

The framework is that of the thriller-detective story. A gang of terrorists are systematically assassinating key-figures in the country; not famous men, but important, lesser-known people. The scene is set in an unnamed provincial town where Professor Dupont, an economist, has been shot at in his study by a hired gunman. Dupont has only been wounded in the arm but in agreement with the Minister of the Interior he lets it be known that he has died of his wound in a private nursing-home. He is actually hidden in the nursing-home and is scheduled to leave for Paris the next day in an official car. The local police are instructed not to pursue their inquiry and are kept in ignorance of the real events. A special agent, Wallas, is sent from Paris to take up the case, but he too, incomprehensibly, is unaware of the real situation. We see the action mainly through his eyes as he wanders around the town trying to pick up the threads. He eventually finds his way into the professor's house on the next evening, at seven-thirty, which is the time at which all the previous assassinations have taken place. The professor has arranged that a friend should go to the house to collect some important papers needed in Paris. But this friend has received a threatening letter and has left the town in a panic, so the professor has to call at the house himself. Wallas, thinking presumably that he is another assassin, fires at him and kills him, just at the moment when the local police inspector is trying to get in touch with him, Wallas, to put forward the theory that Dupont was not assassinated after all, but has just disappeared. The professor is therefore genuinely killed, although twenty-four hours late. Wallas has shot the man whose murder he was investigating.

There is a marked comic element in *Les Gommes*, which might be taken at first sight as a parody of a detective story. We know from the start that the victim has not been killed and that the police and the special agent are fumbling in the dark. Robbe-Grillet seems to have set himself the task of maintaining suspense when the solution has already been given. He does this mainly by telling the story from Wallas's limited viewpoint and hinting at mysterious connexions. Some of the other characters are suspicious of Wallas, who bears a puzzling resemblance to the supposed murderer. We know that Wallas came to the town years ago with his mother to visit someone. It is rumoured that Dupont had an illegitimate son with whom he was on bad terms. Is Wallas the assassin and the son? He cannot be, because we have already been introduced to the gunman and the leader of his gang, yet the doubt persists to the end.

The action also involves various loose ends. Wallas is constantly getting lost in the town and coming to a swing-bridge (can the link be 'du pont' = of the bridge?).[3] Stranger still, he goes into a stationer's shop, which happens to be kept by Dupont's estranged wife, and asks for a soft indiarubber of a particular kind. While he is in the back of this same shop on a later occasion, someone else, apparently the real gunman, also comes in and buys an

---

[3] I have also heard it suggested that the bridge, when down and closed, is a symbol of infinity, because it then allows endless movement. It is true that a raised swing-bridge—and this bridge is often raised—can be profoundly disturbing, because it indicates a break in the continuity of life, and a neurotic, such as Wallas apparently is, must often have the feeling that the thread of intelligibility in life has snapped.

indiarubber. We are never told why these indiarubbers were purchased and they are not referred to again. They can hardly be symbols since Robbe-Grillet's declared policy, as we have seen, is to divest inanimate matter of its psychological accretions. Barthes speaks of 'the mysterious gratuity of the object which gives its title to the book like a paradox or an enigma'. The indiarubbers must be anti-symbols, put in to show that we should not go looking for symbols. The French have a jocular, untranslatable phrase: *Mystère et boule de gomme*; it occurs to me that Robbe-Grillet, engaged on writing a false mystery story, may have indulged in a play on the word *gomme* purely as a mystification, in the hope of teasing earnest academic minds. Or perhaps he was fascinated by the texture of soft rubber and just wanted to describe it, irrespective of the plot, as a painter will put in an extraneous object because of its surface quality. I detect a strongly sensuous note in the apparent austereness of his description of the various types of rubber, and I completely disagree with Barthes who maintains that Robbe-Grillet's style is 'the opposite of poetic writing'.

This brings me back to a question I raised earlier. When Robbe-Grillet gives a carefully non-metaphorical, or apparently non-metaphorical description of an object, what exactly is he doing? He makes two statements, which may be rather contradictory: (*a*) that he is showing things as they are, shorn of human associations; (*b*) that he is bringing out their true strangeness. But if things just are, they are not strange. Strangeness is a human emotion. If we were God, creation would not be strange; it would be ordinary to us, coterminous with us. But we are not God, and therefore consciousness, our awareness of creation, is a perpetual sensation of attempted adjustment and always involves emotion. Robbe-Grillet does not want this emotion to be sloppy or untidy and so, in his most characteristic passages, he rejects all openly emotional words. Yet when his descriptions are good they are emotional though austere, and successful both for himself and for the reader. When they are tedious it seems to be because he is doggedly applying his rule of 'no emotion' with a literalism that tells against himself; or because the particular reader who is bored does not happen to be fascinated, as he is, by the details he is noting down. The descriptions in *Les Gommes* do not bore me and I think it would be easy to prove that all the best ones are metaphorical, poetic, and often humorous. For instance, when Wallas goes into an automatic snack-bar and helps himself to a dish of cold herring, hard-boiled egg, and sliced tomato, there is obvious satire, of a rather geometrical nature, in the vision of identical diners consuming identical sets of food. A separate paragraph, which is in fact a prose poem, is devoted to one piece of tomato; the segment of lovingly described vegetable flesh blooms with comical inappropriateness in the middle of the murder-story.

My objection to *Les Gommes* is that the book is basically frivolous, in spite of the exquisite care that has gone into the writing. The plot might be described as an elaborate open puzzle, full of false trails, blind alleys, and apparently meaningless symmetries. Robbe-Grillet can describe the human, psychological world very well when he wants to, or at least certain incidental aspects of it, but he seems to be mainly interested in building up his complex structure of wilful enigmas and engineered surprises. As a serious novel on the usual level this structure does not constitute a dense artistic object; the conspiracy, the detective work, the personal relationships are all flimsy. If the book is serious, it is a form of literary nightmare, and such a nightmare would result from, and appeal to, psychological complexities that Robbe-Grillet is not prepared to discuss.

*   *   *

With *Le Voyeur*, Robbe-Grillet's personal style of writing is fully established. The title must be a pun on *voyeur*, in the sexual sense, and the act of seeing, but is perhaps not quite appropriate because the hero seems to be a doer rather than a watcher. He is a commercial traveller, Mathias, who returns for a day to his native island off the mainland to sell watches. The country is not specified; the local money is 'crowns', yet the family names are French. We can perhaps assume that we are in Robbe-Grillet's native Brittany and that the exotic currency is just a way of indicating a lack of relationship with contemporary life. As in

Les Gommes, the action is circular and seems to be about to take place in twenty-four hours. As the boat is putting in to land Mathias picks up a looped piece of string from the deck, catches the eye of a little girl who is one of the passengers, and sees gulls floating overhead. These three objects are to occur again and again in the narrative because they provide links with Mathias's childhood; he had a passion for collecting pieces of string; he once spent many hours drawing a gull in profile; and a girl called Violette has some unexplained meaning for him. Once on the island, he hires a bicycle and goes off to sell his wares. Up to about eleven-thirty his movements are clear, and then again a few minutes later. During the gap in the action a girl called Jacqueline, who had been minding sheep on a lonely cliff-top, disappears. She is eventually found, naked, and dead, at the bottom of the cliff. Mathias, after the break, appears very anxious and does not seem at first to be able to remember what has happened. Gradually we realize that he has committed a sadistic murder, using the string and establishing an equivalence between Violette and Jacqueline, who are interchangeable in his mind. Or, if he is not guilty, he imagines the crime very vividly and behaves like a guilty person. In spite of making a violent attempt to get back to the harbour before the boat leaves on the return voyage, he arrives too late and has to wait two days longer until the next boat arrives. He gets a chance to sail on a cargo-boat but does not take it, apparently because he does not want to give the impression that he is running away. During the two days, he returns to the scene of the crime (or imagines he does) to remove some shreds of the girl's clothes and the half-consumed cigarettes that he used to torture her with. It is assumed by the islanders that the girl fell over the cliff and that the waves stripped her bare and the fish damaged her body. Mathias takes the regular boat back to the mainland.

It is impossible to be sure what 'really' happens and what is imaginary, since we are inside Mathias's mind, which oscillates between present, past, and future, between the positive and the hypothetical, as if it were a cinema-screen on which various episodes, true or false, were being projected in a jumbled chronological sequence, yet all with equal brilliance. The fact that everything is seen in the same bright light is at first novel and attractive; then, for me at any rate, it begins to pall, because I feel mental reality to be much more complex than the simple snapping backwards or forwards into reminiscence or supposition. Then again, the structure of the book is ingenious rather than enlightening. All we know about Mathias is that he has an obsession with string, girls—particularly the napes of their necks—and sea-gulls. These motifs occur in different guises, but they do not develop. The figure-eight shape of the loop of string is repeated by two nails in the harbour-wall and by two knots in the wood of an imaginary door; Violette-Jacqueline is, at the same time, a girl glimpsed through an open window on the way to the boat, the little girl on the boat, a girl on a cinema-poster, a waitress in a café, and so on. It may be that a sadistic murderer sees the same few monotonous patterns repeating themselves on all sides; if so, his mind is not, in that respect, very interesting. However, if Robbe-Grillet is working off genuine obsessions, well and good. But my guess is that he has taken hints from elementary psychiatry and is seeing how cleverly he can ring the changes on them. He is again constructing an open puzzle, rather than writing a novel. It is hardly possible to consider Mathias as a character who 'stays put' and admits of an indefinite number of interpretations. At any moment, he is what he sees, either in actual fact or in his mind's eye. Most of what he sees merely defines the setting (I say 'merely', but these are the best parts in my view, because they often consist of Robbe-Grillet's peculiar brand of prose poetry, which has no necessary connexion with being a sadistic murderer); sometimes what he sees is meant to indicate his mental reality, but these indications are rudimentary. If Robbe-Grillet is prepared to suggest a link between a passion for bits of string and a tendency to sadistic murder, he is accepting the beginnings of a psychological theory. Why, then, does he not carry it farther? Perhaps because he does not claim to know very much about the inner workings of a sadistic murderer. But in that case, why write a story about one? I can only repeat that he seems to me to be constructing a puzzle, which has some of the peculiarities of a dream or a nightmare.

On re-reading *Le Voyeur*, I am struck by a paradoxical quality of the writing. The descriptions are at once vivid and uncanny, as if there were no reliable links between phenomena. A scene I particularly like is Mathias's lunch on the first day. He is in a café when he is hailed as a childhood friend by a sailor whom he does not recognize. This sailor, with a bottle of wine in either hand, leads him along the seashore to a house where they eat crabs and potatoes boiled in their jackets, served by a mysterious girl with a scratch on the nape of her neck. The sailor is ebullient and incoherent, jovial and yet incomprehensibly cross. At the end of the meal, Mathias gives the girl a watch and murmurs in her ear some words that he himself does not understand (we are inside his mind and the words are not made comprehensible to us). On the sailor's door is the name 'Jean Robin', but we have already learned that this person died years before. To me the effect is exactly that of a dream, because it is only in dreams that I see things in patches, with exaggerated realism, accompanied by the sensation that all logical connexions have dissolved. I enjoy the episode, I admire the writing, yet I cannot take the passage quite seriously because after a while I want to wake up and escape from the gratuitousness of the dream. But it must be precisely to create this dream-like atmosphere that Robbe-Grillet writes, since it surrounds Wallas's wanderings in *Les Gommes* and recurs in *La Jalousie* and *Dans le labyrinthe*.

* * *

In *La Jalousie*, which shows a still greater novelty of technique, the musicality of construction, already noticeable in the earlier books, becomes clearer. *Le Voyeur* has a narrative in which Mathias's obsessions keep recurring with something like a rhythm, between the initial blast on the ship's siren and a corresponding blast at the finale. *La Jalousie* opens and closes with the shadow of a pillar on a tropical balcony, and has no consecutive narrative at all. It is divided up into what one might call 'movements'. This time, so the summary on the back-cover informs us, we are inside the mind of a jealous husband, a colonial banana-grower, who is watching, and reflecting on, the behaviour of his wife whom he suspects of having an affair with a neighbouring planter. The wife is referred to by her initial, A; the suspected neighbour is called Frank; the husband has no name and neither speaks nor refers to himself internally as 'I'. But for the indication on the back-cover, we might have some difficulty at first in guessing that the book consists of visions succeeding each other in the husband's mind. Like Mathias, he is sometimes watching actual happenings and sometimes living or reliving the future and the past in his imagination. Once we have gone through the book we can reconstitute the story, which is comparatively simple. There is a suspicious air of connivance between A and Frank as they sip their drinks or discuss a book they have been reading; Frank says he has to go down to the coast on business; A says she will go with him to do some shopping; they fail to return at the expected time and spend the night in a hotel; perhaps they committed adultery, perhaps not; they come back with the explanation that the car broke down; life resumes its normal course, except that the relationship between A and Frank now seems less close.

As has been excellently shown by Bruce Morrissette, a great admirer of Robbe-Grillet,[4] the husband's visions are arranged in a pattern of increasing intensity up to the point at which the supposed adultery is imagined as taking place, and then they go on repeating with diminishing force and less coherence until the book stops. Mr. Morrissette does not go so far as to say that the whole pattern of the book is supposed to indicate the rise and fall of sexuality, but this may very well be so. Perhaps it is all the retrospective, auto-erotic meditation of a jealous man who has never made up his mind what to think about his wife's behaviour. More likely, the meditation is roughly contemporaneous with the action. But, in either case, the pulsation is intended to be an important part of the aesthetic effect.

The word 'meditation' is really inappropriate, because the hero is not thinking in words nor is he controlling the flow of images in any way or passing judgement on them. Very precise words are being used to describe the setting and the movements of the

[4] 'En relisant Robbe-Grillet', *Critique*, July 1959, pp. 579-608.

characters, but they belong to the author's language, not to the hero's, and their purpose is, ostensibly, to translate as accurately as possible a succession of visual experiences. As in the previous novels, certain objects have an obsessive force; the cubes of ice that go into the drinks are loaded with the ambiguities of the conversation, of which we hear only a few banal snatches; a centipede, which Frank crushes on the wall, is connected with A's supposed sexual excitement, so much so that the husband imagines Frank crushing another centipede on the bedroom wall in the hotel before consummating the adultery; the husband's passion for his wife seems to be concentrated in the act of watching her brush her hair. Just as the image of the murdered girl echoes through *Le Voyeur* in various forms, so in *La Jalousie* the sound of the brush on A's hair is linked with the sizzling noise made by the centipede and the distant roar of cars and lorries as the husband is waiting for the couple to return.

Although, from the technical point of view, these elements are impeccably woven together, the book is, for me, frankly boring, except in those places where I can enjoy the delicious pedanticism of a description—that of the ice-cubes, for instance, or of a constellation of midges. I much prefer a comparable story, such as Somerset Maugham's *The Painted Veil*, written without any technical innovation. Robbe-Grillet's conventions here seem to be strangling the human interest of the situation and creating limitations which are more damaging than those of the 'traditional' novel. I had doubts about the bits of string in *Le Voyeur*; I have even graver doubts about the sound-associations between hair-brushing, the centipede, and the motorcar. Once more, Robbe-Grillet is building a structure which has its own rigidly respected laws, but these laws seem to be ingenious rather than true. Nor can I feel the presence of the husband as a jealous man. Like Wallas and Mathias, he is a sort of numb centre to the action. The note on the back-cover says:

The character has neither name nor face. He is a void at the heart of the world, a hollow set amongst objects. But since all the lines start from him or converge on him, the hollow becomes as concrete, as solid as the objects, if not more so.

Not for me, I am sorry to say, even after more than one reading. I would expect a jealous man to argue with himself, to use language to some extent even in his private thoughts, to debate the moral issue, to be tempted even to some degree of inner eloquence by the very fact of his jealousy. Obsessional images connected with personal relationships are surely always accompanied by a fringe of rhetoric, even in comparatively inarticulate minds. Robbe-Grillet has amputated language from his hero's consciousness and has reduced it to a patterned flow of images. The interior monologue has been replaced by an interior film with a few sound effects and an occasional snatch of dialogue. For all the apparent austerity, this may be a facile solution. At first, one is inclined to think that it must be a difficult exercise to write a novel in the first person without using the pronoun 'I'. Actually, it may be a way of avoiding the most difficult aspect of writing because it removes the central part of consciousness where value judgements are made. It is this book which should be called *Le Voyeur*, since the hero does not engage with reality at all. Mr. Morrissette claims that he does, because we can deduce from the text that he is present at the dinner-table and makes an occasional remark. However, he is hardly more operative than an observant mute, and although he watches the other two characters, they have no relationship with him, or if they have, it has all been left out as if it were not relevant. He himself may 'act' slightly, in an inward fashion; he imagines, for instance, at the peak of his jealousy that the guilty couple have crashed on the road and are being burned to death, but this again is very simple psychology. A pair of eyes, backed by a crude and obvious surge of resentment, is not much of a man. I should say that the charge of dehumanization is justified here. Robbe-Grillet's brain is working first on the autonomous plan of the structure and secondly on the meticulous definition of certain portions of the external world. It is not working on the emotion of jealousy; he deliberately leaves off before the point at which Proust begins. Admittedly, he creates 'a something which is not the traditional novel', as Geoffrey Grigson has said; I appreciate the technical interest of the 'something', but for the rest I am reminded of Orwell's judgement on

Charles Morgan's novels: 'The furniture is more alive than the people.'

*   *   *

The latest work, *Dans le labyrinthe*, is perhaps the most curious of all. The dream-like atmosphere is still more pronounced than before, yet the book opens with a preface stating that it deals with concrete fact:

> The subject . . . is a strictly material reality, in the sense that this reality does not claim to have any allegorical value. The reader is therefore invited to see in it only the things, gestures, words and events that he is informed about, without seeking to give them either more or less significance than in his own life or his own death.

However, the word 'death' has an ominous ring, which is borne out by the dark and brooding atmosphere of the story. The main part of the plot concerns a soldier who is wandering through a snow-covered town at night, to find a certain street, the name of which he has forgotten. He is carrying a cardboard box, which he is to hand over to a relative of one of his fallen comrades. He is haunted by a small boy, who keeps appearing and disappearing in the lamp-light like a will-o'-the-wisp. The soldier goes into a private house, a café, and a sort of barracks, and everywhere the air is heavy with foreboding because the army has been defeated and the enemy occupation forces are expected to arrive at any moment. In the end, the soldier appears to be shot accidentally by a military patrol and he dies after a period of delirium; or perhaps he is still alive and starts walking the streets again.

The book is, in the first place, a conundrum, and since the note on the back-cover does not supply the key this time, we have to guess at a solution. There is an 'I' in the story, at the beginning and the end, and here again the conclusion echoes the opening. This 'I' is in a closed room where there is a picture of a café-scene entitled 'The Defeat of Reichenfels' and containing some of the characters who figure in the story: the soldier, the little boy, a café-proprietor, etc. The 'I' also says at the end that he arrived too late to give the soldier a third injection, so he is presumably a doctor. The only explanation I can think of is that the doctor has been attending a real soldier after a real defeat, and that the body of the book is a dream or day-dream in which the characters of the picture come alive and are fused with the events of his immediate life. The main ambiguity arises from the fact that sometimes we seem to be inside the soldier and sometimes watching him from outside. It is only in dreams that we can both watch a person and be that person.

Despite Robbe-Grillet's preliminary warning, some critics at once suggested that the soldier wandering through the labyrinthine streets and carrying a box under his arm was man, lost in the trackless world and looking for God in order to hand back his soul to Him. It is difficult to tell whether the author was flattered or exasperated by this interpretation. In either case, since he had put only a few banal letters in the box, the human soul could not be said, on this view, to be a very precious object. I imagine that he honestly did not intend any allegorical meaning. Like *Les Gommes* and *Le Voyeur*, the book is to some extent a mystification, which is a different thing from an allegory. At the same time it is, more clearly than the three other books, a prose poem. The themes are snow, silent houses, light and darkness and receding perspectives. The language is not quite so sober as before because it has acquired a rhythm, and there are some fine bravura passages, in particular a wonderful description of a woman taking flight and disappearing up an echoing staircase. The soldier, the little boy, and what must be the most cherished lamp-post in all literature keep floating in and out of the reader's ken like visions in a crystal ball. As a 'Tale of Mystery and Imagination' the book is undoubtedly a success. I cannot imagine how Robbe-Grillet thought up the details, yet I can see that they all have a compulsive force. But, much as I admire the virtuosity of the writing, I cannot get any general satisfaction from the book because the structure and the meaning elude my intellectual grasp. Robbe-Grillet might say that this is precisely a proof of its being a work of art, that is an irreducible aesthetic object. I should have to answer that subjective fantasy, however compulsive and however severely ordered according to self-invented rules, may be simply the opposite extreme from the *roman à thèse*. I can only record my, perhaps obtuse, impression that *Dans le labyrinthe* remains wraith-like and, no less than *La Jalousie*, involves considerable tedium.

*   *   *

If I have not completely misunderstood him, Robbe-Grillet appears, then, to be established on two major intellectual contradictions.

He wants to cleanse the external world of the pathetic fallacy and show us things as they are, independently of human emotions. In fact, his descriptions are prose poetry and, in his view of the world, objects are apprehended with an unusual, almost mad, intensity. Although he uses accurate, quasi-scientific language, he bears less resemblance to a scientist than to a painter with a strong personal vision, such as Van Gogh. The three most characteristic books are like paintings of different atmospheric conditions: *Le Voyeur* shows Brittany in sunlight flecked with clouds, *La Jalousie* has a tropical monotony and rigidity, *Dans le labyrinthe* is a snowscape, dissolving at the end into rain. Because of his minute descriptions, Robbe-Grillet has been called a neo-realist, and he himself claims to be simply describing that which is. However, his rejection of the pathetic fallacy is not accompanied by any full-scale discussion of the central problem of 'realism', which is that all description involves a choice, since no total, or objectively adequate, description is possible. The dogmatic decision to avoid one form of overtly emotive description may be determined by another, although less explicit, emotional attitude. We can only suppose that, in Robbe-Grillet's case, his conviction is related to his anti-religious feelings.

He dismisses analytical psychology as being beneath contempt and argues that the inner reality of a character can be made immediately present by a description of the visual experiences of that character. Yet on the one hand, he borrows occasional hints from psychology while, on the other, the inner reality of his characters, even in an implied form, does not constitute the substance of his books. Their subject-matter is, in each case, an elaborate system of suggestions and correspondences whose deliberate opaqueness contrasts with his positivistic assertions.

Since the features of this system recur from book to book—Wallas, Mathias, the unnamed husband, and the narrator of *Dans le labyrinthe* are, in fact, all the same numb, mysterious centre, linked to an abnormally sensitive eye—we can only suppose that in each instance Robbe-Grillet is celebrating some private psychological rite. Perhaps this is why he quotes Raymond Roussel as his master. The reader's appreciation will obviously vary according to the degree to which he can respond, instinctively and temperamentally, to this rite.

Novels by Robbe-Grillet:

Les Gommes, Paris, Éd. de Minuit, 1953.

Le Voyeur, Paris, Éd. de Minuit, 1955.
> *The Voyeur* (trs. Richard Howard), London, Calder, 1959; New York, Grove Press, 1958.

La Jalousie, Paris, Éd. de Minuit, 1957.
> *Jealousy* (trs. Richard Howard), London, Calder, 1959; New York Grove Press, 1959.

Dans le labyrinthe, Paris, Éd. de Minuit, 1959.
> *In the Labyrinth* (trs. Richard Howard), New York, Grove Press, 1960.

INDEX

Absurd, the, 212-13, 216, 218, 221, 224, 228
Albérès, R.-M., 184
American novels, effect in France, 15-18, 21
Aminadab, 148, 165
Aragon, Louis, 195
Aristotle, 168
Arnaud, Georges, 16-17, 19, 21
Art, and consciousness, 149-50, 158-9, 161-3; view of, 217-18
Ayer, Professor A. J., 170

Balthasar, Hans Urs von, 31
Balzac, Honoré de, 14, 22, 33, 53, 155, 183, 195, 203, 230-1
Barbey d'Aurevilly, Jules, 37
Barthes, Roland, 183, 233, 236-7, 239, 241
Bataille, Georges, 148, 160
Baudelaire, Charles, 33, 148, 195
Beauvoir, Simone de, 5, 8, 11-13, 109, 111, 121-2, 166-82, 206; career, 166-7; and metaphysical novel, 8, 11-13, 168-9; autobiography, 109, 166, 168, 176, 179, 181; and Sartre, 166, 168, 169, 172, 175-81; and existentialism, 168, 169, 170, 172; on woman, 181; list of novels, 182
Beckett, Samuel, 5, 12, 13, 20, 21, 51, 128-46, 162; career, 128; prenatal memories, 130-1; plays, 133, 135, 143; and names beginning with M, 142; list of works of fiction, 145-6
Béguin, Albert, 30, 187
Behaviourist character, 17-18
Being and non-being, 82-84, 92
Bergson, Henri, 169
Bernanos, Georges, 3, 5, 6, 15, 29-54, 187, 188, 193; and freedom, 30-31; and death, 32; and self-hatred, 34-35; and Satan, 35-

Bernanos, Georges (*contd.*)
36, 41-43; and Substitution, 37-40, 43, 47-50; aesthetic structure of works, 48-51; latent presence of Christ in novels, 50-51, 54; his books embody his own experience of life, 52-54; list of novels, 54
Blanchot, Maurice, 5, 7, 12, 13, 19, 147-65; use of *récits*, 148, 155-6, 161, 164; emphasis on forgetfulness, 151-2; defines the novel, 183-4; list of novels, 165
Bloom, Harold, 163-4
Bloy, Léon, 38, 40
Blum, Léon, 55
Bonnier, Henry, 207
Boswell, James, 171
Breton, André, 80, 88, 148, 155, 187, 195, 204
Broch, Hermann, 162
Buber, Martin, 161, 163
Butor, Michel, 22, 230-1

Cain, James M., 16
Caldwell, Erskine, 15, 16
Camus, Albert, 5, 7, 11, 12, 19-21, 24, 29, 54, 177, 195, 206-29, 234; American influence, 16, 18; as moralist, 206-7, 214; essays, 207, 210, 215-16; dualism, 208-9; and the absurd, 212-14, 216, 218, 221, 224, 228; notion of 'rebellion', 214-16, 218-19, 225; Robbe-Grillet and, 231, 232, 238; list of novels, 229
Carroll, Lewis, 170
Cassirer, Ernst, 163
Cayrol, Jean, 5, 13, 20-21, 23, 183-205; career, 185-6; poems, 185; Lazarus myth, 185-6, 188, 189, 191, 195, 198; list of novels, 205
Celui qui ne m'accompagnait pas, 153-6, 158-60, 165

Cendrars, Blaise, 6
Chamberlain, Neville, 124
Champigny, Professor Robert, 222
Char, René, 204
Character analysis, rejection of, 13–22
Chase, J. H., *No Orchids*, 15, 96
Chaucer, 154
Chemins de la liberté, Les, 16, 103–5, 108, 120–7, 179
Chêne et chien, 87, 89, 97
Chiendent, Le, 81–85, 94, 100
Chinese Revolution, 57, 60, 62–65
Chute, La, 217, 220–1, 226–7, 229
Cinema, 235–6
Claudel, Paul, 181
Colette, 111
Comment c'est, 130, 143–4, 146
Communism, 67, 68, 69
Concentration camps, 185–8
Condition humaine, La, 5, 55, 57, 63, 64–66, 68, 74
Conquérants, Les, 55, 57, 60, 62, 63, 74
Corps étrangers, Les, 186, 202, 203, 205
Crime, Un, 37, 54

Daiches, David, 4
Dans le labyrinthe, 230, 245, 249–52
Defoe, Daniel, 177
Dehumanization of fiction, 13–15, 20–23, 230, 236, 248
de la Mare, Walter, 234
Déménagement, Le, 186, 200–2, 205
De Quincey, Thomas, 153
Dernier homme, Le, 159–61, 162, 165
Derniers jours, Les, 87, 100
Descartes, René, 82, 170
Dialectical relation to consciousness, 163–4
Dialogues d'ombres, 30, 54
Dickens, Charles, 14
Diéguez, Manuel de, 202–3
Dimanche de la vie, Le, 83, 88, 92–94, 100
Dort, Bernard, 201
Dos Passos, John, 16, 124, 177, 179
Dostoievsky, F. M., 14, 155, 162, 174, 195

Duhamel, Georges, 4, 15, 195

Eliot, George, 166
Eliot, T. S., 114, 163, 171, 190
Éluard, Paul, 204
Encyclopédie de la Pléiade, 80
Enfants du Limon, Les, 88
Enfants humiliés, Les, 30–34
English, and existentialism, 170
'Error', 151, 152, 156
Espace d'une nuit, L', 186, 199–201, 205
Espace Littéraire, L', 152, 162, 163
Espoir, L', 55, 59, 60, 67–69, 75
Étranger, L', 5, 16, 18, 217, 220–6, 229, 231, 232, 238
Être et le néant, L', 74, 83, 104–6, 168
Evil, writers' attitude to, 41–43, 46
Exercices de style, 94–95, 101
Exil et le royaume, L', 221, 227–9
Existentialism, 84, 98, 111–14, 117, 121, 124–6, 143, 168–72
Existentialisme et la sagesse des nations, L', 8, 11, 168, 174

Fascism, 67
Faulkner, William, 16, 57, 199
Feidelson, Charles, 164
Feu qui prend, Le, 192, 193, 205
Flaubert, Gustave, 14, 22, 98, 111, 148, 203
Forgetfulness, emphasis on, 151–2
Fraternity, 68–70
Freedom, 30–31
French language, written and spoken, 80–81, 85–86, 96, 99–100
Freud, Sigmund, 11, 87, 169, 180, 234
Fučík, Julius, 67

Gaffe, La, 186, 201–2, 205
Gallimard (publishers), 90, 96
Gaulle, General de, 55, 56, 72
Genet, Jean, 122
Gide, André, 3, 15, 53, 55, 57, 90, 148, 155
Gommes, Les, 230, 233, 236, 239–43, 245, 250, 252

INDEX

Goth, M., 148
Gréco, Juliette, 86
Green, Julien, 3
Greene, Graham, 188, 232
Grenier, Jean, 212
Grigson, Geoffrey, 248
Gueule de Pierre, 86–87, 100
Guggenheim, Peggy, 130–1

Hegel, 9, 97, 147, 151, 152, 157–9, 162, 164, 168
Heidegger, Martin, 58, 73, 106, 151–4, 163
Heller, Erich, 164
Hello, Ernest, 53
Hemingway, Ernest, 15, 16, 18, 238
Hölderlin, J. C. F., 151, 163
Homme révolté, L', 7, 207, 214–20, 224
Huis Clos, 109, 175
Human beings, 'negation' of, 13–15, 20–23
Hume, David, 169–72
Husserl, Edmund, 9
Huysmans, Joris-Karl, 38

Immortality, 171–2
Imposture, L', 32, 34, 37, 42, 43, 44, 47, 53, 54
Innommable, L', 135, 139–43, 146
Invitée, L', 175–6, 182

Jalousie, La, 230, 245–9, 251, 252
James, William, 17
Jarry, Alfred, 98
J'irai cracher sur vos tombes, 97
Je vivrai l'amour des autres, 20–21, 185–6, 189–95, 197, 198, 202, 203, 205
Jeanson, Francis, 109
Joie, La, 31, 32, 35, 36, 43–47, 54
Journal d'un curé de campagne, 5, 32, 37, 39, 42, 45, 48, 50, 54
Journal intime, 97, 100
Joyce, James, 14, 81–82, 96, 97, 128, 129

Kafka, Franz, 128, 133, 147–8, 156, 232

Kantianism, 176
Kast, Pierre, 98
Kierkegaard, Sören, 8, 104, 159, 160, 168

Lalou, René, 183
Lawrence, D. H., 6, 57, 181
Lawrence, T. E. (of Arabia), 71, 74
Lazarus myth, 185, 186, 188, 189, 191, 195, 198
Leavis, F. R., 149
Leibniz, G. W. von, 168
Leiris, Michel, 6, 148
Leopardi, Giacomo, 143
Loin de Rueil, 92, 94, 100, 195

Magny, Claude-Edmonde, 51
Maistre, Joseph de, 38
Majault, Joseph, 12–13
Mallarmé, Stéphane, 148
Malle, Louis, 96
Malone meurt, 135, 138, 146
Malraux, André, 3, 5, 15, 24, 55–75, 116, 204; career, 55–57, 66–67; on the novel, 6–7; and revolution 55–57, 60, 62–66, 69; and Spanish Civil War, 55, 57, 60, 63, 67, 69–70; effect of experiences in the East, 55, 62–65; 'man of action', 57, 60–61; anti-Fascist, 67; and fraternity, 68–70; list of novels, 74–75
Man, Paul de, 164
Mandarins, Les, 176–9, 182
'Mara, Sally' (pseudonym of Queneau), 96, 97, 100
Marcel, Gabriel, 10, 66
Martin du Gard, Roger, 15
Marxism, 164, 176, 233–4
Massis, Henri, 59
Material objects, portrayal of, 13–14, 20–21, 190
Maugham, Somerset, 247
Mauriac, François, 3, 230
Maurois, André, 15
Mauvais rêve, Un, 31, 35, 36, 47, 54
'Mauvaise foi, La', 102, 110, 111, 113, 114, 117, 120

Mercier et Camier, 135
Merle, Robert, 16, 17, 19
Merleau-Ponty, Maurice, 9
Metaphors, 232–5, 239
Metaphysical fiction, 6–7, 11, 12, 13, 21, 168–9
Miner, W. L., 15
Mocky, J.-P., 98
Molloy, 134, 135–8, 143, 145
'Monde distrait', 198, 203
Monnerot, Jules, 184
Monnier, Henri, 80
Monsieur Ouine, 36, 42–43, 45, 46, 50–51, 54
Montherlant, Henry de, 3, 181
Moral uncertainty, 3–5
More Pricks than Kicks, 130, 145
Morgan, Charles, 249
Morrissette, Bruce, 246, 248
Mounier, Emmanuel, 60
Mur, Le, 12, 103–12, 127
Murdoch, Iris, 119
Murphy, 131–3, 145
Mythe de Sisyphe, Le, 20, 24, 207, 211–15, 218, 228

Nausée, La, 5, 12, 20, 103–6, 109, 112–21, 123, 126, 190, 233
Nazism, 214
Nerval, Gérard de, 148, 204
Nietzsche, F. W., 8, 151, 167
Nizan, Paul, 122
No Orchids for Miss Blandish, 15, 96
Noire, La, 185, 195–8, 202, 205
Nouveau roman, Le, 230, 231
Nouvelle histoire de Mouchette, 48–50, 54
Nouvelles et Textes pour rien, 135, 139, 143, 146
Novalis, 148, 153
Novel, writers' views on the, 5–7; defined, 183–4
Noyers de l'Altenburg, Les, 55, 60, 70–71, 75

Objects: *see* Material objects
Odile, 87–88, 100

On est toujours trop bon avec les femmes, 96–97, 100
On vous parle, 189–90, 192, 202, 205
Ortega y Gasset, José, 154
Orwell, George, 248

Pascal, Blaise, 65
Pataphysics, 98, 99
Peste, La, 215, 217, 220, 224–6, 229
Petite cosmogonie portative, 97, 99
Phenomenology, 9, 12, 158, 200
Philosophy and fiction, relationship between, 7–12, 103–5
Picon, Gaëtan, 6, 59, 185
Pierrot mon ami, 19, 90–92, 94, 100, 195
Plato, 152–3, 164, 168
Poe, Edgar Allan, 148
Poetic novels, 79, 82, 86–87, 94, 183, 204
Ponge, Francis, 25
Pound, Ezra, 163
Pragmatism, 17, 21
Premiers jours, Les, 190–2, 205
Pre-natal memories, 130–1
Proust, Marcel, 14, 31, 96, 129, 143, 154, 202–3, 238, 248
Psychology, 11, 14, 17–18, 169, 236–8

Queneau, Raymond, 3, 5, 19, 79–101, 195; career, 80, 88, 90, 97–98; and French language, 80–81, 85–86, 96, 99–100; phonetic spelling, 85–86; poetry, 86–87, 97, 99; pseudonym 'Sally Mara', 96, 97, 100; list of novels, 100–1
Quilliot, R., 218, 223

Reader-writer relationship, 4–6
Rebellion, 214–16, 218–19, 225
Récits, use of, 148, 155–6, 161, 164
Resistance, the, 213–14
Resnais, Alain, 186
Restif de la Bretonne, 195
Revolution, 55–57, 60, 62–66, 69
Ribot, T. A., 169
Rictus, Jehan, 80

INDEX

Rilke, R. M., 151, 162, 164
Robbe-Grillet, Alain, 3, 5, 13, 51, 230–52; portrayal of material things, 13, 22–26; influences, 231–2; and metaphors, 232–5, 239; list of novels, 252
Roblès, Emmanuel, 207
Romantics, 148, 151–3, 155
Roussel, Raymond, 231, 252
Rude hiver, Un, 88–90, 100

Sade, Marquis de, 174
St. Glinglin, 86, 87, 94, 100
Sang des autres, Le, 172–4, 176, 182
Sarraute, Nathalie, 19, 230
Sartre, Jean-Paul, 3, 5, 11–13, 15, 19–21, 29–30, 74, 102–27, 195, 206; on novelists, 6; influences, 9, 16; interest in material objects, 19–21, 23, 190; Being-for-Itself, 84, 142–3; summary of philosophy, 102; *la mauvaise foi*, 102, 110, 111, 113, 114, 117, 120; and Blanchot, 148–9, 151; de Beauvoir and, 166, 168, 169, 172, 175–81; Robbe-Grillet and, 231–4; and the cinema, 236; list of novels, 126–7
Satan, Bernanos and, 35–36, 41, 42, 43
Schiller, J. C. F. von, 164
Schorer, Mark, 202
Scudéry, Mlle de, 148
Self-hatred, 34–35
Séquestrés d'Altona, Les, 109, 126
Shelley, P. B., 163–4
Simenon, Georges, 96, 232, 239
Simon, Claude, 230
Smith, T. M., 15
Sous le soleil de Satan, 34, 37, 40, 41, 43, 48, 52, 54
Spanish Civil War, 55, 57, 60, 63, 67, 69–70, 107–8, 122
Spector, Robert D., 221

Spelling, phonetic, 85–86
Spengler, Oswald, 70, 72–74
Spinoza, B., 168
Steinbeck, John, 15, 16
Stendhal, 183, 238
Substitution, 37–40, 43, 47–50
Surrealism, 80, 86–88, 155, 195, 198
Swift, Jonathan, 133, 143
Symbolists, 151, 164

Temps du mépris, Le, 55, 60, 67, 75
Temps mêlés, Les, 87, 100
Tentation de l'Occident, La, 58, 60, 61
Thody, Philip, 105–6
Thomas l'obscur, 19, 148–50, 154, 155, 157, 162, 165
Tipasa, Camus and, 208, 209, 215
Tolstoy, Leo, 14, 238
Tous les hommes sont mortels, 171–2, 176, 179, 182
Tragedy, 233–4

Valéry, Paul, 164
Vendryes, J., 80–81
Vent de la mémoire, Le, 186, 199, 200, 202, 205
Vian, Boris, 97
Voie Royale, La, 55, 60, 62, 63, 74
Voix du silence, Les, 56–58, 65, 70, 72
Voyeur, Le, 23–24, 230, 242–5, 247, 248, 250, 251, 252

Waiting for Godot, 133, 135, 136, 143
War experiences, effect of, 14
Watt, 130, 133–5, 143, 145
Weil, Simone, 167
Williams, Charles, 38, 53
Woman, de Beauvoir on, 181

Yeats, W. B., 163

Zazie dans le Métro, 79, 95–96, 101
Zola, Émile, 174

Printed in Great Britain by
The Camelot Press Ltd., London and Southampton